The Normal Christian Birth

The Normal Christian Birth

J. David Pawson, MA, BSc

Hodder & Stoughton
LONDON SYDNEY AUCKLAND

Copyright © 1989 by David Pawson

First published in Great Britain in 1989
This edition 1997

The right of David Pawson to be identified as the Author of
the Work has been asserted by him in accordance with the
Copyright, Designs and Patents Act 1988.

11

Unless otherwise indicated, Scripture quotations are taken from
the HOLY BIBLE, NEW INTERNATIONAL VERSION,
copyright © 1973, 1978, 1984 by the International Bible Society.
Used by permission.

British Library Cataloguing in Publication Data
A record for this book is available from the British Library

ISBN 0 340 48972 3

Printed and bound in Great Britain by
Clays Ltd, St Ives plc

The paper and board used in this paperback are natural recyclable
products made from wood grown in sustainable forests.
The manufacturing processes conform to the environmental
regulations of the country of origin.

Hodder and Stoughton
A division of Hodder Headline Ltd
338 Euston Road
London NW1 3BH

'But the gate is narrow – contracted by pressure – and the way is straitened *and* compressed that leads away to life, and few are they who find it.' (Matt 7:14, Amplified Bible)

'Jesus answered, "In truth I tell you, no one can enter the kingdom of God without being born from water and spirit."' (John 3:5, New English Bible)

'Peter said to them, "Each one of you must turn away from his sins and be baptised in the name of Jesus Christ, so that your sins will be forgiven; and you will receive God's gift, the Holy Spirit."' (Acts 2:38, Good News Bible)

CONTENTS

PROLOGUE: A word to the midwife   1

PART ONE: YESTERDAY'S NORMAL DELIVERY –
            The theological dimension   9
1 Four spiritual doors   11
2 Repent of your sins towards God   23
3 Believe in the Lord Jesus   31
4 Be baptised in water   44
5 Receive the Holy Spirit   57
6 Born again   79

PART TWO: THE 'WHAT ABOUT . . . ?' PASSAGES –
            The biblical dimension   91
7   The great commission (Matt 28:19–20)   93
8   The Markan postscript (Mark 16:9–20)   100
9   The dying thief (Luke 23:40–43)   103
10 The second birth (John 3:3–8)   108
11 The living streams (John 7:37–39)   116
12 The known stranger (John 14:17)   120
13 The first eleven (John 20:22)   125
14 The fiftieth day (Acts 1:4–5; 2:1–4)   132
15 The three thousand (Acts 2:38–41)   143
16 The Samaritan converts (Acts 8:4–25)   152
17 The Ethiopian eunuch (Acts 8:36–39)   159
18 The Roman centurion (Acts 10:44–48; 11:11–18;
    15:7–11)   162
19 The whole households (Acts 11:14; 16:15, 31;
    18:8)   169
20 The Ephesian disciples (Acts 19:1–6)   177
21 The acid test (Rom 8:9)   189
22 The holy family (1 Cor 7:14)   197

23   The disjointed body (1 Cor 12:13)   200
24   The baptised dead (1 Cor 15:29)   210
25   The new circumcision (Col 2:9–12)   213
26   The regenerating bath (Tit 3:5)   220
27   The elementary teaching (Heb 6:1–6)   223
28   The working faith (Jas 2:14–26)   230
29   The saving flood (1 Pet 3:18–22)   235
30   The shut door (Rev 3:20)   242

PART THREE: TODAY'S TYPICAL DECISION – The
                        pastoral dimension   247
31   One standard decision   249
32   Helping disciples to repent   258
33   Helping disciples to believe   268
34   Helping disciples to be baptised   276
35   Helping disciples to receive   283
36   Saved at last   294

EPILOGUE: A word to the family   303

APPENDICES
 1   Infant baptism   309
 2   'Spirit' without the definite article   320
 3   Trinity or tritheism?   325

The Normal Christian Birth

PROLOGUE: A WORD TO THE MIDWIVES

This is a handbook on spiritual obstetrics. It is not just for evangelists, though it is particularly relevant to their ministry. It is for pastors, youth leaders, church workers and, indeed, all Christians who have a heart to win others for Christ, all who at some time find themselves 'assisting' when a person is 'born again'.

Basically, this book is about how to become a 'Christian'. It is written out of a burden for a better quality of 'conversion' (as well as a bigger quantity, which all long to see).

Birth affects life. This is true of physical birth. A good 'delivery', quick, clean and free from complications, produces a healthy baby. A protracted, painful and complicated birth can have a damaging effect, both physiological and psychological, leading to poor health and slow development.

This is just as true of spiritual birth. Many 'Christians', including myself, were badly delivered. Initiation either took years to be completed or has remained incomplete. In many cases an umbilical cord to the past has never been cut and tied off. Some have never been washed. Others never had hands laid on them in order to breathe in and cry out! Some are barely alive or soon abandoned (as was the people Israel, according to Ezek 15:4–5).

There is a noticeable gap in the literature on this subject. On the one hand, there are many small booklets to give to 'enquirers', explaining how they can respond to the gospel. Most, as we shall see, have over-simplified the procedure to the point of distortion and misdirection, usually based on a misinterpretation of two solitary texts: John 1:12 and Revelation 3:20 (see chapters 5 and 30). The typical 'sinner's prayer' is seriously inadequate (see chapter 31).

On the other hand, recent years have seen a spate of erudite tomes on the 'initiation-complex', written by scholars for scholars (the names of Frederick Dale Bruner, James D. G. Dunn and George R. Beasley-Murray spring to mind). The challenge to integrate sacramental or Pentecostal insights with the traditional evangelical outlook has stimulated these publications. The objective is one I share, though I have reached my own conclusions about the blend!

Between the needs of the enquirer and the scholar there is a void which this book seeks to fill. It is a serious study for those who are prepared to sit down with an open Bible and an open mind, who are not afraid to enter unexplored territory and love God with all their mind. It is not an academic treatise, requires no knowledge of Greek or Hebrew (though some points will be mentioned and explained), contains few references to other works (though a discerning reader will realise many have been studied in the preparation of this volume), and requires average intelligence to grasp the real issues. However, a willingness to *un*learn will be essential, since many traditional assumptions will be questioned.

I have a particular concern to see the 'evangelical' and 'Pentecostal' streams flowing together. These are the two major growing-points on the Christian scene, and (according to some statistical surveys) their integration usually quintuples evangelistic effectiveness. Yet present relationships between the two seem to be based on sympathetic tolerance rather than shared truth. Though there is now much less disagreement or disturbance over 'gifts of the Spirit', there is still a deep gulf over 'baptism in the Spirit', the latter being more directly relevant to our subject.

Readers who like to know the worst quickly may be helped by a summary of the primary challenges in these pages (though they are urged not to dismiss the whole because they disagree with parts!).

Evangelical tradition is asked to reconsider its assumption that 'believing in Jesus' and 'receiving the Spirit' are synonymous and simultaneous (usually lumped together in the phrase 'receiving Jesus'). Pentecostal tradition is asked to reconsider its assumption that 'receiving the Spirit' and being 'baptised in the Spirit' are *not* synonymous or simultaneous (the latter usually being regarded as some kind of 'second' stage or blessing). Both streams are asked to reconsider their assumption that baptism in water is a symbolic rather than a sacramental act (the fear of 'baptismal regeneration' can become irrational and unscriptural).

The position I have taken is midway between the evangelical and the Pentecostal. This could simply upset both and finish up in no man's land! Or it could be seen as a genuine meeting-point where a truly biblical amalgamation can take place.

In a nutshell, I believe that the 'normal Christian birth' consists of true repentance and genuine faith, expressed and effected in water-baptism, with a conscious reception of the person of the Spirit with power. This understanding of 'initiation' is developed in three dimensions:

Theological. The first section comprises a statement about the whole process, followed by an examination of its four elements, and concludes with a chapter relating it all to the doctrine of regeneration.

Biblical. Normally, a study of the relevant scriptures should precede any statement of conclusions. Though this section of the book was actually written first (and some keen Bible students might well begin here), it has been placed second so that readers may see the wood before examining the trees! The passages have been chosen for detailed study because they are crucial or controversial. It is not necessary (and may not be helpful) to work through all of them at the first reading. However, the reader is encouraged to look at chapters 9, 10, 13, 16, 20, 21, 23, 27 and 30, which are fundamental to the whole presentation. No doubt each reader will have his or her own favourite test-text as well!

Pastoral. The temptation to rush on to the practical application must be resisted! To attempt to apply this teaching before being convinced by the Spirit that it is true to scripture could be disastrous. Unfortunately, a pragmatic age is more interested in the question 'Does it work?' than the more important question 'Is it right?' Pragmatic Christians ask 'Is it blessed?' rather than 'Is it biblical?' A true disciple learns to grasp principles first, before putting them into practice. It is morally wrong to use human beings as guinea-pigs! Nevertheless, I hope this study will do more than change opinions – hence this last section is full of practical hints and tips for the 'soul-winner'.

The Appendices cover some specialised topics not essential to the main argument, but of interest and concern to some readers. I have had to be totally honest in stating my conviction that infant baptism cannot be integrated into the understanding of spiritual birth presented here. My hope is that those who find this offensive will not dismiss the whole book on that ground, but will still find much to help them in their ministry. Regarding the definite article ('the'), I am not the first to notice its conspicuous absence from many N.T. statements about the Holy Spirit (as in 'baptised in Holy Spirit', 'filled with Spirit' and 'Did you receive Spirit?'). While, with others, I find this usage has theological as well as grammatical significance, my main argument does not rest on this point – hence its relegation to an appendix. Yet it provides an interesting confirmation of my thesis that receiving (the) Spirit is a conscious experience with audible evidence.

As with any serious writing, this book has been many years in the making. It was hammered out on the twin anvils of biblical study and pastoral care. The basic thesis was first published in 1977 in my *Truth to Tell* (Hodder & Stoughton), chapter 9 of which ('Got a conversion complex?') contains the essence of this book. A promise was made then to provide a 'deeper and more detailed treatment later'. That pledge, recalled by my wife, is now fulfilled in this book. The material presented here has been refined by use in seminars for church leaders of many denominations in this and other countries.

I want to dedicate this book to a host of friends who share my conviction that 'evangelical' and 'charismatic' belong together. To Gordon Bailey, John Barr, Alex Buchanan, Clive Calver (who invited me to proclaim this message on a Youth for Christ tour of twenty-one cities entitled 'Let God speak'), Michael Cassidy, Gerald Coates, Michael Cole, Barney Coombs, Derek Copley, Nick Cuthbert, Don

PROLOGUE

Double, Bryan Gilbert, Bob Gordon, Jim Graham (my
successor at Gold Hill, Chalfont St Peter), Ian Grant, Lynn
Green, Michael Green, Michael Griffiths, Chris Hill, Graham
Kendrick, Cecil Kerr, Gilbert Kirby, Douglas McBain,
David McInnes, Brian Mills, John Noble, Ian Petit, Derek
Prince, Ian Smale ('Ishmael'), Colin Urquhart, Terry Virgo,
Philip Vogel, Rob White and so many more who have sought
in their own ways a synthesis of charismatic experience of the
Spirit with evangelical exegesis of scripture, and by their
personal affection have stimulated me to 'go and do likewise'.
It need hardly be added that none of them must be held
responsible for the views expressed here (I want to keep their
friendship!).

Last, but by no means least, I want to mention my wife,
who gave me the courage and the coffee to keep at it, believing
it to be the most important thing I may ever do in my ministry.
She has humbly taken the role of 'your average reader' and
carefully studied each chapter from that perspective. Without
her support it would not have been written.

Sherborne St. John

Part One

YESTERDAY'S NORMAL DELIVERY – The theological dimension

1 FOUR SPIRITUAL DOORS

The thesis offered in this book can be simply stated: *Christian initiation is a complex of four elements – repenting towards God, believing in the Lord Jesus, being baptised in water and receiving the Holy Spirit.* Each of these is quite distinct from the others. All of them are essential to entering the kingdom of God. They are not mutually exclusive, but are fully complementary and together constitute the process of 'becoming a Christian'. They may occur very close together or over a period of time. The important thing is their completion rather than their coincidence.

A BALANCED APPROACH

Since all four elements are necessary, it is a futile exercise to grade them in importance. Yet different streams of church life have tended to emphasise one, sometimes at the expense of others. *Liberal* thought has concentrated on repentance, especially in terms of radically changed attitudes and lifestyles, though in recent years the emphasis has been on social injustice rather than personal immorality. *Evangelical* thought has focused most attention on faith, particularly its individual and inward aspects, though sometimes stressing doctrinal truth rather than personal trust. *Sacramental* thought has emphasised water-baptism, though it has usually felt the need to add a rite of 'confirmation' where the subjects have been babies (rather than believers). *Pentecostal* thought has rediscovered Spirit-baptism, though it has seen this as a subsequent experience rather than an integral part of initiation.

I believe these four streams are right in what they affirm but wrong in what they tend to undervalue, ignore or even deny.

We shall attempt a synthesis of all that is best in each view. Yet this is not undertaken as an ecumenical enterprise: it is more a biblical exegesis that could provide a base for true integration, based on honest correction rather than dishonest compromise.

All four strands are woven together in the New Testament: Christian initiation is there understood as a combination of ethical reform, eternal relationship, external rite and existential renewal.

It is the essence of heresy to take part of the truth and make it the whole. So often the whole biblical truth on a subject is only understood when different, even disparate, aspects are held together in proper tension. For example, this book must inevitably major on the *human* aspects of the new birth – on the need to repent, be baptised and receive the Spirit, as well as on the need to 'believe in the Lord Jesus' – which may cause some readers to wonder if this is compatible with the Reformation principle of 'justification by faith *alone*'.

Two convictions which underlie every statement in this book must therefore be categorically stated at the outset:

First, Christ's finished work on the cross is *objectively sufficient*, in and of itself, to save the *world* from sin. Nothing can, much less need, be added to it. Through his death, burial and resurrection, he has accomplished everything that needed to be done 'for us men and our salvation'. He has made atonement for sin and reconciled us to the Father. We are assuming that all this has already been made perfectly clear to the one who wants to be saved.

Second, his completed work is not *subjectively efficient*, in the sense of saving any particular *individual* from their sins. It must be personally appropriated and applied. The recipient of these 'benefits of his passion' is active rather than passive. The gospel demands a response. A person may be entitled to an inheritance but will not possess it until it is claimed; their active appropriation of it in no way implies that it has been earned.

The controversy is not therefore over anything that needs to be *added* to faith but how faith is to be *exercised* in order to appropriate what grace is offering. To see water-baptism, for example, as an addition to faith whereby people make themselves more worthy or deserving of salvation is a dreadful travesty. To see it as an expression and consummation of faith whereby the penitent believer is identified with Christ in his death, burial and resurrection is a totally different approach. Baptism is then seen as the means of *experiencing*, not earning, the deliverance those events achieved.

From this point of view, faith is the most fundamental of the four elements and actually underlies the other three. Repentance is linked to faith from the beginning of Mark's gospel (Mark 1:15). Baptism is linked to faith at the end of the same gospel (Mark 16:16). The Spirit is received by faith, not works (Gal 3:2). In a real sense, therefore, to have faith is to repent, be baptised and receive the Spirit (Acts 2:38; see chapter 15).

A SCRIPTURAL APPROACH

We have already begun to include scripture references. Yet stating a thesis and supporting it with proof-texts collected at random is not a valid procedure for establishing biblical truth. A proper overall study strategy needs to be matched with a contextual analysis of particular passages. Conclusions should be reached *after* this process, even though they may be stated at the beginning of a full presentation.

The subject of *Christian* initiation itself dictated some of the basic guidelines. In particular, the starting-point of biblical investigation was indicated. Obviously, this meant concentrating on the *New Testament*, even if there were some 'foreshadowing' references in the Old. But where to start in the New Testament?

Unsuitable candidates
Surprisingly, the events related in the gospels are too *early* for our purpose. Covering the period between the advent and ascension of Jesus, the gospels cannot give us a full picture of the normal pattern of initiation as understood by the

post-Pentecost church (which is the precedent for the 'age' in which we also live). Though repentance, faith, baptism and the Spirit are all mentioned, with some helpful insights into their meaning, none of them could take on that full 'Christian' significance they acquired after the events of Easter and Pentecost. For example, the baptism practised by John (and by Jesus' disciples) was so different from later baptism into the name of Jesus that re-baptism would be necessary (Acts 19:1–6; see chapter 20). Again, the Holy Spirit had been 'with' the disciples during the gospel period, but could only be 'in' them after Pentecost (when they 'received' him), which could only happen after Jesus was 'glorified' (John 7:39; 14:17; see chapters 11 and 12). Even faith could only centre in the ability of Jesus to heal and deliver as the Messiah; it could not yet encompass him as the Saviour of the world (delivered by his death) or the Son of God (declared by his resurrection), much less Lord of all. This is one reason why the dying thief should not be regarded as a model of Christian conversion (see chapter 9). Paradoxically, the full gospel cannot be found in the four gospels! While all the elements are present in embryo, their gestation is far from complete (which, presumably, is why God gave us the rest of the New Testament!).

But the epistles and Revelation are too *late* for our purpose. All of these writings were addressed to believers, who had already been initiated! There is therefore no direct or systematic treatment of our subject. Failure to realise this has led to the misuse of texts. (Revelation 3:20 is a classic example. A rebuke to believers, it has been used almost universally as an invitation to unbelievers; see chapter 30.) However, there are frequent reminders in the epistles and Revelation of the different facets of initiation, the selection depending on their relevance to the immediate needs of the believers being addressed (see below for some examples); but it is almost impossible to reconstruct an adequate survey from these incidental references. As we shall see, the writers of the epistles everywhere take the water-baptism and Spirit-baptism of their readers for granted – but nowhere do they describe or define either event! Only their effects or implications are mentioned.

A good starting-point

So, if the gospels are too early and the epistles too late for our starting-point, what are we left with? The book of Acts! It is the only book in the New Testament to major on post-Pentecost evangelism. It is full of detail about how unbelievers became believers, how sinners became saints. It is a record of the divine and human aspects of salvation, telling us about the acts of the apostles in bringing Christ to people and the acts of the Spirit in bringing people to Christ. Most of the teaching transcribed by Luke is addressed to the unsaved. Not only do we gain valuable insights into how the message was communicated; we are shown the response that was expected and obtained. Only here can we study Peter, John and Paul actually engaged in evangelism. In the examples of counselling enquirers we can discern their understanding of initiation.

Some objections to using Acts

Some Bible scholars would, however, take strong exception to the use of Acts as a source of doctrine. Their objection has taken two forms. The *general* criticism is that doctrine can only be based on the didactic (teaching) portions of scripture (like the epistles) and must not be built on narratives (like Acts). The *particular* criticism is that Luke was a historian, but not a theologian. For both these reasons, it is said that we must begin with the epistles, particularly those of Paul (who *was* a theologian!) and read Acts in the light of his theology. Apart from the difficulties of this approach in relation to initiation (outlined above), there are serious flaws in both objections.

It is the 'genius' of revelation in scripture that truth is embodied in concrete situations rather than abstract propositions. The whole Bible is a narrative – from the garden of Eden to the new Jerusalem. The great truths of creation and redemption are wrapped up in the recital of events. Most of the Old Testament and much of the New is in narrative form. The Bible is not so much a book of systematic theology as a history of situational theism. And all this 'narrative' was written so we could 'learn' from it (Rom 15:4; 1 Cor 10:6). *All* scripture is useful for teaching, because it is all inspired by God (2 Tim

3:16). We can learn as much from God's deeds as his words; indeed, they belong together and illuminate each other. The record of happenings is for instruction as well as information. The Bible does not present a comprehensive history of the world, the nation of Israel or the church. It is a *selection* of significant events accompanied by a prophetic *interpretation* of those events, both being the work of the Spirit of God. (Acts 15 itself contains a perfect example of resolving a doctrinal dispute by the narrative of divine activity, confirmed by scripture.)

Luke is not just a historian, though he claims the integrity of accurate reporting in the first volume of his works (Luke 1:1–4). He selects the events he records and the details within those events. Then he weaves them into an overall pattern based on his profound insights. If theology means understanding God, Luke was quite a theologian! The idea that it is impossible to extract a 'theology of Luke' from his writings as one can with Paul is a myth that needs exploding. (On the issue of Luke as a *theologian*, readers are recommended to sample Roger Stronstad's *The Charismatic Theology of Luke* (Hendrickson, 1984).)

The attempt to drive a wedge between the descriptive narrative of Acts and the didactic nature of the epistles is quite unrealistic. Both were written at the same time about the same situations (remember Paul and Luke were travelling companions). Acts contains 'didactic' passages and the epistles contain narrative (compare Acts 15 with Gal 1–2). There is a unity of outlook between them that outweighs the variety of expression.

Using Acts as a source for a theology of initiation

We may, then, approach Acts with confidence. It has the great advantage of being written 'on location', as one writer has put it. These are eyewitness accounts, at both first hand and second hand, of how the apostles set about evangelising the world. What they said and did gives us our basic material for a theology of initiation.

Where should we begin within Acts? Surely with those

passages containing the most detailed accounts of what happened when people became Christians. The two that spring most readily to mind are to be found in Acts 8 and 19. Events at Samaria and Ephesus are related in great detail for a reason. In both cases the initiation had been incomplete, causing the concerned apostles to take the necessary steps to make good the omissions. The only real difference between the two groups involved was that the Samaritans were much 'further on' than the Ephesians when the apostles came on the scene and therefore needed less 'supplementary' ministry. But the basic content and sequence of their initiations was identical: a fourfold pattern of repentance, faith, baptism and reception of the Spirit. Since three key apostles (Peter, John and Paul) were involved, we are entirely warranted in assuming that their 'technique' on these occasions reflected their general practice and represents the response to the gospel expected by the early church.

It is frequently objected that the circumstances were exceptional in both cases and that the initiation was therefore 'abnormal'. Since evangelism today is neither directed to Samaritans nor to disciples of John the Baptist, we are told we cannot use these events as a precedent. Such criticism fails to distinguish between those features which were exceptional and those which were normal. It misses the point that the apostles were concerned to bring an *abnormal* situation into line with the *normal* pattern. These converts' introduction may have been different from others, but their initiation was the same (some readers may find it helpful at this point to refer to the detailed exegesis of the two passages, in chapters 16 and 20).

With this fourfold framework in the back of our minds, we can look at Luke's record of other 'conversions', noting how many elements are mentioned each time:

Acts 2   Peter mentioned repentance, baptism and reception of Spirit but not faith (though this may be implied in the enquirers' question and deduced from the phrase 'received the word').

Acts 8   The Ethiopian was only 'baptised' according to the best text (some manuscripts add a profession of faith and one adds the reception of the Spirit; see chapter 17).

Acts 9   Paul is 'baptised' and 'receives the Spirit' three days after his Damascus road encounter with the Lord (cf. v.18 with 22:16). But there is no specific reference to his repentance or faith (though both are clearly implied in his conversation with Jesus and his subsequent comments and actions).

Acts 10   Cornelius clearly 'repented' (cf. 10:35 with 11:18) and 'believed' (cf. 10:43 with 11:1 and 15:7), but he received the Spirit' *before* he was 'baptised in water' (the *only* example of this sequence; see chapter 18 for an explanation).

Acts 16   The Philippian jailer 'believed' (with all his household) and was 'baptised' (with all his household), but there is no mention of his 'repenting' or 'receiving' (see chapter 19 for the meaning and implications of 'household').

Other occasions scattered through the Acts account limit the initiation to 'believed'. The *four* elements are not explicitly listed outside the Samaritan and Ephesian cases, though Cornelius and his household come close. Baptism is the one most frequently included; repentance is the one most frequently excluded.

What are we to make of all this? Why does Luke not mention all four every time? Apart from any other reason, his literary skill would prevent him from being so boringly repetitious! But there is a rationale behind his selectiveness: in each situation he brought out the most striking or significant features. The sight of three thousand baptisms at one time and in one pool (Bethesda?) or the sound of a whole household receiving a Pentecostal outpouring in the middle of a sermon could understandably crowd other details into the background! What was a perfectly normal experience for Jewish believers becomes 'news' when it happens to Samaritans and even Gentiles!

It would be erroneous to conclude that the omissions indicate that all four elements are not necessary for every individual. If Acts were taken that way, it would mean that most converts don't need to repent, many do not need to believe, some do not need to receive the Spirit and a few don't need to be baptised! However, it is clear that all four constituted 'normal' initiation for Luke, while he selects from them the most relevant for his purpose in recording particular events. The same procedure of selection by relevance occurs in the epistles, as we shall see.

One further point needs to be made: the whole process of initiation, from 'repenting' to 'receiving' took time, sometimes short and sometimes quite long:

for the twelve apostles, it took some *years*;

for the Ephesian disciples, probably *months*;

for the Samaritan converts, perhaps *weeks*;

for the apostle Paul, a few *days*;

for the Philippian jailer, only *hours*; and

for the Cornelius household, apparently *minutes*.

Clearly the speed of the process is irrelevant, but its completion is vital. Luke and the apostles were far more concerned about validity than velocity!

Initiation in the gospels

With this fourfold framework derived from Acts we can now turn to the gospels. The first discovery is that the ministry of John the Baptist covered all of them! He taught the need for repentance from sins (Luke 3:8); he came so that through him all might believe (John 1:7); he inaugurated water-baptism (Matt 3:11) and predicted Spirit-baptism (the last is emphasised in all four gospels – Matt 3:11; Mark 1:8; Luke 3:16; John 1:33). John was fully aware of his own inadequacy and the limitations of his ministry. His baptism could deal with the past, but not with the future; for that, his followers would need a power which he could not mediate (and which he may not have had himself, being less than the least in the kingdom and not working any miracles – see Luke 7:28 and John 10:41; but cf. Luke 1:15).

Jesus picked up where John left off, preaching repentance and faith (Mark 1:15), practising baptism (John 4:1–2) and promising the Holy Spirit (John 7:37–39). However, there has already been some development in the concepts. Faith in the kingdom 'at hand' (i.e. within reach) is now much more personal, since the King is also 'at hand' and his name is Jesus. Faith has become 'believing in his name' (John 1:12; 2:23). The coming 'immersion' in the Holy Spirit will also be a 'drink' that will produce a spring from the depths of a person's being (there is a remarkable parallel between John 4:14 and 1 Cor 12:13; see chapters 11 and 23); above all, this Spirit-baptism will not just bring a *power* into human lives – 'Holy Spirit' is a *person*, 'another stand-by', just like Jesus (John 14:16).

It is even more significant that the four aspects of initiation all figure prominently in the brief summaries of Jesus' post-resurrection, pre-ascension instruction of the apostles. A composite of the four gospels produces a comprehensive missionary mandate, which fully explains the pattern of apostolic ministry we have already observed in Acts. They were to preach repentance (Luke 24:47), preach the gospel so that people might believe (Mark 16:15–16) and baptise them when they did (Mark 16:16; Matt 28:19). Above all, this ministry could not even be begun without Spirit-baptism for the apostles themselves (Luke 24:49; John 20:22; Acts 1:5) and the same power was promised to their converts as well (Mark 16:17, which explains Peter's confident offer to his hearers in Acts 2:39).

Initiation in the epistles

This seems a good point to turn to the epistles. In the light of the careful counselling of enquirers we have seen him give at Ephesus (Acts 19:1–6; see chapter 20), it should not surprise us in the slightest that Paul takes all four elements for granted when writing to the churches he himself founded. There are scattered references throughout his letters to his readers having

repented (2 Cor 7:9; 1 Thess 1:9);
believed (1 Cor 15:11; Eph 1:13);
been baptised (Gal 3:27; Eph 5:26);
received (2 Cor 1:22; Gal 3:2).

He even refers to these elements when writing to a church he had not himself planted (Rom 2:4; 3:26; 6:3; 8:9). It is true that he never mentions all four together in the same context (for the same reason that Luke rarely does in Acts; he is selecting the most relevant aspects for his immediate purpose). What is significant is that whenever he mentions *any* of them, he assumes that *all* his readers know from their own experience what he is talking about. (Some have claimed an exception to this 'rule' in his references to water-baptism in Romans 6:3 and Galatians 3:27. However, although his words could imply that some have not been baptised, his phrase 'all of us', rather than 'those of us', indicates that the contrast is with unbaptised unbelievers, not unbaptised believers.)

It is precisely because he can take these four things for granted with all his readers that there is neither a command nor an exhortation anywhere in Paul's letters to be baptised in water or in the Spirit. But it is quite wrong to conclude from this that all four can be taken for granted *today*, as is often assumed by those who separate Paul's epistles from Luke's Acts, building their doctrine of initiation on the former, in isolation from the latter. Though Paul takes them for granted in the epistles, he himself, with the other apostles, did *not* take them for granted in Acts! On the contrary, in their evangelism they insisted on checking and then completing an initiation that was lacking any vital component. For example, Paul could only take it for granted that all his Corinthian readers had been 'baptised in one Spirit' because he had planted their church and had made very sure that they were all fully initiated (1 Cor 12:13; see chapter 23 for a fuller treatment of this vital point). Were he to visit many churches today he might be much more likely to ask 'Did you receive the Holy Spirit when you believed?' (Acts 19:2) than to affirm that all have been 'baptised in the Spirit'!

There is a more subtle reason why Paul's epistles must be studied in the light of Acts: some of his 'didactic' instruction cannot be fully understood without the descriptive information Luke provides. Paul *never* links the verb 'baptise' or the noun 'baptism' to the word 'water'! This has led some reputable scholars, who study Paul's theology in isolation, to claim that his concept of baptism (in such verses as Rom 6:4; Gal 3:27; Eph 4:5) has nothing to do with water at all! It is only from his experience in Acts, both in his being baptised himself and in baptising others, together with Luke's clear references to water (Acts 8:36, for example), that we can assume Paul linked the two (there is one context where he uses the word 'water' but not 'baptism' – Eph 5:26).

Similarly, Paul uses the phrase 'baptised in the Spirit' (in 1 Cor 12:13) without any definition or description of what he means. The same is true of its use in all four gospels. It is *only* from Luke's record of events in Acts that we can know exactly what is involved in being 'baptised in the Spirit'. Once such Pauline phrases are separated from their Lukan content they can be given entirely different meanings, which can be arbitrarily inserted from a preconceived theological outlook (a hermeneutical liberty which has the effect of distorting doctrine).

The other New Testament authors also refer to initiation. Peter, for example, is the only letter-writer to use the words 'baptism' and 'water' together (1 Pet 3:21; see chapter 29). John majors on believing in Jesus and receiving the Spirit (1 John 3:24; 4:13; 5:1–5). But the anonymous author of the epistle to the Hebrews lists all four parts of initiation in a single sentence and in their normal sequence (Heb 6:1–2; see chapter 27). On the basis of the material considered in this chapter, we may conclude that there is a fourfold pattern of Christian initiation which is carefully *articulated* in Acts, clearly *anticipated* in the Gospels and consistently *assumed* in the Epistles. Let us now look at these 'four spiritual doors' which lead into the kingdom of God on earth.

2 REPENT OF YOUR SINS TOWARDS GOD

Repentance is probably the least controversial of the four parts of initiation, but for that very reason it is probably the least considered and the most neglected!

The word is more easily understood by Jews than Gentiles. It was woven into the history of Israel, particularly during the times leading up to her exile, when prophet after prophet sought to avert the impending disaster by calling for national repentance. Anyone familiar with Amos 4 or Jeremiah 18–19 would know perfectly well what repentance meant. Perhaps this is why it is rarely defined in the New Testament.

It has become almost a cliché to say that repentance is not just 'feeling sorry'. Such a feeling can express a variety of attitudes. Sometimes it is simply regret that our actions have brought such consequences on *ourselves*; this is little more than self-pity and reveals that the heart is still egocentric (Cain and Esau are good examples of this emotion – Gen 4:13 and Heb 12:17). More commendable is that overwhelming remorse at the consequences of our actions on *others*, which is at least less self-centred (Paul must have felt this when he recalled his persecution of the church – cf. Acts 9:1–2 with Phil 3:6). Real repentance, however, begins when we realise the consequences for *God* (and his Son); this is that 'godly sorrow' which does not of itself constitute repentance, but which can lead to it (2 Cor 7:9). Light dawns when we realise we have 'sinned against heaven', as well as against others and, in a sense, against ourselves (Luke 15:18, 21). Only then are we able to grasp that we have defied God's authority, broken his laws, polluted his creation, spoiled his pleasure, provoked his anger and deserved his judgement. Our unhappiness will then be more than tinged with fear.

Given this emotional background, the strength of which will vary enormously according to individual temperament and the circumstances of enlightenment, let us look at that true repentance to which such feelings can and should progress.

Scriptural repentance involves three dimensions: thought, word and deed. In passing through these mental, verbal and practical phases, there is a movement from the 'inward heart' to the 'outward life'. To express the latter without the former is morally offensive ('Rend your heart and not your garments' is a typical prophetic admonition – Joel 2:13). To profess the former without the latter is hypocrisy. A simple illustration may help; a London taxi driver takes an overseas visitor a very long way round to Heathrow Airport in order to make some much-needed extra money; conscience-stricken at exploiting the stranger's ignorance, he apologises and returns the whole fare. He has *changed* – in thought, word and deed; he has repented of his sin.

THOUGHT – CONVICTION OF PAST SINS

The word 'repent' (Greek: *metanoeō*) means literally to change one's mind. It means to think again, particularly with reference to past behaviour. A typical example from the New Testament would be Peter's demand that his Jewish hearers reconsider the crucifixion of Jesus and realise it had been a judicial murder of no less a person than the Messiah, God's own Son (Acts 2:32–38; 3:13–19).

To repent means to think about things from God's point of view, to agree with his analysis and accept his verdict. It is to say 'Yes' to God's 'Yes', and assent to his 'No'. It is to learn to say 'Amen' to God's word. It is to have a clear vision of human sin, measured by the standard of divine righteousness and the inevitable judgement that must take place when the two meet (John 16:8). It is to come to a 'knowledge of the truth' (2 Tim 2:25) about God and about one's self.

At one level, this discovery will be in *general* terms. On the one hand, a person will become deeply aware that God is much *better* than he is generally thought to be. The Lord is absolutely holy, absolutely pure, absolutely just. On the other hand, a person will become painfully aware that he himself is much, much *worse* than he thought he was. Instead of thinking of himself as basically a good person who has done bad things from time to time (the 'humanist' view), he discovers he is basically a bad person who has managed to do some good things from time to time (Jesus' view of human nature – Luke 11:13; cf. John 2:24). Worse than that, even the good things he has done can be as offensive to God as the bad and need also to be repented of (Isa 64:6 describes human righteousness as a menstrual cloth; Phil 3:8 describes it in terms of human excreta!). This discovery, that God finds self-righteousness more offensive and intractable than crude sin, comes as a great shock to human pride and completes the revolution in thought inherent in true repentance.

Once this stage is reached, the new way of thinking turns to the level of the *particular*. This is the most important feature of repentance: that it is related to specific 'sins' (plural), rather than general 'sin' (singular). Until the somewhat abstract concept of 'sin' is translated into detailed and concrete terms, it is difficult to proceed to further stages of repentance. Jesus came to save us from our sins, not our sin (Matt 1:21). It is vital to know what those sins are from which we need to be saved.

So far we have considered only the *inward* aspects of repentance. But this needs to be followed by two *outward* aspects. One makes repentance *audible*; the other makes it *visible!*

WORD – CONFESSION OF PAST SINS

Thinking differently about former actions needs to be followed by *speaking* differently about them. The mouth is usually the channel of communication between the inside and the outside of a person (Matt 12:37; Mark 7:18–23; Jas 3:9–12).

John the Baptist's ministry centred on that repentance which was crucial to the approaching kingdom. Baptism in water was the culmination or consummation of the repentance

(Matt 3:11; note the significance of the preposition: '*into* repentance'). Confession of sins (plural) was a vital accompaniment of baptism (Matt 3:6). This was no formalised liturgy, no comprehensive 'general' confession (it is possible to confess having left undone what ought to have been done and having done what ought not to be done without thinking of a single specific wrong!). John the Baptist expected verbalised public admission of personal guilt in specific matters. Deeds of darkness were to be brought into the light before God and man.

Such confession of sins (as distinct from sin) has two great benefits. The first has already been touched upon, but needs to be repeated: namely, *particularity*. Naming sins involves identifying them first. Vague generalities will simply not do ('Well, I'm sure I must have sinned at some time, somewhere; after all, hasn't everybody?'). The reality of our sins is acknowledged when specific confession is made ('I have done this . . . and this . . . and this!). Of course, such self-disclosure involves the swallowing of pride; to admit one has been in the wrong is never easy. However, it is far better to do it now voluntarily than to have it done involuntarily later. What is uncovered by man now will be covered by God's mercy; what is covered by man now will be uncovered by God's judgement.

The second benefit of verbal confession is the acceptance of *responsibility*. Excuses cannot be included in a confession; extenuating circumstances cannot be pleaded. The individual is accepting both his accountability to God and his responsibility for himself. It is comparatively easy to acknowledge the need for help (or, these days, for 'inner healing'); that leaves much of our self-respect intact! True confession admits that the real problem is wilful guilt and that the real need is for undeserved forgiveness. Confession opens up the channel for grace to flow (1 John 1:9).

It is often helpful to add *renunciation* to the verbal part of repentance, especially where sins have been obsessional or occultic. It can be therapeutic and liberating to verbalise repudiation in this way. The *Oxford English Dictionary* defines the verb 'renounce' as 'to abandon, surrender, give up, repudiate, refuse to recognise, decline association with, disdain fellowship with, withdraw from, discontinue, forsake'. A schoolboy described it rather more succinctly as being 'sorry enough to stop'! By a natural progression we have already reached the third dimension of repentance.

DEED – CORRECTION OF PAST SINS

Words of repentance need to be followed by *works* of repentance. John insisted that candidates for his baptism should first 'produce fruit in keeping with repentance' (Luke 3:8). When asked to explain what he expected them to *do*, he was both specific and practical in his reply: they were to distribute their surplus clothing to the poor, make sure their financial accounts were ready for the auditor, cease taking advantage of their authority and stop agitating for higher wages! It is interesting to note that none of these sins were 'religious' or 'spiritual'.

An example from Jesus' ministry (Luke 19:1–10) is the case of Zacchaeus, who promised not only to 'go straight' in the *future*, but also to repay those he had defrauded in the *past* (with interest and a large bonus): Jesus joyfully announced that salvation had entered the house with himself.

Paul, likewise, expected repentance to be demonstrated in practical ways. The 'heavenly vision', to which he was not disobedient, was a mission to the Gentiles, calling on them to 'repent and turn to God and prove their repentance by their deeds' (Acts 26:20).

John the Baptist, Jesus and Paul all demonstrate that repentance involves putting the past right wherever this is possible.

Some of this putting right will take the form of *negative* action. The destruction of sources of temptation may be involved (the Ephesians burned a huge amount of occult literature, for example – Acts 19:19). Wrong relationships will need to be ended, especially where extramarital or homosexual intercourse are involved ('such *were* some of you', 1 Cor 6:11). Any umbilical cord which is a link to past sin must be tied off and cut. The past must be brought to a conclusion.

Much of the putting right will take the form of *positive* action, as it did with Zacchaeus. The word for this is *restitution*, which involves adequate compensation for those who have been wronged. Forgiveness restores the relationship with God as if it had never been broken; so far as he is concerned the past is forgotten as well as forgiven (what an amazing control God has over his own memory!). The reason we find it so difficult to 'forgive ourselves' is that we do not have this ability to 'blot out' such memories. At the level of human relationships, forgiveness from God does not set a person free from obligation to others, whether these are marital, commercial or even criminal. God's grace has led many to repay their debts, restore their marriages and even confess to crimes for which they have never been punished. In many cases, *reconciliation* will be another 'fruit' of repentance, both with those who have been wronged and with those who have done the wrong (Matt 5:23–24).

All this is the hardest part of true repentance. Some doubt whether a sinner is capable of such deeds when he first turns to God and imply that such repentance will follow initiation rather than constitute its first part. They forget that divine help will always be made available to anyone who truly desires to repent (note that God 'granted' repentance to Cornelius and his household, which enabled them to 'do what was right' even before they heard the gospel – Acts 10:35). It cannot have been easy for Paul to send Onesimus (his name means 'Useful') back to his master, or for him to go, or even for Philemon to have him back (notice that Paul offers to make restitution on his behalf – Philm 12–14, 19).

If putting things right is the hardest part of repentance, it is also the most rewarding. There is deep relief to be found in putting right a wrong (a joy shared by the Redeemer, though he never needed to do it for himself). The father's joy when the prodigal returned was reflected in the prodigal's joy at having done the right thing at last.

This 'turning' from sins to God is the essence of the New Testament word 'conversion'. The word means to turn around, change course, reverse direction. It is therefore very near to the word repentance, but is particularly related to this third aspect of it. A changed life is evidence of repentance, though not necessarily proof of regeneration (see chapter 6). Such evidence of repentance was expected *before* baptism was administered – for this rite marked the final break with the old life of sin and the climax of God's cleansing forgiveness (Mark 1:4; Acts 2:38).

Even natural disasters may be seen as calls to repentance, for they remind us that we shall all unexpectedly come to ruin unless we repent of our sins (Luke 13:1–9). The horror of this future judgement of God makes any present sacrifice worthwhile – of things we want to gaze at, touch or go to (Matt 5:29–30). Better to turn away from sins now than have God turn away from us then.

Turning to God now means that he can turn to us! The Bible dares to say that when we repent towards him, he repents towards us! When the word is used of God, it is, of course, in its mental rather than moral sense – he 'thinks again'. When we change our minds about sins, he can change his mind about us. One of the clearest statements about this in the Bible is Jeremiah's observation of the potter and his clay (Jer 18:1–10). Few metaphors have been so misunderstood! Most exegetes suggest that the clay has no part to play in its own ultimate shape (a notion that is much nearer Islamic than Judeo-Christian philosophy!). Actually, it is the clay that is choosing what kind of vessel it becomes. When it does not respond to the potter's original intention, he decides to make it a crude pot instead of a slender vase. The clay is in an active and dynamic relationship with the potter; each affects the other, though the potter has the last word, since he has overall control of the situation (the clay cannot make anything of itself without him). It is a picture of God's people, Israel. If the nation repents, God will repent and make her a beautiful vessel filled with his mercy; if she does not repent, he will make her an ugly vessel filled with his judgement.

It is repentance, therefore, that makes it possible for forgiveness to be given. This is true even at the human level. Jesus told his disciples that a sinning brother must first be rebuked, but then forgiven – seven times a day, forty-nine times a week, one thousand four hundred and seventy times a month . . . *if he repents* (Luke 17:3–4). In the same way, God can 'change his mind' from judgement to mercy for us only if we truly repent of those things which deserve the one but need the other. That is the strongest motive anyone could have for repenting of their sins. 'Repent, then, and turn to God, so that your sins may be wiped out, that times of refreshing may come from the Lord, and that he may send the Christ, who has been appointed for you – even Jesus' (Acts 3:19–20).

Yet to make repentance the only, or even the primary factor, would be to fall into the trap of do-it-yourself salvation. The emphasis would then be on what man does for God rather than what God does for man. A 'Christian' would be defined in terms of moral reformation: the 'do-gooder' version of Christianity which is the most common one encountered outside the church and is not unknown inside!

The Bible does not teach justification by repentance, but justification by faith. Turning from sin in repentance is the proper prelude to turning to Christ in faith, to which topic we must now address ourselves.

3   BELIEVE IN THE LORD JESUS

The importance of faith to initiation can hardly be over-estimated, unless it is taken to such an extreme as to render the other components optional or unessential. Of the 'four spiritual doors', this is undoubtedly the most crucial, and without it the other three lose their significance and effectiveness. It is doubtful if anyone would truly repent of their sins unless they already 'believed' in the certainty of judgement and the possibility of salvation (which may explain why Peter didn't mention faith when the crowd at Pentecost asked him what they should do; see chapter 15). An essential element in water-baptism is the candidate's faith in the power of God to raise someone who is dead and buried (Col 2:12; see chapter 25). The Holy Spirit is received by faith (Gal 3:2). So the whole process of initiation is an exercise and expression of faith. No wonder, then, that the simplest answer ever given to the question 'What must I do to be saved?' was 'Believe in the Lord Jesus, and you will be saved' (Acts 16:30–31).

Can we take it for granted, even among evangelicals, that faith is understood? Probably not in all its fullness. For there are a number of different dimensions to the New Testament concept, any of which can be exaggerated at the expense of the others. For example, the verbal expression of faith is vital (Rom 10:9); but if a *profession* of faith' is taken as sufficient evidence for 'believing', serious misjudgements can result, to the detriment of the church as well as the individual. It is not *saying* we have faith that saves us, but actually having it. Faith needs to be possessed and practised, as well as professed and proclaimed!

There are five fundamental facets which together constitute full faith, according to apostolic doctrine: historical, personal, verbal, practical and continual.

FAITH IS HISTORICAL

It is a truism that faith is based on facts, not feelings. But it cannot be repeated too often, especially in an existential culture where subjective experience is regarded as the touchstone of reality. This has led to the extraordinary extreme of having faith in faith itself! Many believe it is the *act* of believing, not the *facts* that are believed, which makes faith effective. Believing anything is far superior to believing nothing. In colloquial terms, 'It doesn't matter what you believe, so long as you are sincere.' Religion becomes a placebo!

In this atmosphere of relativism and credulity, it is offensive to claim that the validity of faith depends on objective reality rather than subjective sincerity. Yet that is the Christian assertion, which must be made in the face of the contrary spirit of our age. The only *saving* faith (whatever the other sorts may or may not achieve) is based on historical events, which have already taken place or will yet do so.

The Bible is basically a history of the world. It begins earlier and ends later than all other such annals, primarily because its writers had access (by divine revelation) to those eras (past and future) which no man has been able to observe and record. Only God can know how it began and how it will end, since he is the cause of both.

It is all the more necessary today to begin with this large framework of faith than ever before. Formerly, there may have been a time when faith in one God as past Creator and future Judge could be taken for granted in a 'Christian' country. That is no longer the case, in view of the secularist philosophy and religious pluralism of contemporary society. It has become necessary not only to enquire whether people believe in God, but also what kind of a God they believe in!

Fortunately, the Bible anticipated this need to begin with a basic faith in a 'good God'. Whoever is looking for God must first 'believe' that he really does exist and that he wants to be found (Heb 11:6). It is significant that when the apostles preached to Gentile (as distinct from Jewish) audiences, they invariably sought to establish this 'God-framework' *before* mentioning Jesus Christ (Acts 14:15–17; 17:22–31).

However, faith in God is not only concerned with his activity at the inauguration and climax of history. It must also accept the fact of his intervention in the middle of history (dividing it into BC and AD), for the salvation of a rebellious race. Faith involves recognition of God's decision to reach all nations through one nation (the Jews) and all individuals through one individual (the Jew called Jesus). A relativist age, in which all are considered to have *some* truth and none is considered to have *all* truth, finds this 'scandal of particularity' deeply offensive. That Jews in general and one Jew in particular should have a monopoly on salvation (John 4:22; 14:6; Acts 4:12; etc.) could hardly be more alien to modern thought. Yet this, too, is essential to saving faith.

The heart of it, however, lies in those crucial events which constitute the true 'hinge of history': namely, the death on a cross, the burial in a tomb (notice how prominent this is in scripture and the creeds) and the resurrection with a body – all of which happened over the space of a few days to the historical human being called Jesus of Nazareth (1 Cor 15:3–4 lists these three facts as the most fundamental of the Christian faith). However, historical events are explained as well as recorded in the Bible. Faith includes an acceptance of the *significance* of events as well as their *occurrence*. Since the Jesus who was crucified, buried and raised was thus proved to be what he claimed to be, the incarnate Son of God, these events take on an importance for the whole of history and the whole human race.

If God is thus in control of history, its course is determined by personal choices rather than impersonal chance and by moral judgements rather than material forces, as against the popular view that history is a haphazard cycle of arbitrary happenings. However, since God is eternal, his hand is more easily seen in the long term than the short. The exception to this is to be seen in the brief period during which his Son was on earth. If his judgements operate slowly in history, his acts of mercy were swiftly achieved (this difference is itself a clue to his character – Jonah 4:2). The death and resurrection of Jesus, by atoning for sin and overcoming death, have become the heart of salvation-history.

This progression from the God of all history to the Jesus of history was the framework of faith preached by the apostles. For example, the twin poles of Paul's proclamation were the 'kingdom of God' and the 'name of Jesus' (Acts 28:31); the same is true of Philip (Acts 8:12). Thus, this 'historical' gospel was both *extensive* (the 'rule' of God is universal – Ps 103:19) and *intensive* (the authority of God is 'focused' in Jesus, who is now 'Lord' of all). It is also *exclusive* of other faiths and religions.

It is vital to emphasise this historical basis for saving faith. The social pressures against such a claim are today as great as they were in the days of the Roman Empire, if not greater. Yet this faith overcame the world then (1 John 5:5) and it can do so again!

FAITH IS PERSONAL

To stop at the historical dimension would turn faith into a credal confession, an intellectual acceptance. True, the creeds were composed for this precise purpose – to safeguard the vital historical element (both the facts and their meaning) for future generations. Yet it is possible to recite the creeds with sincerity and even conviction without that relationship and commitment which are essential ingredients of saving faith. The creeds certainly begin in a personal way ('*I* believe . . .'), but they fail to apply the confession in a personal manner. To say 'I believe that is true' is not the same as saying 'That is true for me.' To believe that Jesus is the Saviour of the world is not the same thing as believing that he is my Saviour. To bear 'witness' to Jesus involves a firsthand testimony as well as a second-hand creed!

Christian faith is believing in a single person rather than a series of propositions. It is not just believing *that* Jesus died and rose again; it is believing *in* the Jesus who died and rose again.

The change of preposition is crucial, transferring faith from the mind, where it rightly begins, to the will (which is the citadel of our personality and very close to what the Bible means by 'heart'). It is a shift from the objective (information about Jesus) to the subjective (confidence in Jesus). Whereas in the previous section we highlighted the danger of a subjective faith without any objective content, we must now be aware of the opposite peril!

It is perhaps significant that the New Testament writers (and particularly John) usually prefer the verb 'believe' to the noun 'faith', emphasising that it is something to do rather than something to have (see pp. 38–40 below). Though they sometimes refer to faith as a 'body of truth' (usually with the definite article, as in 'the faith', quite common in the 'pastoral' epistles of Paul to Timothy and Titus), the usual connotation of faith is as an 'attitude of trust'.

Such a trusting attitude involves obedient action. Mary's word to the servants at Cana ('Do whatever he tells you' – John 2:5) is a profound expression of faith in her son. To put it in a rather more theological way: faith in Jesus involves obeying him as Lord as well as trusting him as Saviour. If we really trust someone, we will not hesitate to do whatever they tell us. (This is one reason why baptism is essential to faith and therefore to salvation; to profess that we trust him when we have not even done the first thing he commanded is a contradiction in terms, if not sheer hypocrisy.)

Yet even obedience can be quite impersonal, if it is limited to the 'law of Christ' recorded in the New Testament. If the essence of faith is a personal relationship with the risen Jesus, best expressed in the biblical concept of 'knowing' a person (John 17:3; cf. Gen 4:1), then obeying his written commands or even believing that his atoning death is personally applicable and effective is not likely to foster such intimacy. Something else is needed . . .

FAITH IS VERBAL

It is a modern heresy that the expression of a desire in words can actually bring it about ('Name it, claim it!'), either psychologically in ourselves or parapsychologically in others. This has more to do with the pagan notion of the so-called divine powers inherent in man than with faith in the biblical God. However, there is an element of truth in such a philosophy – namely, our words reinforce as well as reflect our thoughts.

The New Testament clearly teaches that faith needs to be put into words. But the emphasis is not on the persons *by* whom they are expressed; it is on the persons *to* whom they are addressed. Mere verbalisation can be done in solitude, but talking to one's self (however edifying or profitable!) is not usually a sign of mental stability, much less spiritual benefit. Saving faith is expressed by talking to others. It is only spoken aloud in their hearing and it is only because they are listening that the words of faith become effective.

The first and foremost example of this verbal expression is the direct address of Jesus by name when seeking salvation. Peter quoted Joel to this effect in his first sermon at Pentecost ('. . . everyone who calls on the name of the Lord will be saved' – Joel 2:32 in Acts 2:21), and it was soon obvious that he interpreted this prediction as a reference to Jesus. It is very striking how frequently the '*name*' of Jesus is referred to thereafter in the book of Acts (2:38; 3:6; 4:7, 10, 12, 17, 18, 30; 5:28, 40, 41; etc.). Other incidental references indicate that new disciples were encouraged to 'call on' Jesus by name, particularly at the time of their baptism (Acts 22:16).

The gospels are full of examples of men and women who did just this. A classic case is the blind man who refused to keep quiet until Jesus heard him (Mark 10:46–52); Jesus' statement to him, 'Go, your faith has healed you,' must not be taken to mean that by shouting he had healed himself – but that his determined words had been the means of releasing the healing power of Jesus into his body. Perhaps the very reason why the gospel writers have recorded so many stories like this was to encourage later generations to do likewise, even though they would not be in a position to see or hear him physically – after all, the blind man at Jericho couldn't see him either!

To address Jesus aloud by name is to express belief in his presence as well as his continued existence. It is precisely because he is alive and around (by his Spirit) that such words of faith are so effective. 'I cried unto the Lord and he heard me . . .' is as true of Jesus in the New Testament as of Yahweh in the Old.

It is highly unlikely that liturgical recitation qualifies as a 'word of faith'. The Lord alone knows how many members of a congregation, repeating 'Christ, have mercy upon us' at the appropriate stage in a service, are really seeking his mercy (or even realising how much they need it). Repetition of another's words, unless they spring spontaneously to mind, is not usually a genuine cry from the heart for help (see chapter 31 for a critique of the use of 'the sinner's prayer' in evangelism). To 'call' is associated with that raised tone of voice natural to a mood of acute anxiety, due to a realisation of real peril. In a word, it is the cry of someone in urgent need of being 'saved'.

Paul's statement about the need to verbalise faith is probably the most widely quoted ('If you confess with your mouth, "Jesus is Lord," and believe in your heart that God raised him from the dead, you will be saved. For it is with your heart that you believe and are justified, and it is with your mouth that you confess and are saved' – Rom 10:9–10). But it needs careful unpacking. He is applying to the gospel a principle originally attributed by Moses to the law (Deut 30:11–14). The link between the two is 'righteousness', demanded by the law and offered by the gospel. In both cases this 'righteousness' is not a distant standard far beyond reach, but as near to a person as the words on their lips; indeed, to express it in speech is the first step to attaining it (cf. Josh 1:8). In the case of law-righteousness, this involved recitation of the laws of Moses; but in the case of faith-righteousness it involves confession of the Lordship of Jesus. Note that the commandments have been replaced by the Christ as 'the way' of righteousness.

But 'confess' to whom? Most Bible students have too readily assumed that this refers to a confession before men,

37

either as a credal statement with believers (translations which put 'Jesus is Lord' in inverted commas invite this interpretation) or as a simple testimony to unbelievers. But the context is one of trusting in the Lord and calling on his name (see v. 11–13), and the primary reference could therefore be to addressing Jesus himself as Lord (as Paul himself had done on the Damascus road – Acts 22:8, 10).

However, the two directions of such 'confession' are not mutually exclusive. Maybe Paul himself had a double application in mind. To confess Jesus as Lord to his face needs to be followed by the same confession in the face of others, especially those who do not believe it yet, though one day they will have to acknowledge his position (Phil 2:9–11). It is a common motif in the gospels and the epistles that our confessing a relationship with Christ before men and his confessing a relationship with us before his Father are inextricably linked (Mark 8:38; 2 Tim 2:11–13).

Confessing our recognition of his Lordship to Jesus himself is an act of faith that makes it possible to have his righteousness in our lives; confessing it to others is an act of faith that makes it very necessary! Such confession may be the very first real 'act' of faith a disciple takes, but it must not be the last.

FAITH IS PRACTICAL

We have already noted that faith is something we do rather than something we have (hence the New Testament preference for the verb rather than the noun). John records an interesting exchange between Jesus and the crowd – they asked him 'What must we do to do the works God requires?' and got the reply 'The work of God is this: to believe in the one he has sent' (John 6:28–29). A modern evangelical might have replied 'You mustn't even try to do any works; simply believe'! But that would be an over-simplification. To believe is to be 'obedient to the faith' (Acts 6:7). New Testament faith is very practical.

It is a great pity that the word 'works' has taken on such a negative connotation, especially so among those who build their theology largely, if not entirely, on Paul's teaching. The word is actually quite neutral, and takes on a positive or negative flavour only by association with other concepts. It is vital to realise that Paul usually refers to 'works of the law' and emphatically discourages any thought that these can bring merit (or even be properly achieved!), especially in relation to justification (acceptability to God). But though we cannot possibly be saved *by* such works (Eph 2:9), Paul is equally emphatic that we are saved *for* 'good works' (Eph 2:10). We can become so obsessed with the wrong concept of 'works of the law' that we become blind to the right place of 'works of love', 'good works' and, in the present discussion, 'works of faith'.

For the word 'works' simply means 'actions'. It refers to putting something into practice. It is in this sense that James rightly says that 'faith without works [actions] is dead' (Jas 2:20), that it is quite useless to save anyone! He is not contradicting Paul, but is complementing him, when he adds 'You see that a person is justified by what he does and not by faith alone' (Jas 2:24; quite wrongly thought to be in conflict with such texts as Gal 2:16). Paul is thinking about 'works of law'; James is thinking about 'works of faith'. The examples James chooses to illustrate his point (the prostitute Rahab and the patriarch Abraham) show that he is not even considering moral achievements. Both were risking their whole future because they trusted God (all this is fully developed in chapter 28). James is forcefully underlining the point he has made earlier in the same chapter – that credal confession by itself falls short of saving faith, if nothing is done about it. He points out that the demons are also sound monotheists yet are not believers (Jas 2:19)! Paul and James would agree that '*justification is by works of faith alone*'. It is faith in action that saves.

There is another New Testament writer who makes a profound contribution to our understanding of this practical aspect of faith: the anonymous author of the epistle to the Hebrews (see chapter 27 for the background and purpose of this unique letter). Hebrews 11 is a classic exposition of the nature of faith – not just what it is ('being sure of what we hope for and certain of what we do not see' – v. 1), but mostly what it does: translating the invisible into the visible, the future into the present, the heavenly into the earthly, the there-and-then into the here-and-now. The examples he takes are all 'works of faith', what men and women *did* because they trusted the Lord: Abel offered the right sacrifice; Enoch walked with God (all the way into heaven!); Noah built an ark; Abraham left his home for a tent at eighty years of age, made love to his elderly wife and was willing to kill his son; Isaac and Jacob both left property to their sons which was not yet theirs; Joseph made arrangements for his own funeral in a land he had not seen since his youth; Moses' parents risked their lives to hide their baby; Moses himself left a palace to lead his enslaved relatives into a trap between an army and the sea; Joshua marched round city walls; Rahab hid the spies; etc. Not a word about how they thought or felt about their faith, just what they did about it. Though all these examples are from Jewish history (appropriate for a letter to 'Hebrews'), they are models for Christian faith also – and, indeed, are waiting for Christians to catch them up (v. 40)! Their inward confidence in the future was proved by their outward conduct in the present.

In other words, faith is not just *accepting* the truth of God's word; it is *acting* on that truth. There is always an element of risk involved: if it is not true, there will be future loss; if it is true, there will be future gain. But the actions of trust and obedience must be maintained until faith turns into sight (note the wonderful statement in v. 13, 'All these people were still living by faith when they died'), which means that:

FAITH IS CONTINUAL

It is also of the essence of faith to *go on* acting on God's word, however long it may take for his promises to be fulfilled. That is why the same letter to the Hebrews continues by exhorting Christians to follow the example of Old Testament saints and 'run with *perseverance*', fixing their eyes on Jesus, the pioneer and perfecter of their faith (i.e. the one who starts if off and finishes it off), the one who went to and through the bitter end for the joy that lay beyond (Heb 12:1–2).

The emphasis on the continuity of faith begins in the Old Testament. When Habakkuk feared that the impending judgement of God in the form of a Babylonian invasion would fail to discriminate between the few righteous and the many wicked people in Israel, God assured him that 'the just shall live by faith' (Hab 2:4). The word translated 'faith' is not frequent in the Old Testament, and in every other context it means 'faithfulness, fidelity, keeping faith with someone' (the Hebrew word is *emunah*); it is something that is said to be 'broken' if it is not maintained. The word 'live' in this context means simply 'survive the coming judgement'. 'Just' refers to those whom God (not man) accounts as righteous in his sight. So we may paraphrase the text in Habakkuk: 'Those whom God accounts as righteous will survive the coming judgement by *keeping faith* in him.' The prophet himself was one of those who kept faith with the God of Israel throughout the disaster, even when the Babylonian invaders destroyed all the trees and animals, as was their ruthless custom (Hab 2:17; 3:17–18).

This 'golden text' of Habakkuk is frequently quoted in the New Testament (and became the rallying-cry of the Reformation, centuries later). When used by apostolic writers, the stress is always on the continuity of faith, keeping faith with God. It is for this reason that Paul quotes it ('by faith from first to last' or, more literally, 'from faith to faith' – Rom 1:17) and the author of Hebrews makes the same point ('and if he shrinks back', a nautical term for lowering sails – Heb 10:38).

As in the Hebrew language, so in the Greek – 'faith' and 'faithfulness' are exactly the same word (*pistis*). It is translated one way as a gift of the Spirit (1 Cor 12:9) and the other as a fruit of the Spirit (Gal 5:22). Indeed, it is sometimes difficult to know which to use, and the meaning has to be gauged from the context. To be full of faith is the same as being 'faithful'.

Another pointer to the continuity of faith is to be found in the Greek tenses used for the verb 'believe'. When the initial step of faith that inaugurates the life of a believer is referred to, the aorist tense is used, referring to a single event or moment (examples may be found in Acts 16:31; 19:2). But on many occasions the present tense is used, indicating a continuous action or present, as distinct from a past, condition. John is particularly fond of this second form: 'For God so loved the world that he gave his one and only Son, that whoever believes [i.e. *goes on* believing, or is believing *now*] in him shall not perish but have [i.e. here and now, not just in the future – see v. 36] eternal life' (John 3:16); 'The work of God is this: to believe [i.e. to *go on* believing, or to be believing] in the one he has sent' (John 6:29); 'But these are written that you may believe [i.e. *go on* believing, or be believing] that Jesus is the Christ, the Son of God, and that by [*going on*] believing you may have [i.e. go on having] life in his name' (John 20:31). (Note that this makes John's gospel more suitable for believers than unbelievers, since its aim is to keep readers in faith rather than bring them to faith, which explains why it was written later than the three synoptics.)

Paul never rested on his *past* step of faith on the Damascus road. In the middle of his pilgrimage he relied on a *present* faith: 'The life I am living in the body I am living by faith in the Son of God . . .' (Gal 2:20). At the end of his life he was able to claim 'I have kept the faith' (2 Tim 4:7). His teaching is full of warnings about the need to 'continue' in the faith (Acts 11:23; 14:22; Rom 11:22; 1 Cor 15:2; Col 1:23; 1 Tim 2:15). There is sad news of those who have 'wandered' from the faith (1 Tim 6:10, 21) and even 'shipwrecked' their faith (1 Tim 1:19). No wonder he exhorts the Corinthians to 'Examine yourselves to see whether you *are* [i.e. now] in the faith; test yourselves' (2 Cor 13:5).

The implication of this testimony is clear: true faith means 'keeping faith'. True faith is what we finish with, not what we start with. Justification may be ours in a moment of faith; sanctification and glorification are the results of a lifetime of faith. (The bearing of this on the 'once saved, always saved' notion will be discussed more fully in chapter 27, which considers the 'apostasy' passages in Hebrews, and in chapter 36, which asks when a person is 'saved'.)

Saving faith is not just a *step*; it is a *walk*, a series of steps stretching from this life into the next (1 Cor 13:13). Once a person has put their trust in the Lord Jesus Christ, the next step of faith is to be baptised in water . . .

4 BE BAPTISED IN WATER

The inclusion of baptism as an essential element in Christian initiation causes widespread uneasiness. Some fear that this emphasis on what is obviously a *human* act opens the door to 'salvation by works' and compromises the doctrine of 'justification by faith alone'. But, as we have already pointed out, they do not seem so worried about 'adding' repentance to faith or confession with the mouth. The truth is that the real disturbance over baptism lies deeper and is the more common concern about the 'necessity' of baptism.

The basic problem is that it is such a *physical* act, whereas Christian initiation is supposed to be essentially 'spiritual'. How can a material rite affect moral realities (or even represent them)? Of course, a moment's reflection will confirm that the other three elements all have some physical connections. Repentance may involve clothes (Luke 3:11), money (Luke 19:8) and books (Acts 19:19). Faith involves use of the mouth (Rom 10:10, which makes this 'essential' to being saved). Reception of the Spirit often comes through the laying-on of hands (Acts 8:17; 9:17; 19:6). But these three still 'feel' more spiritual than physical, whereas baptism 'feels' more physical than spiritual! But why should this be such a problem?

The inability to relate the physical to the spiritual is endemic to the Western world and stems from the roots of Occidental thinking in Greek philosophy, in which the separation of the physical and spiritual 'worlds' was fundamental. This profoundly affected Greek behaviour, leading to extremes of both indulgence and asceticism. It affected their beliefs, too, leading to the great debate as to whether the physical world was more 'real' (Aristotle) or the spiritual (Plato). In the West, 'secular' thought has followed Aristotle, while 'sacred' thought has followed Plato. This has led to an excessive 'spiritualising' in

Christianity (which has more in common with Eastern mysticism, by a strange irony). This kind of thinking lies behind the definition of a 'sacrament' as 'an outward and visible sign of an inward and spiritual grace'. So many see the water of baptism as a 'mere' symbol, whereas the 'real' part is entirely 'spiritual'. This separation between the 'outward' and 'inward' aspects even suggests the possibility of having the 'spiritual reality' of baptism without the physical rite.

There are those who sincerely believe that the New Testament itself fosters this dichotomy between the physical and spiritual 'worlds'. Picking up the prophetic emphasis on reality rather than ritual in the Old Testament (see, for example, Isa 58:6–7 and Hos 6:6), they see the climax of this trend in Jesus' indifference to external rites of cleansing (Mark 7:1–23) and his insistence on cleanliness of the heart. Similarly, the prophetic notion of heart-circumcision (Deut 10:6) is picked up by the apostle (Col 2:11). Above all, the epistle to the Hebrews contrasts the 'earthly' physical 'types' of the 'old' covenant (temples, altars, sacrifices, priesthood, vestments, incense, etc.) with the 'heavenly' spiritual 'anti-types' of the 'new' covenant. Surely, therefore, Christians should concentrate on the spiritual and leave the physical behind.

But this is not the whole truth about the 'new' covenant. The same Jesus who criticised ritual washing before meals commanded baptism for all his followers (Matt 28:19; see chapter 7). The same Paul who spoke of circumcision of the heart linked it to baptism (Col 2:11–12; see chapter 25). The same writer to the Hebrews spoke of the need to come to God with *bodies* washed in pure water (Heb 10:22; see chapter 27). For all of them were Jews, not Greeks. Hebrew thought never made the mistake of separating the spiritual and the physical, since the God who was Spirit created the material world, which was to be affirmed and enjoyed. The Bible condemns asceticism as heresy! Sexual relationships have spiritual significance (it is only in 'Greek' thinking that celibacy is regarded as a nobler state than marriage).

In scripture physical things are not only apt metaphors and appropriate analogies of spiritual things; the physical can be the actual means of communicating the spiritual. This principle held good from the very beginning, from the trees of life and knowledge in Eden, right through to the clay and spittle used by Jesus to cure blindness. It finds supreme expression in the incarnation itself, the Word made flesh. It was in his *body* that Jesus bore our sins on the tree (1 Pet 2:24), and it was the resurrection of his *body* that brought the hope of eternal life. No wonder Christianity has been called 'the most materialist of all the world religions' (a remark attributed to Archbishop William Temple).

It is not surprising to find that the Lord commanded his followers to engage in two physical acts, one to begin the life of a disciple and the other to continue it. Both would have profound effects. In relation to the Lord's Supper, Paul describes in detail the positive effects of 'communion' and the negative effects of 'condemnation' that can flow from this 'sacrament' (1 Cor 10–11).

Having quoted a 'Greek' definition of a 'sacrament', we will now attempt a 'Hebrew' one! It is *a physical event with a spiritual effect*. With this in mind, we can approach our study of baptism and its part in Christian initiation, asking four basic questions: where, how, why and when was it done?

WHERE WAS IT DONE?

Where did the practice originate? Who began it?

The idea of ritual cleansing is almost universal – from bathing the bridegroom before marriage, an ancient and widespread practice, to the obsessive hand-washing familiar to modern psychiatrists. But when did it become specifically religious, and what are the roots of the Christian rite?

It is unlikely that the roots of New Testament baptism will be found in pagan religion (though there may be a reference to such in the mention of baptism 'for the dead' in 1 Cor 15:29; see chapter 24). It is far more probable that the background is Jewish. Certainly the Old Testament contains details of ritual washings, particularly in connection with the priesthood. The prophets, too, looked forward to a deep cleansing of the people (note the 'clean water' of Ezek 36:25).

The ritual baths discovered in the Essene community at Qumran also bear witness to the place in at least one strand of Jewish tradition of regular cleansing by immersion; the proximity of this practice in both time and place to the ministry of John and Jesus is striking. However, while there may be an association of ideas, there is no evidence of any direct link, particularly in the minds of the people who were baptised in the Jordan. They did not see themselves separating from their society, but from their sins – in response to the first prophetic voice for centuries (note John's adoption of Elijah's manner of dress) and the announcement of the Messiah's imminent advent.

Many scholars have seen a precedent in Jewish 'proselyte' baptism, which developed in the Diaspora (the 'dispersion' of Jews outside their own country) as a means of preparing Gentile adherents for full membership of the Jewish people. But the earliest concrete evidence for the practice comes from the end of the first century AD, so we do not know whether it was already familiar in Jesus' day. In any case, there were real differences between this and Christian baptism. It was accompanied by circumcision; it was self-administered; it was administered to whole families but *not* to any babies born subsequently; and, above all, it was designed to remove racial defilement, not moral guilt. If it was already known before John the Baptist began his ministry, how offensive it must have been to demand it of *Jews*!

In spite of all this background, we shall not be misled if we regard baptism as an original practice introduced by John at the direct revelation and command of God, though one which would be easily understood against the back-cloth of all physical and spiritual cleansings with water.

The outstanding feature of John's preaching and practice of baptism was the strong emphasis on *moral* content. He announced the long-awaited news that the kingdom (rule, not realm) of God was on the verge of breaking into history, bringing such standards of righteousness to the affairs of men that the urgent prerequisites for citizenship were repentance and forgiveness. John understood the act of immersion (see the next section) in the Jordan river to be both the consummation of repentance and the communication of forgiveness (Matt 3:11; Mark 1:4; Luke 3:3).

The link between John's baptism and the later Christian practice is twofold. First, Jesus himself submitted to John, though for him it was an act of 'righteousness' rather than repentance (Matt 3:15). His submission and comment are a standing rebuke to any of his followers who consider it unnecessary! Second, Jesus himself continued to baptise others, after he began his own ministry. Indeed, at one time both John and Jesus were using the same river, a few miles apart, causing odious comparisons to be made between the respective numbers (John 3:22–26). Actually, Jesus did not do it himself, but left it to his disciples (probably for the same reason that Peter and Paul left it to their helpers – cf. John 4:2 with Acts 10:48 and 1 Cor 1:14–17).

Surprisingly, for most of Jesus' ministry there is no mention of any baptising, even when the twelve and the seventy are sent on missionary tours. However, it is right in the forefront of Jesus' final instructions to the apostles between his resurrection and ascension. His clear inclusion of it in the missionary mandate (Matt 28:19; cf. Mark 16:16) is more than an adequate explanation for its universal application in the early church. By then, as we shall see, the meaning of the practice had undergone considerable development, but the mode or method remained the same.

HOW WAS IT DONE?

Representations of John at the Jordan by Christian artists of later centuries have often portrayed candidates standing in water up to their knees, thighs or even waists, while John sprinkles a few drops from a scallop shell on their heads; the pictures are a compromise between the biblical record and later liturgical practice (immersion of the bottom half and affusion for the top half!). How important it is to read scripture without putting on the spectacles of tradition!

The New Testament makes it clear that the baptisms of John and the apostles were by total immersion in water ('submersion' might be a better word). John chose a particular stretch of the Jordan river precisely because of its adequate depth (John 3:23). Philip took the Ethiopian 'down into' the water (Acts 8:38). It has been objected that there would not be enough water in Jerusalem to baptise three thousand at once; this overlooks the pools of Bethesda and Siloam – and of course the biblical record does not claim they were all in the water at the same time!

The very word 'baptise' implies such total immersion. It had not, in New Testament days, become a *definitive* term for an ecclesiastical rite. It was an ordinary Greek word (*baptizein*) of a *descriptive* nature. It was used for the sinking of a ship (not its launching!), the dipping of a cup in a bowl of wine, the soaking of cloth in a vat of dye. It was used where in English we would say drench, dip, dunk, duck, douse, deluge or soak, sink, swamp, steep, saturate. It was also used more generally as a metaphor meaning to 'overwhelm'. That John was called 'the Baptist' was not because it was a title, much less the denominational label it has become; it was a descriptive nickname, meaning the Plunger, the Dipper (the same descriptive phrase was applied to Jesus as the 'baptiser' in Holy Spirit – John 1:33; so Jesus was as much a Baptist as John!).

For centuries this notion of baptism was understood. Even when baptism was later applied to babies (see Appendix 1), they were immersed (witness the dimensions of medieval fonts). Greek Orthodox churches still *immerse* infants (three times in the name of the Trinity!), perhaps because they know Greek! It is a tragedy that the word is rarely translated into an English equivalent in our Bible versions, but merely transliterated into English spelling. In fact, its meaning is now so technical that it has all but lost its original connotation. To talk about 'baptising by sprinkling' would make as much sense to a Greek as drawing a square circle or frying snow!

New Testament baptism needed water and 'lots of it'. But it

also needed *words*. In John's baptism, the candidate was required to make a verbal confession of particular sins (as was mentioned in chapter 2). In the apostles' baptism, the candidate was expected to 'call on' the name of Jesus. The baptiser was also required to baptise *into* his name (Acts 19:5). There does not seem to have been a fixed formula, such as is often insisted on today, but the inclusion of the name of 'Jesus' was the important thing (see chapter 7 for a discussion about the strange discrepancy between the trinitarian 'name' of Matt 28:19 and the 'unitarian' use of the name of Jesus throughout Acts).

Finally, as regards mode, while baptism was never self-administered, its effectiveness seems to have depended much more on the spiritual state of the baptised than the baptiser (Jesus was baptised by someone who was not himself baptised – Matt 3:14).

WHY WAS IT DONE?

We have already noted that John's baptism was intended to consummate repentance and communicate forgiveness. This twofold purpose was clearly carried forward into Christian baptism (Acts 2:39). But a new emphasis was added after the death, burial and resurrection of Jesus.

Baptism is a bath for those who are dirty

It is for the washing away of sins (Acts 22:16, Eph 5:26, Heb 10:22). Its cleansing action is inward rather than outward, of the conscience rather than the body (1 Pet 3:21). Even this language is moving beyond John's understanding. But a whole new dimension is added with the following concept.

Baptism is a burial for those who are dead

The necessary prelude to baptism is to 'put off the flesh' as Jesus did, to be crucified with him; this is the 'circumcision' made without hands to which Paul refers (Col 2:9–12; see chapter 25). The 'burial' in water is the vital link between the believer's death to his old life and his resurrection to new life

(Rom 6:4; Col 2:12; 1 Pet 3:21). How appropriate to this meaning is the act of total immersion – submerging and emerging, buried and raised (all other modes concentrate attention on the bath rather than the burial aspect).

It is very noticeable that in most of the references to baptism in the New Testament, the language is instrumental rather than symbolic. It is not just like a bath; it *is* a bath. It is not just like a burial; it *is* a burial. The 'sign' actually accomplishes what it signifies. When baptism is thought of as a 'mere' symbol, pointing to a spiritual reality outside itself, that opens the way to thinking that it can point to something that can 'happen' at another time, either some time before the baptism (in the case of believers) or a long time afterwards (in the case of babies). (One of the best books on this 'instrumental' understanding of baptism is G. R. Beasley-Murray's *Baptism in the New Testament* (Eerdmans, 1962), though he does not distinguish water-baptism from Spirit-baptism too clearly.)

But the New Testament language is *coincidental* as well as instrumental, describing what actually happens at the time of the baptism itself. This puts the emphasis on the *divine* activity in baptism rather than on the human act. To see it only as an 'act of obedience' or 'testimony' (a kind of wet witness) is to miss its essential purpose. It is a 'means of grace', a means of *saving* grace. The New Testament writers do not hesitate to use the word 'save' in connection with baptism (Mark 16:16; Acts 2:40–41; 1 Pet 3:21 – this last being the strongest statement of all, with its assertion that 'baptism now saves you'). In this 'bath of regeneration' (Tit 3:5; see chapter 26) a person is 'born of water' (John 3:5; see chapter 10).

No wonder that the apostles associated the act with some of the great redeeming events in previous history. Peter saw a type of Christian baptism in Noah's flood, in that he and seven of his near relatives were separated from their old evil environment by the water (1 Pet 3:20; see chapter 29). Paul saw the crossing of the Red Sea as a type of Christian baptism (1 Cor 10:1–2) – it is tempting to draw the conclusion that what passing through that water meant to the Jew in relation to

Pharaoh, passing through baptism means to the Christian in relation to Satan (certainly, after baptism 'sin has no more dominion' – Rom 6:11–14). It is the sacrament of breaking with the past and making a clean start.

Some readers will find all this rather difficult to accept, and will no doubt suspect me of teaching the dreaded doctrine of 'baptismal regeneration'. But the fear of this distortion can reduce the rite to a mere symbol. The error is avoided by remembering that the New Testament nowhere implies that baptism achieves any of the above results in and of itself (the technical description for this mechanical, even magical, view is the Latin phrase *ex opere operato*). Only in certain spiritual conditions is baptism 'effective'. The water by itself can do nothing more than wash dirt off the body. It is the power of God through his Spirit in response to human repentance and faith which enables the physical act to have such a spiritual effect. Which brings us by a simple progression of thought to our final question.

WHEN WAS IT DONE?

When were people baptised in the days of the apostles? The simple answer is: as soon as they could convince others that they had truly repented and believed. It could therefore happen on the same day as they first heard the gospel (Acts 10:48), or even the same night (Acts 16:33).

Of course, human judgment was involved in this, and the occasional mistake was made (Acts 8:13), though it was firmly corrected as soon as it was discovered (Acts 8:18–23). The important thing is that proof rather than profession was the criterion for gauging repentance (Acts 26:20). However, whereas repentance was the only condition required for John's baptism, Christian baptism required faith in the Lord Jesus Christ as well (Acts 19:4–5).

From this perspective, the spiritual state of the candidate was a far more important factor than the amount of water or form of words used in the rite, since without this penitent faith it was ineffective for man and unacceptable to God (if baptism shares the same sacramental character as the Lord's Supper, it could even be positively harmful if administered to an impenitent unbeliever). It is therefore a *voluntary* step to be taken by morally responsible people (1 Pet 3:21; see chapter 29). There can be no *vicarious* repentance or faith in the case of personal salvation. Every individual must make his own response to the gospel and his own request for baptism (notice that 'each one of you' qualifies both 'repent' and 'be baptised' in Acts 2:38; see chapter 15).

This explains the unusual use of the middle voice of the verb 'baptise' (for example, in Acts 22:16). The active voice would mean 'Baptise yourself.' The passive voice would mean 'Be baptised.' The middle voice means 'Get yourself baptised' (i.e. by someone else). While it is done by others, it is decided by *one's self*. Both the will and the conscience of the individual are involved. Baptism is a conscious and a conscientious action.

'INFANT' BAPTISM

All of which inevitably raises the question of baptising 'infants' (it would clarify the debate to use the word 'baby' rather than 'infant', making it quite clear that the issue is about those who are quite incapable of repenting or believing for themselves – indeed, quite incapable of committing the sins which baptism washes away!). The question will be dealt with more fully under other heads (see chapters 15, 19, 34 and Appendix 1); here we are only concerned with the New Testament references to baptism.

Most scholars accept that there is no explicit record of the baptism of a baby (of either believing or unbelieving parents) in the New Testament, either by John the Baptist or the early church. Many go on to explain this 'silence' by saying that this was the 'first generation' of Christians, who would all be *adult* converts. However, it is inconceivable that none of those first converts were parents or even grandparents, that none of the thousands who flocked to John at the Jordan or to the apostles at Pentecost had any family! The silence becomes deafening.

However, there is more positive evidence that babies were not included. It is said of John's baptism that it was for repentance and that candidates confessed their sins – neither of which could possibly apply to babies. At Pentecost it is specifically stated that those who were baptised were those who 'received the word' (Acts 2:41; exactly the same language is used of the 'households' that were baptised – see chapter 19 for a detailed study).

Other passages have been used as indirect evidence for the inclusion of babies. Peter's claim that the 'promise is for you and your children' is, however, a reference to Spirit-baptism, not water-baptism, and is clearly qualified by the reception of and response to a divine call and is equally offered to 'all who are far off' (Acts 2:39; see chapter 15). Paul tells a believing wife that her 'children . . . are holy' (1 Cor 7:14; see chapter 22); but by the same token, so is the unbelieving husband, and the context of Paul's statement is the topic of divorce, not baptism. Children are addressed in the epistles of Paul as 'in the Lord' (Eph 6:1; Col 3:20); but they are clearly old enough to be faced with moral responsibility.

Most scholars admit that there is no direct evidence for the baptism of babies in the New Testament; but some want to make the opposite point, that there is nothing against it either. However, that is not the case. The problem is that it is impossible to apply the New Testament theory of baptism (i.e. its meaning and significance as outlined above) to babies without the practice becoming at best merely symbolic (of future hopes) or at worst downright superstitious (saving the baby from hell), with the mildly sentimental somewhere in between (the baby's 'coming out ceremony'). To see it as a bath to wash away sins or as the burial of a sinner requires a faith that goes beyond the words of scripture. For the simple fact is that the New Testament language about baptism *cannot* be applied to the baptism of babies as it stands. Either its conditions or its effects have to be severely modified or even discarded in order to 'fit' it to the situation of the newly born.

The real grounds for baptising babies are theological rather than textual (as we seek to make clear in Appendix 1). What happens is this: a biblical concept, which may be valid within its own context, is exalted into a principle that is used to interpret matters beyond its proper sphere. The three doctrines which have been used in this way (on which see Appendix 1 for a fuller explanation) are those of original sin, hereditary covenant and prevenient grace – not one of which is directly related to baptism in the New Testament (baptism is for the cleansing of actual sins, not original sin; it is for those who are born of the Spirit, not for those born of the flesh; it is the sacrament of appropriated grace, not the symbol of prevenient grace).

WHAT IT CANNOT DO

Baptism marks the end of the old life and the beginning of a new life, the death of a sinner and the birth of a saint, the burial of the old man and the resurrection of the new man. It is the 'bath of regeneration', bringing about not just a new start in life but a new life to start with!

But such talk can raise hopes too high! Many have anticipated that their baptism would not only enable them to *start* the new life clean but also to stay *clean*, that it would deal with their future as well as their past, that it would prove to be 'the double cure' from the dominion as well as the defilement of sin. The first sin we commit after baptism is terribly traumatic! Have I undone my baptism? Will I need another baptism? Was I really ready for it? Actually, we probably just need our feet washing (John 13:10)!

The real situation is that water-baptism was not designed to do all this for us. It can deal with our past, but not our future. We need to remember that John the Baptist recognised the limitations of water-baptism. He recognised the need for power as well as purity. By revelation he knew that another 'baptism' was required – and that it would very shortly be available. He even knew who would be the one to administer it. His prophetic insight comprehended the twofold ministry of the Messiah, to 'take away the sin of the world' (John 1:29) and to 'baptise' in the Holy Spirit' (John 1:33) – and the person to do this was his own cousin, Jesus!

Every believer needs to receive *both* baptisms, one from a Christian and the other from Christ. In the one we receive the gift of God's Son in his death, burial and resurrection; in the other we receive the gift of God's Spirit in his power and purity. The Levitical priests of the old covenant were consecrated by being washed in water and anointed with oil (Exod 29:4,7; Lev 8:6,12). In the new covenant all God's people are priests and need this dual consecration. From our study of the 'washing' we turn to consider the 'anointing'.

5 RECEIVE THE HOLY SPIRIT

Though the early believers never used the name 'Christian' of themselves, they would probably not have considered it appropriate for anyone until they had received the Holy Spirit. 'Christ' means 'anointed one' and it originated in the practice of anointing a new king with oil (in our own coronation service, this particular part is still known as 'the Chrism'). Biblically, oil was a symbol of the Spirit of God, so the expected Messiah, the 'Anointed One' (Ps 2:2 is the only explicit use of the phrase), the Christ (Greek: *christos*), would be anointed by the Spirit (Isa 61:1). Jesus was recognised as the Christ (by Peter, in Matt 16:16; by Martha, in John 11:27).

By a natural extension, his followers were nicknamed 'Christians'; but it is significant that this first happened in a Gentile city (Antioch), where they were first perceived as a new religion (whose 'god' was called 'Christ') rather than as a Jewish sect (as had been the case in Jerusalem).

However, had the disciples adopted this term for themselves, as later generations clearly did, it would almost certainly have deepened in meaning. Instead of just signifying 'a follower of the anointed one', it would have conveyed the further thought of 'an anointed follower of the anointed one', or, literally, someone who had been 'Christ-ened' (in modern terms, christened!). For it was fundamental to the gospel that the One anointed by the Spirit would then anoint others, thus multiplying his ministry through them (Matt 3:11; Mark 1:8; Luke 3:16; John 1:33; esp. John 14:12). Had the early church used the word 'christening', they would have applied it not to water-baptism, as is customary today, but to Spirit-baptism. It would have brought the fourth stage of initiation to mind, not the third.

The reception of the Spirit may also be considered a 'confirmation', as well as a 'christening'! The apostles Peter, John and Paul were not content with a response to the gospel until the Holy Spirit was received (see chapter 16 on Acts 8 and chapter 20 on Acts 19). They were not content because they were not convinced! The gift of the Spirit, received in an audible and visible manner, was the divine 'confirmation', the proof, that the penitent, baptised believer had been accepted by God and now belonged to him. The 'charismatic' experience of Paul's Corinthian converts, which had released all the spiritual gifts among them, was regarded by him as the 'confirmation' of his preaching, as well as of their conversion (1 Cor 1:6–7). Thus, the possession of the Spirit was the mark of the Christian (see chapter 21 on Rom 8:9), the visible seal of divine ownership (see below), the basic ground of assurance (1 John 3:24; 4:13). It was fundamental to entrance into the kingdom (see chapter 10 on John 3:5) and to living in the 'new' covenant (2 Cor 3).

The reception of the Spirit needs to be studied from three points of view. First, it must be clearly distinguished from the other three components of initiation. Second, the variety of language used about it needs to be surveyed. Third, it is necessary to ask exactly how this occurs in the individual disciple's experience.

ITS DISTINCTIVE NECESSITY

It is absolutely vital to notice that in the New Testament the reception of the Spirit is *never* identified or confused with repentance, faith or water-baptism. All four are quite distinct, and all four are needed.

Few confuse repentance with reception of the Spirit

It seems obvious in scripture that the one is a prelude to the other. It is necessary to get *sins* out of the way before the *Holy* Spirit can take up residence. Conversely, it is dangerous to clear out evil without filling the vacuum that is left (Matt 12:43–45)!

Thus, the ministry of John the Baptist is misunderstood if seen as complete in itself, even though he brought many through repentance for their sins to an experience of real forgiveness in water-baptism (Mark 1:4). Recognising the inadequacy of his ministry, he clearly pointed his disciples to a Spirit-baptism so different that he himself could not give it to them. However, there is never a hint that this superior baptism, administered by a far superior baptiser, would render repentance or water-baptism obsolete.

Many confuse faith with reception of the Spirit

'Believing in Jesus' and 'receiving the Spirit' are so widely assumed to be synonymous (and therefore simultaneous) that the two phrases, always distinct in the New Testament, have been run together in most evangelistic appeals, exhorting the hearers to 'receive Jesus'. It is presumed without question that anyone who has 'received Jesus' has also and automatically 'received the Spirit', whether this was accompanied by any conscious experience and outward evidence or not! But this thinking is contrary to New Testament teaching in two major respects:

First, *it is obvious that on a number of occasions 'believing' and 'receiving' were not simultaneous and are therefore not synonymous.* It is accepted that this was the case with the twelve apostles, for instance. Clearly, they believed in Jesus some years before receiving the Spirit (John 7:39; note that 'believed' is an aorist participle, indicating here a once-for-all step of faith already taken). However, this case is often dismissed because it was 'pre-Pentecost'; they could not receive the Spirit when they believed because 'he was not yet (given)'. This argument would be valid were there no 'post-Pentecost' examples, but this is not the case. There were, in fact, a number of later situations in which people 'believed' some time before they 'received'. The clearest example is Samaria, where people 'believed' (aorist tense again) without 'receiving' (Acts 8:17). Some have tried to get round this by questioning whether their 'believing' was 'full' Christian faith; but Luke never says this, and neither Peter nor John made any corrections on this score. Others point out the unique circumstances that can explain the 'delay', but that does not begin to answer the real questions raised by this incident (for example, how did anyone know that they had not received?). The fact remains that their 'believing' and 'receiving' *were* separated in time (see chapter 16 for a fuller examination of this event). Even *one* case of such a separation *after* Pentecost would be sufficient to uphold the distinction, but there are others in the book of Acts, notably at Ephesus (see chapter 20). Paul's own question to the 'disciples' there, 'Did you receive the Holy Spirit when you believed?' (Acts 19:2; aorist participle again), reveals that he himself understood that they could be distinguished from each other, both in thought and experience. While it is true that he subsequently discovered that even their faith was deficient, the implications of his original question remain valid. And the 'fuller' faith to which he brought them *before* baptising them into the name of Jesus was still not the same as receiving the Spirit, which happened *after* their baptism. This sequence of faith–baptism–reception seems to have been the usual pattern for most of the New Testament disciples (see chapter 27 on Heb 6:1–6; the *sole* recorded exception was Cornelius' household, where the sequence was faith–reception–baptism – see chapter 18).

Second, the phrase 'receive Jesus' was never *used in apostolic evangelism.* Its almost universal usage today is assumed to be scriptural, but is based on a superficial reading rather than a careful study. There is a definite change in the application of the word 'receive' between the four gospels on the one hand and the Acts and epistles on the other, corresponding to the pre-Easter and post-Pentecost periods. Few seem to have noticed this shift, though it has profound theological significance, as well as historical interest. While the Son of God was here on earth, in the flesh and among 'his own' people, he was rejected by many but 'received' by some; those who thus received him were given the 'authority' (*exousia*, not yet the power, *dunamis*, for that was not available before Pentecost) to be God's children, since their receiving/believing meant that they had been 'born of God' (John 1:11–13; note carefully the *aorist* tenses of the verbs, which limit the statement to the historical period of the incarnation). The word 'receive' continues to be used of Jesus, both by himself and about himself, during the remainder of his ministry (e.g. John 5:43). However, after his ascension into heaven and his sending of 'another' person to take his place on earth, the verb 'receive' is consistently transferred from the second person of the Trinity to the third, the Holy Spirit (Acts 2:38; 8:17; 10:47; 19:2; 1 Cor 2:12; Gal 3:2; etc.).

There are only two apparent exceptions to this 'rule'. Jesus on one occasion stated that receiving one of his apostles would be equivalent to receiving himself, which in turn would be equivalent to receiving the one (his Father) for whom Jesus had been an 'apostle', a 'sent-one' (John 13:20; the verb *apostellein*, 'to send', and the noun *apostolos*, 'sent-one', are virtually the same). Since this was said on the last night of his life, it presumably referred to the post-Pentecost mission of the apostles. But it is important to note that he is not saying 'Whoever believes the gospel is receiving me', but 'Whoever receives you as persons is welcoming me, for you are my representatives' (a principle Jesus had already expounded in relation to the final judgement – Matt 25:31–46). Paul was to discover the negative side of this truth when he persecuted the church (Acts 9:4). The text does not equate 'believing' and 'receiving' and does not mention the Holy Spirit at all.

The other 'exception' is in Paul's exhortation to the Colossians: 'So then, just as you received Christ Jesus as Lord, continue to live [lit. 'to walk'] in him, rooted and built up in him, strengthened in the faith as you were taught, and over-flowing with thankfulness' (Col 2:6–7). The first thing to note is that this is not in the context of evangelising unbelievers but of edifying believers; there is no record of Paul, or any other apostles, exhorting a sinner to 'receive' the Saviour. More significant is the word translated 'received'; it is not the simple Greek word *lambanein* ('to receive'), but *paralambanein*, a compound verb with a prefix meaning 'beside'. To 'beside-receive' was a less direct word, meaning to receive through someone else – to hear about someone, to be taught about someone, to be given insight or information concerning them. This 'indirect' reception fits Paul's point and the context of his remark exactly. He is reminding the Colossians of the original instruction they had 'received' about the implications of daily life lived in the Lordship of Jesus Christ. If they were to remain 'in him', that original teaching must be maintained and applied or their relationship with him would deteriorate, especially if they listened to other philosophies (v. 8). This indirect verb for 'receive' is also used in a passage considered earlier (John 1:11–12; here those 'who did not receive' [*paralambanein*], indicating those who had *heard* about him but not met him personally – probably referring to the priests and national leaders – are distinguished from those who did receive [*lambanein*], indicating those who had direct personal contact with Jesus).

We conclude that there is no post-Pentecost ground for using the term 'receiving Jesus' of Christian initiation. In its use today, it should be regarded as a misleading equivalent of 'believing in Jesus', but it should not be understood to encompass 'receiving the Spirit'. Much confusion of thought and experience has resulted from this amalgam of two quite distinct entities. In 'believing' the primary reference is to human activity; in 'receiving' it is to divine activity. In 'normal' initiation one precedes water-baptism and the other follows it.

Some confuse water-baptism with reception of the Spirit

Those who rightly want to give baptism its full sacramental significance (rather than a mere symbolism) are particularly prone to this error. Correctly perceiving regeneration as the end of the old life and the beginning of the new, water-baptism (which has primary reference to the past) and Spirit-baptism (which has primary reference to the future) are run together into a single event and experience. The close conjunction of 'water-and-Spirit' in Jesus' own teaching on the new birth has probably encouraged this mistake (see chapter 10). Paul's habit of using the verb 'baptised' (e.g. Gal 3:27) and the noun 'baptism' (e.g. Eph 4:5) without further qualification has led a few scholars to imagine that the apostle himself had rolled the two baptisms into one. However, two pieces of New Testament evidence point in the opposite direction.

First, there is no record of anyone receiving the Spirit *during* their baptism in water. Once it was just *before* (Acts 10:47). Usually, however, it was just *after* (e.g. Acts 19.6), though once it was long after (Acts 8:16). This pattern followed the experience of Jesus himself, who 'received' after he came up out of the water (Matt 3:16).

Second, the New Testament clearly teaches that it is possible to have one baptism without the other. Those who have received the Spirit also need to be baptised in water (like Cornelius and his household); those who have been baptised in water also need to receive the Spirit (like the Samaritans). Neither renders the other obsolete.

This said, there does seem to be a real link between the two. Water-baptism usually, though not invariably, led on to Spirit-baptism. When Paul discovered that the Ephesian disciples had not received the Spirit, he immediately suspected the validity of their water-baptism (Acts 19:3; see chapter 20)! Perhaps the connection may be found in the concept of resurrection. As the death and burial of Jesus led to his emergence from the grave by the power of the Spirit (Rom 8:11), so the burial of a penitent believer in the watery grave of baptism may be expected to lead into an experience of resurrection life by that same power of the Spirit (this note is clearly sounded in such passages as Rom 6:3–4; Col 2:9–12 – see chapter 25; 1 Pet 3:18–22 – see chapter 29). As the death, burial and resurrection of Jesus present an integrated whole in the gospel, so water-baptism and Spirit-baptism belong together in the response to that gospel, though in both cases the parts are not identified or confused with each other.

But what exactly is 'Spirit-baptism'? We can begin to answer that question by considering the words used in the New Testament to describe it.

ITS DESCRIPTIVE NUANCE

If the vocabulary used to describe the reception of the Spirit is anything to go by, it must be a very rich experience indeed! Many metaphors and similes are used, in addition to straight-forward nouns and verbs. Before any are studied in detail, it cannot be too strongly emphasised that the words are descriptive (which expand our understanding) rather than definitive (which limit the meaning). They need to be treated as dynamic rather than doctrinal terms, to be appreciated existentially in life rather than intellectually in logic. The verbs are more vivid, but we shall begin with the nouns.

Promise

This is the word that links prophecy to fulfilment. It affirms an event that has been predicted and is therefore to be expected. Above all, it indicates an example of God's trustworthiness in keeping his word. Since the Bible contains over seven hundred separate predictions (over eighty per cent of which have already been fulfilled!), the word plays a large role in scripture and has even been claimed as the key to Old Testament theology. Luke uses the noun on the day of Pentecost, for the experience of both the 120 and the 3,000 (Acts 2:33, 39). The Holy Spirit was of course promised by Jesus himself, both before his death (John 7:37–39) and after his resurrection (Acts 1:5). But he was only repeating a promise already made by his Father (Luke 24:49) centuries earlier through the prophets of Israel (supremely in Joel 2:28–29; but also in Isa 32:15; Ezek 36:27 and elsewhere). Indeed, Paul hints that this outpouring of the Spirit was implicit in the promise made to Abraham, right at the beginning (Gal 3:14)!

Gift

Closely linked to 'promise' (often in the same context – Acts 1:4), this word underlines both the divine source and gratuitous nature of the outpoured Spirit. It cannot be earned, bargained for or worked for; it can only be 'received' with gratitude (or refused!). Scholars have argued about the significance of the genitive in Acts 2:38 – whether the 'of' means the gift consisting of the Holy Spirit or the gift communicated by the Holy Spirit; the former seems more likely (cf. Acts 10:45 and 11:17) and thus the gift *of* the Spirit himself then releases the other gifts *from* the Spirit (1 Cor 1:7). The 'charisma' (singular) of the Spirit brings the 'charismata' (plural). There is an interesting conjunction of phrases in the epistle to the Hebrews, 'tasted the heavenly gift . . . shared in the Holy Spirit' (6:4; see chapter 27), which emphasises the experiential nature of the gift.

Deposit

The Greek word (*arrabon*) is variously translated: 'earnest, pledge, foretaste, instalment, guarantee, first-fruits' are just some of the alternatives. It is of course a commercial term. Today it would be used primarily about money and describes the first down-payment which secures a total purchase (hence 'deposit'). In New Testament times it was more generally used of goods and represented the first delivery of an extensive order, as a guarantee that the rest was on its way (hence 'earnest'). Both applications would be covered by the phrase 'first instalment'. Paul uses the word three times (Rom 8:23; 2 Cor 1:22; Eph 1:14).

As 'promise' gives the gift a *past* reference, 'deposit' turns it to the *future*. To receive the Spirit is only just the beginning! Not only will there be *more* to have on earth; there will be *much* more in heaven. In fact, living in the Spirit is a foretaste of heaven! One sign of this is the joy that expresses itself in music (Eph 5:18–20). Another is the fellowship experienced by the people of God with each other and with him. Yet another is the increasing knowledge of God's mind and heart (through words of wisdom, knowledge, prophecy and interpretation).

Renewal

Used only once of 'receiving the Spirit' (Tit 3:5; see chapter 26), 'renewal' is an illuminating word, speaking of returning something to its original condition, restoring that which has been lost. The Bible teaches that the image of God in man has been marred and that the influence of the Spirit can be removed (Gen 6:3; note that universal violence was the result). It is through the Spirit that the image is now in the process of being restored (2 Cor 3:17–18). The process begins when the Spirit is 'poured out' upon us (see below).

From these nouns, we now turn to a consideration of the verbs.

Given/Received

These two words simply correspond to the noun 'gift', though the first describes God's side of the event and the second man's. 'Received' is not entirely passive, however; there is an active co-operation required in accepting this gift, as there is in all giving and receiving (see chapter 13, on John 20:22, and chapter 35).

If anything, the verb 'given' is used more widely than the noun 'gift' (see Acts 8:19; 11:17; 15:8; Rom 5:5; 2 Cor 1:22; 5:5; 1 John 3:24; 4:13). One of the features which makes the word of God 'living and active' is this more frequent use of verbs than nouns, which tend to be too 'static' – and the even rarer use of adjectives (cf. 1 Cor 13:4–7; 'love' is not just something you *have*, but something you *do!*).

Baptised

This is sometimes used as a synonym for 'received' (cf. Acts 10:47 with 11:16). The noun 'baptism' is *never* used of the reception of the Spirit (unlike modern Pentecostal preaching); only the verb 'baptised' is used, followed by the preposition 'in' (Greek: *en*) and the words 'Holy Spirit' (in the dative case *pneumati* and without the definite article 'the' – for the significance of this last point, see Appendix 2). The whole phrase 'baptised in Holy Spirit' is used by John the forerunner, Jesus himself and the apostle Paul (see chapter 23 for the reasons why 1 Cor 12:13 is believed to contain this exact phrase, though most English translations obscure it by translating '*en*' with 'by', making the Spirit the agent rather than the medium of the baptism).

All baptisms require an *agent* (who does the baptising), a *medium* (in which the baptising is done) and a *purpose* (for which it is done). As John was the 'agent' of water-baptism, Jesus is the 'agent' of Spirit-baptism; hence both are given the title 'the baptist' or 'the baptiser' (Greek: *ho baptizon* – Matt 3:1; John 1:33). But the title is descriptive rather than denominative!

The medium was quite different: 'in water' and 'in Holy Spirit'. But the action was similar. The significance of the word 'baptised' is the same in both cases. David Watson, in his *One in the Spirit* (Hodder & Stoughton, 1973), p. 68, puts it very clearly:

> *The term 'baptism' or 'baptise' is a rich word, and in secular literature it meant 'plunge, sink, drown, drench, overwhelm'.* A person could be overwhelmed (lit, baptised) by debts, sorrow, calamity; or overcome (lit, baptised) by wine or sleep. Euripides in the Orestes uses *bapto* when water is splashing into a ship, but *baptizo* when the ship is water-logged or sinks.

It would certainly be the most natural word for the New Testament writers to use, in view of the experiences described in the book of Acts.

The purpose of the two baptisms was quite different. The one is concerned with purity, with starting clean in the Christian life, cut off from a past that is now dead and buried. The other is concerned with power (Acts 1:8; 10:38), not just to continue the Christian life (2 Tim 1:6), but to take an active role as a member of the body of Christ (1 Cor 12:13) and, above all, to be a witness to Jesus in the whole world (Acts 1:8). Note that the purpose of a baptism is expressed in the preposition 'into' (Greek: *eis*); John's baptism was 'into repentance' (Matt 3:11), Christian water-baptism is 'into the name of Jesus' (Acts 19:5) and Spirit-baptism is 'into one body' (1 Cor

12:13; but see chapter 23 for an explanation that 'into' means 'consummation of' rather than 'introduction to').

Filled

Again, the equivalent noun 'fullness' is never used in the New Testament and can be misleading when it is used today. That 'filled with' is synonymous with 'baptised in' is clear from textual comparison (cf. Acts 1:5 with 2:4, for example). Yet there is a difference of flavour. 'Baptised' has an initiatory nuance; it seems to have been used only once in any individual's experience, of their first 'filling' (no one is said to have repeated 'baptisms' in the Spirit). 'Filled', however, is used of subsequent outpourings of the Spirit (e.g. Acts 4:31). In fact, Paul's exhortation to 'be filled with the Spirit' (Eph 5:18) uses the present continuous tense, the preposition 'in' and lacks the definite article – so should be translated 'Go on being filled in Spirit', clearly implying a continual state. 'Baptised' could not be used in this sense, since it refers to a single, initial event.

However, there is another development of the word. A person who has been 'filled' at his initiation (i.e. 'baptised') and has gone on 'being filled' since then deserves to be described as 'full' of Spirit (e.g. Acts 6:3). This form does carry overtones of maturity and sanctification, but is still primarily concerned with power (Acts 6:8); though a person who goes on being filled will produce the fruit as well as the gifts of the Spirit (Gal 5:22–23).

The absence of the definite article 'the' in 'filled with Holy Spirit' centres thought on the subjective power rather than the objective person of the Spirit (again, see Appendix 2). In other words, 'filled' puts the emphasis on his empowering rather than his indwelling.

Finally, 'filled' usually implies an 'overflow'. We shall pick up this aspect later in the chapter. It is sufficient to mention here that wherever the word is used in the New Testament it is followed by an obvious outpouring *from* those who have experienced an outpouring *on* themselves. If the event itself is first 'inward', it always resulted in 'outward' consequences, invariably of a vocal character, as we shall see later (even the exhortation to 'be (being) filled' in Eph 5:18 has in mind the objective of overflowing in 'psalms and hymns and spiritual songs').

Drink

Another 'fluid' word(!), 'drink' was used by Jesus (John 7:37–39) and Paul (1 Cor 12:13) in connection with 'receiving' the Spirit. If 'baptised' conveys the idea of external immersion, 'drink' suggests an internal imbibing. There is also a subtle shift from passive submission to another's action (being submerged) to an active co-operation of one's own activity (swallowing). It is always used in the aorist tense (the single event), never in the present (a continued action) – which links the word to 'baptised' rather than 'filled'. There is therefore no thought of going on drinking in the Spirit. One good draught primes the pump, so to speak! After the drink, spring water continues to flow from within the person (John 4:14; 7:38; see chapter 11). Having *once* been filled from the outside, one can *continue* to be filled from the inside. The Spirit has come in to dwell.

Fall on, come upon, poured out upon

All these dramatic terms come from the Old Testament (probably from the Greek 'Septuagint' version, so called because it was reputedly the work of *seventy* Hebrew scholars) and have a long history behind them. They indicate the sudden appearance of 'charismatic' activity, usually of a prophetic nature.

Luke is particularly fond of these terms and uses them interchangeably with 'received', 'baptised' and 'filled' (Acts 1:8; 2:17, 33; 8:16; 10:44, 45; 11:15; 19:6). Paul also occasionally used them in the same context of initiation (Rom 5:5; Tit 3:6).

They indicate the external source of this experience (as did 'drink'). This means that it has no connection whatever with meditative techniques to release the 'divine' spirit believed by some to be embodied in human nature from birth (John 1:9 refers to the light embodied in the Word, external to but exposing the darkness in 'every man'). The phrases also point to a source in heaven rather than on earth. The experience is both external and eternal.

Finally, we note the dramatic overtones – of something sudden rather than gradual, extraordinary rather than everyday, displayed rather than hidden. Outpourings usually make a splash!

Seal

This vivid metaphor, again taken from the world of commerce (as was 'deposit'), is simple to understand. It is a visible and indelible mark, placed on purchased goods to indicate to other customers that they already belong to another buyer. Today it is used more in connection with documents, as a token that an agreement or transaction has been completed and cannot be altered. While the modern usage is not inappropriate (e.g. in Eph 4:30), the ancient meaning provides the better understanding. Paul is primarily concerned with the clear evidence that faith has been acceptable to God (Eph 1:13). Not surprisingly, he links the word closely to his other commercial metaphors (Eph 1:14; 2 Cor 1:22). John may be using the same concept in his gospel (John 3:34; 6:27).

Anoint

With this word, we have come full circle to the opening paragraphs of the chapter. The word was used of Jesus and by Jesus in connection with his own reception of the Spirit (Luke 4:18; Acts 10:38). Since he was to give the Spirit to others as well as receive the Spirit himself, the word 'anoint' is naturally extended to believers when they share his experience (2 Cor 1:21; 1 John 2:27). As we have said, this 'anointing' is a true 'christening' as the 'sealing' is a true 'confirmation'.

All the words we have examined point to a rich and deep experience of a dynamic kind. Now emphasising the divine and then the human, now the momentary and then the continual, now the external and then the internal, now the personal and then the impersonal – the New Testament writers appear to have ransacked the dictionary for an adequate presentation of the many facets of receiving the Spirit in power. But what exactly is the event in itself? How does it happen and how does anyone know it has happened?

ITS DEFINITIVE NATURE

It is surely inconceivable that an event described in the language just examined could happen to a person without them or anyone else being aware of it! To claim that such terminology could be used where not even the person most affected was conscious of anything happening is to rob language of meaning and reduce it to the level of absurdity.

Yet this is precisely the outlook of those who consider that 'believing in Jesus' and 'receiving the Spirit' are one and the same thing. Since in many, if not most, 'conversions' today there is a total absence of any charismatic manifestation, it is widely (and hopefully!) assumed that the Spirit has been received automatically (and sub-consciously!). To draw the apostolic conclusion that such have believed but not yet received would create such a mountain of pastoral problems that the issue dare not be faced. It is perhaps significant that this rationalisation is invariably accompanied by a reluctance to use the descriptive language of the New Testament for such a 'reception' of the Spirit (words like 'baptised in', 'filled with', 'poured upon' are clearly inappropriate!).

One thing emerges very clearly from a study of the New Testament references to 'receiving' the Spirit, which has been noted by many Bible scholars – namely, the 'peculiar definiteness' of all the records. Others speak of the gift of the Spirit as 'something whose reception may be verified'. Yet another comments that Paul speaks 'as if the reception of the Spirit was something as definite and observable as, for example, an attack of influenza'! Few have put it better than the missionary statesman Roland Allen[1] in his *The Ministry of the Spirit* (World Dominion Press, 1960), pp. 9–10:

> The gift which the apostles received was a definite gift received at a definite time. It was not the experience of a vague influence which they felt more or less markedly at different times: it was a definite fact concerning which they could name the time and the place. Later the Holy Spirit was given to many others, but always this peculiar definiteness marked the coming of the gift. There was always a time and a place at which each convert received the gift. It was perfectly natural for St. Paul to ask certain men at Ephesus of whom he stood in some doubt, 'Did ye receive the Holy Spirit when ye believed?' (Acts 19:2, RV). He asked a definite question expecting an equally definite answer, as a matter of course. He expected Christians to know the Holy Spirit, to know whether they had received Him, and to know when they received Him . . . In this the gift of the Holy Spirit to all the later disciples partook of the same character as the first gift of the day of Pentecost.

This 'peculiar definiteness' is antecedent to Pentecost. Jesus himself 'received' the Spirit with visible and audible accompaniments (Matt 3:16–17), though the bodily form of a dove and the voice from heaven were unique to his 'initiation'. Closer parallels are to be found in the Old Testament, in such events as the 'ordination' of Moses' seventy elders (Num 11:25) and the divine approval of Saul as king (1 Sam 10:6). In these cases the evidence was 'prophesying', which is precisely the sign predicted of the outpouring of the Spirit in the 'last days' (Joel 2:28–29).

[1]After some years in China, Roland Allen became vicar of Chalfont St Peter (where I was a Baptist pastor fifty years later); resigning in 1907 over the scandal of indiscriminate infant baptism, he devoted himself to such major works as *Missionary Methods – St Paul's or Ours?* and *The Spontaneous Expansion of the Church*. He himself predicted that his work on the Holy Spirit would not be appreciated for another fifty years; it was published in 1960! He was truly prophetic and foresaw the need for indigenous missions, church growth and charismatic renewal. I owe an immense debt to his pioneer thinking.

Prophesying

Here, then is the sign of receiving the Spirit common to both Old and New Testaments. But what exactly is 'prophesying'?

It is *speech*. It should not surprise anyone that the evidence comes out of the mouth. We have already seen that 'filled' implies 'overflowing' (that is how we know anything has been filled, as with the petrol tanks of our cars). Throughout scripture the mouth is regarded as the overflow of the heart. This is true at the emotional level – full of fun, we laugh; full of anger, we shout; full of sorrow, we howl; full of fear, we cry out. It is particularly true of our spiritual life. Nothing going into the mouth makes a man sinful; but what comes out reveals the sinful state of the heart. If a person has been filled to overflowing with the Spirit of God, it is entirely to be expected that his mouth will be involved. The tongue, set on fire by hell (Jas 3:2–12), is now set on fire by heaven! The 'unruly member', which no man can tame, is now controlled by supernatural forces!

It is *spontaneous* speech. The prompting to verbalise comes from within the Spirit-filled person. No hymn has been announced, no creed is being recited, no liturgy is being performed. It is the living spring within beginning to bubble up and out. It is characteristically unpremeditated, extemporaneous, unstudied, uncontrived – in a word, impromptu (see chapter 35 for comments on the practice of encouraging people to 'make sounds').

It is spontaneous *spiritual* speech. The words will not be coming from the mind, but from the spirit (1 Cor 14:14–15 makes the clear distinction), bypassing the normal mental process behind verbalisation. The spirit knows just 'what to say', for it is being directed by the Holy Spirit. The Spirit-filled person is still doing the actual speaking (the breathing of the lungs, the vibration of the larynx, the moving of tongue and lips), but there is no deliberate forming of the words. Thus a person will be fully conscious of 'prophesying', while intellectual awareness of what he is saying may be total, partial (1 Pet 1:11–12) or non-existent (if it is not in a language his brain has already learned). The emotional accompaniment may also vary enormously, depending on temperament, circumstances and many other factors. The New English Bible phrase 'ecstatic utterance' (1 Cor 12:10) is grossly misleading: in fact, the Bible is strangely silent about the feelings of being filled, and the only 'excited' experience recorded in Acts 2 was that of the curious bystanders (vv. 6, 12).

This speech may take a number of different forms:

Tongues
This horrible word conveys an impression of 'uncontrolled babbling'. The Greek word (*glossai*) means simply 'languages' (as 'tongue' meant in older English). It implies proper grammar and syntax. Since God gave all the languages on earth (Gen 11:7–9), he can speak any of them – through human beings filled with his Spirit. The purpose of different languages at Babel was destructive, but the gift of tongues at Pentecost was constructive. On the latter occasion it served the useful function of a 'sign', pointing beyond itself to the presence of the God of all nations, seeking to reunite what he had divided. The listeners did not *need* to hear their own languages (Peter only used one to preach to all of them); but to hear them from semi-literate northerners convinced many of them that a supernatural event was taking place before their very eyes. The important thing to note is that Peter understood that 'speaking in unknown languages' was, in fact, 'prophesying', for he readily identified it with Joel's prediction ('This is that . . .', quoting Joel 2:28–39). If the gift was totally new, at least since Babel, Peter could only have made this identification by direct revelation (as with his realisation that Jesus was the Christ – Matt 16:17); but it is just possible that such 'unintelligible' verbalising was already associated with early 'prophesying' in the Old Testament (as in the case of the seventy elders and Saul). The fact remains – for Peter, tongues and prophesying were virtually the same thing.

The same outward manifestation accompanied other occasions when the Spirit was received and, be it noted, when there was neither need for, nor recognition of, the languages given (Acts 10:46; 19:6). But was this the *only* form of 'prophesying' at such times? Is 'tongues' the exclusive evidence to show the Spirit has been received?

On the one hand, it is the only sign that is mentioned on every occasion when the 'evidence' is described. On the other hand, other manifestations are listed – praise on one occasion (Acts 10:46) and prophecy (distinguished from 'tongues' and presumably in their own language) on another (Acts 19:6); on neither occasion is it stated that all spoke in other languages (the more natural interpretation is that some did one thing and some did another). On the basis of this testimony, and in the absence of any clear scriptural statement that it *must* be tongues as the only and necessary sign of having received the Spirit, it would seem unduly dogmatic to demand this on every occasion. To say that 'tongues' *could* always be the evidence seems warranted; to say it *should* be seems unwarranted (more on this in chapter 35). It is safer to say that some form of 'prophesying' must be the evidence of receiving the 'Spirit of prophecy' (Rev 19:10). But what are these other forms?

Praise

This form, which is mentioned along with tongues when Cornelius and his household receive the Spirit (Acts 10:46), is clearly different from tongues, as the word 'and' indicates – even though at Pentecost the content of the tongues had extolled the wonderful works of God (Acts 2:11). It appears to be a spontaneous outburst of worship in their own language (Latin?). True worship is not a 'natural' activity of man (though he can be persuaded to engage in ritual and liturgy when that is socially acceptable); it is a spiritual activity of God in man. An unselfconscious explosion of praise would certainly indicate the Spirit's entrance!

Prophecy

At first sight, it may seem strange to list 'prophecy' as one form of prophesying! However, the word is used in both a broad sense, which includes tongues (as in Acts 2) and a narrow sense, in which it is distinguished from tongues – as when the Ephesian disciples receive the Spirit (Acts 19:6), as it is when Paul lists the gifts of the Spirit (in 1 Cor 12:10) or gives directions for corporate worship (1 Cor 14:5). The two main differences are a) that tongues are normally unintelligible to speaker and hearer alike, while prophecy is intelligible to both and b) that tongues are addressed to God while prophecy is addressed to man (1 Cor 14:2–3). What they have in common is that the content originates with the Lord rather than the speaker.

Other ejaculations
Paul mentions a number of other spontaneous words or phrases in his epistles.

The classic example is 'Abba' (Rom 8:15–16; Gal 4:6). This is grossly misunderstood when it is called 'the inward witness', since the Greek verb (*krazein*) means to cry out involuntarily (cf. its use in Matt 14:26, 30). This word, a Jewish baby's first address to its father (the English equivalent would be 'Dada' or 'Daddy'), was Jesus' favourite and familiar form of prayer to his own Father, but a word he did not use in his public teaching. It would never be used by Jews, even in private prayer; they would not dare to be so familiar with a God who threatened dire punishment for those who took his name in vain! Nor would the Gentiles use it, since it was a Jewish word. Its spontaneous use, by Jew or Gentile, would surely indicate the witness of the Spirit of Jesus that the person 'crying out' in this way was also now entitled to use such a term of endearment!

Another example is the phrase 'Jesus is Lord' (1 Cor 12:3). It must be emphasised that Paul is not referring to a credal recitation, as most commentators seem to assume (a parrot could be trained to say that, without any supernatural help!), but to a spontaneous shout of recognition (similar to the Jewish child shouting 'Abba' when sighting his father). The context includes ejaculations inspired by other supernatural powers ('Jesus is cursed'), which apparently were being called out during worship at Corinth.

There are also 'groans that words cannot express' (Rom 8:26), though it must be added that neither these nor the ejaculations mentioned above are specifically linked to the moment of initiation and too much weight must not be put on them in this connection.

Reception of the Spirit

Finally, we must ask *how* they received the Spirit. Did it happen in a purely arbitrary, unexpected way, or were there human conditions to be fulfilled? Were the recipients totally passive at the time or actively co-operative?

It goes without saying that the gift was not sought before there was clear repentance, faith and baptism. The absence of any of these could block the gift (there were unique reasons why it was given to Cornelius before baptism, so his case provides no precedent).

On the basis of Acts 1, some have taught that it is necessary to 'wait' on the Lord, perhaps implying that the timing of the gift is entirely a matter for his sovereign will to decide. But this was only necessary before Pentecost, which God had marked in his diary for the first outpouring; even so, the period of 'waiting' was only for a few days. Both Peter and Paul obviously expected the gift to be given immediately after the repentance–faith–baptism response to the gospel was complete. However, there is a hint that prayer for the gift needs to be determined and persistent; Jesus, in the context of the gift of Holy Spirit (Luke 11:13), told his disciples to go on asking until they received. Certainly, prayer seems to have been an essential element in 'receiving', even for Jesus himself (Luke 3:21–22), as well as for the apostles (Acts 1:14) and those to whom they later ministered (Acts 8:15). It is necessary to ask for the gift; it is not automatic.

How important was the laying-on of hands? It is an intensive form of prayer-request, both directing and concentrating intercession on a particular person. It has to be said that in the only two recorded cases in the New Testament where the Spirit was received without this act, there were very good reasons for it. On the day of Pentecost there was no one already filled with the Spirit who *could* have laid hands on them (so Jesus himself did so with his own 'fingers' of flame 'touching each one of them'); for the Gentile household of Cornelius there was no one who *would* have done it! In all other recorded cases, hands were laid on, usually as an immediate postscript to baptism (Acts 8:17; 9:17; 19:6). It would seem valid to assume that this physical act was the normal means of communicating the Spirit to others; this is certainly taught in the epistle to the Hebrews (Heb 6:1–6; see chapter 27), where the laying-on of hands is listed among the items of elementary teaching to be given to beginners. Obviously, if the gift is given and received spontaneously (as with Cornelius) this will not be necessary, but it does seem to have been normal.

It is also clear that, as well as those ministering to them, the recipients themselves needed to be active. Prophesying is a human, as well as a divine, activity. As we have already seen, the one receiving the Spirit co-operates by using his lungs, larynx and lips. But is this co-operation voluntary or involuntary? Were New Testament disciples so 'overwhelmed' by this supernatural power that they 'couldn't help' something exploding from their mouths? Unfortunately, they are not available for cross-examination! The Bible merely tells us what they did, not whether they had any choice in the matter! But other scriptures point to an answer. The Holy Spirit is not just a power, he is a person. He is a Comforter to lead and guide. Unlike the Father and Son, he is not a king and does not rule with absolute authority. He can be grieved (Eph 4:30), quenched (1 Thess 5:19) and resisted (Acts 7:51). All this does not convey an impression of an 'irresistible force'. He never violates a human will nor forces his power or gifts on anyone. He even entrusts the control of his gifts to their recipients; they don't 'have' to be used (1 Cor 14:28).

We may therefore conclude that the Spirit will only be given to those who want to receive him and 'set their sails' to move with the wind. It is necessary to be willing in the day of his power! But what an incredible privilege – to have the Spirit of the living God take up residence within us, supplying constant refreshment for ourselves, new abilities for others, an effective witness for Christ and a child's adoration for the Father!

6 BORN AGAIN

Language has been a problem since the Tower of Babel! Words seem to develop a life of their own. Sometimes they become too flexible and acquire too broad a meaning; sometimes they become too fixed and acquire too narrow a meaning. 'Love' is an example of the former trend; 'gay' of the latter.

Biblical words are not exempt from such changes. A teacher using biblical terminology is not necessarily expounding biblical truth (by the same token, the frequent use of scriptural quotations does not make teaching 'biblical', especially if texts are quoted out of context).

It is often necessary to strip words of their modern connotations in order to recover their biblical meaning. But 'unlearning' is always harder than learning. Breaking a habit is much more difficult than making one (as every golfer knows!). Habitual use of words dies hard!

'Conversion' and 'born again' are good examples of this danger, and of the difficulty of avoiding it. They have both moved from flexible descriptions to fixed definitions. To say 'I am a born-again Christian' is almost nonsensical – like talking about a round circle or a four-cornered square! Similarly, the statement that 'I can't remember the day of my conversion' contains a built-in assumption which is quite unbiblical.

The trouble is that the two terms have long been treated as synonymous in evangelical circles. They have been used interchangeably to define that work of God in us which brings us from the death of sin into new life in Christ. Into both words has crept a tacit understanding that this happens instantaneously. For the purpose of effective testimony, it is considered an advantage if the person was conscious of the moment when this happened, or is at least able to pin a date on it, though it is 'allowed' that many believers (perhaps most, according to some surveys) were not aware of what was happening at the time.

If (and it is a very big 'if') it is accepted that both words refer to a supernatural and instantaneous event, then the question naturally arises: How does this relate to the fourfold complex of initiation already outlined in previous chapters? At what stage in the process does conversion/regeneration occur?

But is the generally accepted understanding of the words truly biblical? That is the prior question. In this chapter we shall seek to show that a careful examination of the scriptural use of these terms reveals that both are descriptive rather than definitive, that only one of them describes the supernatural work, and that neither is necessarily instantaneous!

CONVERSION

Who hasn't heard an evangelist say, 'I never converted anyone – only God can convert a human soul'? The remark sounds right, but is quite unbiblical. According to scripture, God never 'converted' anybody!

In modern evangelical parlance, the noun is used frequently ('my conversion'); where the verb is used, it is invariably in the passive voice ('I was converted'). In the New Testament the noun is never used and the verb is usually in the active voice ('convert your brother') or the middle ('convert yourself'). The verb always has a human subject, never the divine. (If this thought is totally unfamiliar, I invite you to work through a sample of texts: Matt 13:15; Mark 4:12; Luke 22:32; Acts 3:19; 2 Cor 3:16; Gal 4:9; Jas 5:20; 1 Pet 2:25.)

The fact is, in New Testament Greek the word 'convert' is not the technical or theological term it has become. It is a very ordinary word, one of a group of words derived from the simple root meaning 'turn' (Greek: *strepho*). The particular form usually translated 'convert' has the added prefix *epi-*, which gives it the meaning of 'turn *around*' or 'turn *back*'. The modern phrase in the Highway Code, 'make a U-turn', is as near an equivalent as one could get.

It is therefore a most appropriate description to use when a sinner turns away from his sins, turns right round and turns back to God. It describes his own action (not God's), whether he has decided by himself to do this or has been persuaded by someone else. Nor is there anything in the word itself to qualify the speed of the turn, whether it is sudden or slow; the word is solely concerned with direction. Whether an about-turn is made in one big movement or a series of smaller ones is quite immaterial. The important thing is that a person who was going one way (to hell) is now travelling in the opposite direction (to heaven). Realisation of all this should be a source of comfort to many Christians formerly embarrassed when asked to 'give a testimony'; the essential element in conversion is the change of direction, not the timing of the change. Some drivers speeding the wrong way have skidded round in a few seconds (the sight and sound are quite sensational and make good entertainment, as Hollywood discovered!). More careful drivers may take their time, and make it safer for others. Either way, the vital thing is to be on the right side of the road! Actually, it is repentance and faith that are more difficult to date; water-baptism and Spirit-baptism are easily remembered and dated.

In passing through the 'four spiritual doors', a person is completing this 'turn' from sin to God. At each of the four stages, human action is necessary and a further 'step' is taken. All four are referred to in the imperative mood in the New Testament, indicating commands to be obeyed:

Repent (Acts 2:38)
Believe (Acts 16:31)
Be baptised (Acts 22:16)
Receive (John 20:22)

Of course, the proportion of human activity required at each stage varies considerably. In water-baptism it is confined to seeking and submitting to it (the middle voice is so significant: 'Get yourself baptised'). In Spirit-baptism God does most of it, though the reception is active rather than passive. In repentance and faith the emphasis is heavily, though not exclusively, on the human part.

It would seem legitimate, therefore, to use the word 'conversion' of the whole process, viewed from the angle of human activity at all four stages. All of them are needed for a *complete* 'turn-around'. In particular, water-baptism marks the final break with sin and Spirit-baptism begins the new life; both are fundamental to 'conversion' and should be included in a testimony to one's introduction to Christ.

However, 'conversion' can be repeated! The same word is used in the New Testament of a believing brother who 'converts' back to sin (Gal 4:9; Tit 3:11). He will need to be 'converted' back to God again (Luke 22:32; Jas 5:20), though in this instance neither water- nor Spirit-baptism will be necessary. The Salvation Army lassie, who reputedly claimed she had been converted ten times and that each time was better than the last, was at least being honest!

The word is obviously much more flexible than we realise. Perhaps it would be safer to use the simple equivalent 'turn around', which is all it originally meant. Testimonies would need to be more explicit and more objective. Instead of telling 'how I was converted', which is a rather convenient shorthand, I would need to describe what sins I repented of, why I believed what I heard, when I was baptised and how I received the Spirit. Such witnessing would be more informative and more inspiring!

REGENERATION

I shall now turn to 'regeneration' – yet another word which suffers from having become a technical term of theology, where it generally denotes that act of divine grace whereby the sinner is given a new nature. It is almost universally assumed that this will therefore be an instantaneous event, of which there may be no subjective consciousness at the time, though an awareness of its having happened will certainly come later.

This 'doctrinal' understanding inevitably raises the problem of relating this moment of regeneration to the process of initiation. At what point does the miracle take place? Three incompatible answers compete for attention: Calvinist, Arminian, Catholic.

Calvinist. A Reformed theology, emphasising the sovereignty of God, usually places the moment of regeneration *before* the whole of initiation, on the 'logical' basis that fallen human nature is utterly incapable of repenting from sin, let alone receiving the Spirit. God exercises his sovereign grace in regeneration first, thus making it possible for the sinner to respond to the gospel. The choice to be born again is therefore entirely God's prerogative.

Arminian. Most evangelicals and Pentecostals seem to work on the assumption that regeneration takes place after repentance and faith but before (or, at least, apart from) water-baptism. Evangelicals often equate regeneration and 'Spirit-baptism' ('born of' and 'baptised in' the Holy Spirit being regarded as synonymous, though the latter term is rarely used). Pentecostals would keep them entirely separate. Either way, the choice to be 'born again' is both human and divine; when man responds to the gospel, God responds by regenerating (hence the emphasis on 'making a decision').

Catholic. A sacramental approach identifies regeneration with water-baptism, whether that follows or precedes (in babies) personal faith. The Anglican service for infant baptism in the Book of Common Prayer embodies this belief, though the Alternative Service Book is ambiguous on the point. In this case, the choice to be 'born again' seems to lie with the parents and the priest.

If the three viewpoints are deeply divided in their conclusions, they are united in the underlying premise that regeneration is virtually instantaneous. But is this assumption borne out by scripture? If not, could this explain the deep divisions between them? And, furthermore, how has the notion arisen?

'Regeneration', like 'conversion', is really quite an 'ordinary' word, descriptive rather than definitive. Its development from a simple root is easily understood. From the verb 'to be' (Greek: *eimi*), a simple prefix produces a verb meaning 'to come to be' or 'to become' (*ginomai*); yet another prefix changes it to 'to become again' (*anagennao*), though when this last is used in the noun form, a different prefix meaning 'again' is used (*palingenesia* – no prizes for guessing how the first book in the Bible got its name!).

The verb for 'come to be' is used over two hundred times in the New Testament, with a great many shades of meaning – from the very ordinary narrative ('John the baptiser came to be in the wilderness' – cf. Mark 1:4), which is little different from our English 'happen', to the extraordinary events of creation ('what cannot be seen came to be what we can see' – cf. Heb. 11:3). The narrower sense of 'become' also has two distinct connotations, both relevant to our study. On the one hand, it can refer to a totally new beginning, something coming to be for the very first time, hence an appropriate word for the creation of the world (and used this way in John 1:3, 4, 10). On the other hand, it can refer to something which already exists taking an entirely new form, whether by natural process (a mustard seed 'becoming' a large tree – Luke 13:19) or by supernatural intervention (water 'becoming' wine – John 2:9).

This double sense of 'become' (in Hebrew and Aramaic, as well as in Greek) made it an ideal word for Jesus to use in his conversation with Nicodemus. It could link the event of physical birth (in which a new person comes to be part of the old creation) with the concept of spiritual birth (in which the same person comes to be part of the new creation). The latter is simply 'coming to be again' (it could be translated 'coming to be from above', since the Greek word can mean again or above – see chapter 10). In any case, a divine act of creation is involved, though this does not exclude an element of manufacture (i.e. starting with some old material). Even a physical birth is not 'from nothing'; it is the product of existing genetic material and the process of gestation. The incarnation itself has this double combination – of a divine being who had existed from all eternity and a human being who began in time. Continuity of identity can coexist with discontinuity of form.

Though the noun for 'becoming again' is only used twice in the New Testament, it is applied significantly both to human beings (Tit 3:5) and to the whole creation (Matt 19:28). The God who is restoring his highest creatures to their original condition intends to do the same for the entire universe! The heavens and the earth are to be 'born again' (Rev 21:1–5), though this will be achieved by a baptism of fire rather than water (2 Pet 3:10–13)!

There is nothing in the word 'regeneration' itself, or in the contexts in which it is used, which implies that 'coming to be' is instantaneous. That it *may* be so is not disputed – and sometimes this is specifically stated, as when the new resurrection body is given 'in a flash [i.e. a moment], in the twinkling of an eye' (1 Cor 15:51–52), though admittedly a different word is used there. But that it *must* be instantaneous is just not true. The original creation (genesis/generation – Gen 2:4) was certainly a process in many stages, whatever view is taken of the length of the six days. The re-creation of the heavens and the earth will obviously have a similar set of phases. Likewise a mustard seed does not 'come to be' a great tree overnight. In fact, the word is used far more frequently in scripture of things that have *taken time* – long or short – to 'become' what they are. Even the incarnation (the Word 'becoming' flesh) took nine months. The cause of how they have become, the nature of what they have become and the purpose of why they have become is of far more consequence than the 'velocity' of becoming!

Why, then, such an emphasis on 'instantaneous' regeneration? It is probably due to a widespread impression that anything that happens slowly or gradually can be 'explained away' in terms of 'natural' causation (like water becoming wine through vine cultivation and fermentation) whereas the same thing happening suddenly demonstrates its 'supernatural' causation (as at Cana).

There is a profound fallacy behind this kind of thinking: namely, that God is not at work in the normal and slower processes of nature. There is also a false assumption that God's nature demands that he do things in a hurry. That could be a bad case of making him in our image, since our most common complaint about his activity in history is that he does not respond to situations quickly enough! From his work in creation we need to learn something of his patience (Jas 5:7–8), especially in an age that demands 'instant' satisfaction.

Once the concept of regeneration has been liberated from its 'instantaneous' associations, we are able to gain a fresh appreciation of its relation to the process of initiation. Both are processes rather than single events, and they correspond to each other in a remarkable way.

To consider the beginning of the Christian life as a birth is fully scriptural and goes back to the words of Jesus himself, though, for the record, it needs to be pointed out that it is not used very frequently (in fact, being 'born' of the Spirit occurs fewer times than being 'baptised' in the Spirit, the ratio being six to seven – not generally reflected in evangelical preaching today!).

There is, therefore, some kind of analogy between physical and spiritual 'birth' (though Nicodemus took it too literally – John 3:4!), which implies that there is a degree of similarity between the two. Now physical birth is certainly a process made up of a series of events. From the first contractions of the uterus, through the emergence of the newly born baby and the cutting of the umbilical cord, to the first breath and cry, the whole sequence has brought a new life into being (though it had existed in darkness for some nine months already). To call any one of these stages the 'birth' is exceedingly difficult. To ask at what particular point the baby was actually 'born' is probably futile and certainly irrelevant. The whole procedure may have been delightfully quick or relatively slow. What matters is that a new life has begun and that everything that is needed for a healthy life to follow has been done, and done properly. Birth has little significance in and of itself; it is the prelude to life and the quality of that life is the important thing.

Scripture encourages us to see in this an analogy of the 'new' birth and to apply the word and concept of 'regeneration' to the whole process of initiation. Apart from some obvious parallels that we can draw (the first pains of 'conviction', the cutting of the umbilical cord in 'repentance', the washing of the baby in 'baptism' and the crying out in the Spirit, with hands laid on!), there is also biblical warrant for doing so.

Just as we can apply the word 'conversion' to all four stages in initiation, since all of them are referred to in the imperative mood, indicating the need for human activity, so we can apply the word 'regeneration' to all four stages of initiation, since all of them are referred to in the indicative mood, indicating the fact of divine activity:

God himself grants repentance (Acts 5:31; 11:18);
God bestows the gift of faith (Eph 2:8);
God raises from the grave of baptism (Col 2:12);
God pours out his Spirit (Tit 3:5).

The whole process is God's doing. Through it he is 'regenerating' (i.e. causing to 'become again') a person. Every stage is necessary to begin the 'normal' Christian life and necessary to healthy growth and development.

As we have already seen, the proportion of human activity varies from stage to stage; and this is usually in inverse ratio to the divine activity at each stage. In the first two (repentance and faith) the primary emphasis is on the human contribution, but in the third and fourth (water- and Spirit-baptism) it switches to the divine. Indeed there seems to be a progressive decrease in human activity and a corresponding increase in the divine through the four stages. This progressive shift of emphasis may be represented diagrammatically:

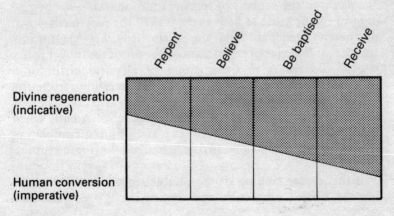

Of course, this chart is a summary of textual statistics rather than a statement of theological concept. Yet the trend may have some spiritual significance: initiation is a separation from the effort of self and an introduction to the energy of God.

So, while the *whole* process may be regarded as both 'conversion' (from the human point of view) and 'regeneration' (from the divine point of view), the latter word is particularly applicable to the second half of the process, the two baptisms in which God is completing the introduction to new life. Before evangelical readers recoil in horror from such a statement, they are urged to look again at those two verses of scripture that define most specifically the nature of the 'new birth'. John 3:5 (rendered literally) states that a person 'comes to be again *out of* water and Spirit' (see chapter 10 for a full examination of this intriguing phrase). Titus 3:5 (again rendered literally) speaks of being 'saved' through the 'bath of regeneration' and the 'outpoured Spirit in renewal' (see chapter 26 for a detailed exegesis of this verse). However much we may wish that Jesus and Paul had attributed regeneration to repentance and faith, we must take scripture as it stands. The wording of these verses presents no problem when we see regeneration as a total process, coterminous with the completion of initiation.

Receiving the Spirit, the fourth and final stage of the new birth, carries a significance absent from the other three. It is the *completion* of the process of regeneration, marking the beginning of the new life as well as the end of the new birth, since this new existence is 'life in the Spirit' (Rom 8:4–5). But it is also the *confirmation* of regeneration, the proof that new life has begun. To revert to the analogy of physical birth for a moment, receiving the Spirit with an overflow from the mouth is equivalent to a baby's first breath and cry. There is also a biblical parallel in the 'coming to be' of Adam, when God 'breathed' into his nostrils (the 'kiss of life'), completing the process of his 'generation' or 'genesis' by bringing him to life.

If this understanding of the double significance of receiving the Spirit (completion and confirmation) is correct, then neither repentance and faith nor baptism provide a proof or guarantee of justification. This is because they can each be professed and practised in a way that is unacceptable to God, who alone knows all that is in the heart. The proof of his approval and acceptance lies in the evidence that he has given his Spirit, this being the 'seal' on the transaction. It is the basic ground of assurance: 'We *know* that we live in him [i.e. God] and he in us, *because* he has given us of his Spirit' (1 John 4:13; cf. 3:24). No wonder the apostles were deeply concerned when such evidence was lacking (see chapters 16 and 20); this was the touchstone of being a 'Christian' (Rom 8:9; see chapter 21 for a criticism of this interpretation).

Two further questions may be raised at this point, though they will be answered more fully in chapter 36. First, why is so much stress put on the *birth* rather than the *life* of spiritual babies (so that our evangelism is more concerned with getting people 'born again' than with making sure they are 'fully alive')? Second, why are evangelicals so reluctant to consider water-baptism (and Pentecostals so reluctant to consider both that *and* Spirit-baptism) as an integral part of the whole process of regeneration?

At root, both questions relate to an over-simplified view of salvation. When salvation is preached primarily in terms of being safe from hell rather than in terms of being salvaged from sins, when it is seen as more relevant to the next world than this, more appropriate to those about to die than to those who expect to go on living – then it becomes more important to have been 'born' of the Spirit than to be 'living' in the Spirit (the need for justification overshadowing the need for sanctification). If our understanding of salvation downplays the 'this-worldly' perspective, then (since they are primarily concerned with this life, liberating us from our sins here and now) both water-baptism and Spirit-baptism decline in relative importance in the Christian life, even becoming optional rather than essential.

This 'ticket to heaven' mentality is unbiblical and indicates an unbalanced view of salvation. Justification and regeneration are viewed as ends in themselves rather than means to that 'holiness without which no one will see the Lord' (Heb 12:14, RSV). But the new birth is neither a discharge certificate from hell nor a season ticket for heaven. It is given to make a sin-free life possible (1 John 3:9), to enjoy eternal life both here and hereafter. Sanctification is the vital link between justification and glorification. Since water-baptism and Spirit-baptism are a vital part of sanctification, they are an integral part of full salvation; that is why Paul uses the word 'saved' of both (Tit 3:5), and why Jesus saw them as fundamental constituents of the new birth (John 3:5).

For far too many converts the process of new birth is long and complicated: faith may come well before repentance; baptism may come long after faith (or, more confusing still, long before); many people are not sure whether they have been 'baptised' in the Spirit or not; some have never even repented; others have never been baptised. It is not usually their fault. They were badly delivered by inexperienced and untrained midwives.

This book has been written to try and improve the situation. Having taken this *topical* overview of the 'normal Christian birth' we need to look at the *practical* ways in which this teaching can be applied in evangelistic and pastoral situations.

However, before we do so, it is necessary to make sure that the general principles outlined already are firmly rooted in scripture. We need to look at a couple of dozen key passages which have a direct bearing on our theme. It will be even more important to have an open Bible at hand – and an open mind, for there are many new things to learn and old things to unlearn!

Part Two

THE 'WHAT ABOUT . . .?' PASSAGES – The biblical dimension

7 THE GREAT COMMISSION
(Matthew 28:19–20)

¹⁹'Therefore go and make disciples of all nations, baptising them in the name of the Father and of the Son and of the Holy Spirit, ²⁰and teaching them to obey everything I have commanded you. And surely I am with you always, to the very end of the age.' (Matt 28:19–20)

This missionary mandate to the apostles, and through them to the whole church, is bracketed by two of the most incredible claims Jesus ever made for himself. He began by asserting his universal authority throughout *space* and ended by promising his perpetual presence throughout *time*. His 'marching orders' can only be fully understood against this background of his comprehensive power and position. He now exercises his rights, both to send out the apostles to recruit an international band of followers and to apply his own absolute standards to them.

'All nations' applies to ethnic groupings rather than to political entities: it springs from God's desire to include every variety of human being ('kindred, tribe, tongue') in his kingdom, though 'nations' or 'peoples' is also a Jewish synonym for 'Gentiles'. It is highly significant that this commission comes in Matthew, the gospel written primarily for *Jewish* readers! It makes absolutely clear that Jesus himself initiated the outreach to the Gentile world, a switch of policy from an exclusive mission to the 'lost sheep of Israel' (Matt 15:24). The change had been anticipated before his death (Matt 21:43 and 24:14).

The grammatical aspect of his instruction is important. One imperative verb ('to disciple') is qualified by two present continuous participles ('baptising' and 'teaching'). They are to do discipling rather than make disciples. Verbs are more dynamic than nouns!

A 'disciple' is a learner, but from a person rather than a book, course or system. He is an apprentice rather than a student. Discipleship involves relationship – with a discipler, a teacher, a leader. So the question is raised, Make disciples *of whom*? Of themselves or of someone else? The transitive form of the verb can favour either application – Peter could make disciples of Peter, or disciples of Jesus. The question is settled by the context: the *name* in which they were to be baptised was not that of an apostle and the *commands* they were to teach were not those of an apostle. They were to make 'disciples of Jesus'. This is confirmed by the care with which Peter and later Paul avoided baptising their own converts (Acts 10:48; 1 Cor 1:13–17); and by the fact that the early Christians were collectively known as 'disciples', but never as 'disciples of . . . Peter, John, Paul, etc.'. However, in so far as the teaching of Jesus is embodied in the lives of the teachers, discipling may be done by imitation as well as by instruction (1 Cor 4:16; 1 Thess 1:6; Heb 6:12; 13:7; 3 John 11).

Some Bible scholars have made much of the fact that the command to 'disciple' comes before the command to 'baptise', deducing from this that baptism should always follow instruction. Surprisingly, this point is often made by paedobaptists (those who baptise babies) – when the logical conclusion of the point is believers' baptism (Charles Simeon, the evangelical Anglican, was one such, as was John Calvin before him – see Appendix 1). Let the saintly Richard Baxter (in his *Disputations of Right to Sacrament*, p. 149f., quoted in T. E. Watson, *Baptism Not For Infants* (Walter, 1967), p. 27) speak for this viewpoint:

> This is not like some occasional historical mention of baptism, but it is the very commission of Christ to His apostles for preaching and baptism, and purposely expresseth their several works in their several places and order. Their first task is by *teaching* to make disciples, which by Mark are called believers. The second work is to baptise them . . . The third work is to teach them all other things which are

afterwards to be learned in the school of Christ. To contemn this order is to renounce all rules of order; for where can we expect to find it if not here?

However, the grammar cannot fully carry this interpretation, since it does not consist of three consecutive imperatives, but of only one with two participles – they are to 'disciple by baptising and teaching'. Not that baptising precedes teaching even in this case, though other paedobaptists use this to justify baptising babies long before they can be 'taught'. This opposite view is equally unjustified from the text, since the verb 'disciple' is nothing if not a fully conscious and voluntary relationship chosen by the person concerned.

'Baptising' is more a transliteration than a translation. As we have already seen, in Greek the word means to dip, plunge, drench, soak or submerge something in a liquid (such as a cloth in a dye, a cup in a bowl of wine or even a ship sunk in the sea; see chapter 4). Most commentators take it as a reference to water-baptism rather than to Spirit-baptism, particularly because of the 'name' element. Confirmation of this may be found in the fact that though the practice of water-baptism seems to have faded away during Jesus' ministry, it became universal in the early church from the day of Pentecost onwards. Only the Lord's command would have ensured such a continuation of a physical rite after the full spiritual baptism of the Messiah had come (cf. Peter's reaction to Cornelius' Spirit-baptism in Acts 10:47). Apostolic insistence on water-baptism can only be explained if the great commission is a genuine recollection of the actual words of Jesus.

It has become fashionable to attribute these words to the early church rather than to Jesus, though in the apparent absence of any other order of Jesus to do it this creates the further problem of finding some other explanation for Peter's insistence on water-baptism on the day of Pentecost! One of the main reasons given for this attribution is that the trinitarian wording of Matthew 28:19–20 is more reminiscent of ecclesiastical formulae and is at variance with the use of the name of Jesus by itself throughout the book of Acts (e.g. Acts 8:16;

19:5). Certainly, there is no direct evidence of the use of the trinitarian formula in baptism until the second century AD.

If the form of immersion in water was the same for the apostles as it had been for John the Baptist, the *formula* used was certainly different. Indeed, the use of a name in baptism was clearly an apostolic innovation. The Matthean formula is usually assumed to contain three names: 'Father', 'Son' and 'Holy Spirit'. But this simple reading of the phrase is, in fact, too simplistic – for the following reasons:

1. Technically, 'Father' and 'Son' are not 'names', but relationships.
2. The 'name' of the Father is 'Yahweh', from which comes 'Jehovah'.
3. The 'name' of the Son is 'Jesus'.
4. The word 'name' is in the singular (one), not the plural (three).

However, the main problem with the 'three names' position comes from the fact that though trinitarian benedictions were known to and used by the apostles (e.g. 2 Cor 13:14), there is no record of any trinitarian baptisms in the New Testament. These, like all healings and deliverances, were done in the single, powerful name of 'Jesus' only. How do we explain this apparent discrepancy?

Many scholars (from MacNeile to Barclay) simply attribute the Matthean formula to a later liturgy of the church that is being read back on to the lips of Jesus. However, since there are no manuscript grounds for regarding this as a later addition to the gospel as written, this supposition questions the integrity of the tax-and-text-collector who penned it, accusing him of inaccurate reporting!

Others have accused Luke of the same misrepresentation, speculating that his literary objective of uplifting Jesus led him to simplify his reporting in Acts, reducing the actual formula used in order to emphasise the name of Jesus. However, Luke shows no other signs of wanting to suppress trinitarian language (see Luke 3:22 and Acts 2:32–33; 20:21–22).

The extreme view would be that *both* Matthew and Luke are

misreporting – in which case there would be little hope of recovering the original baptismal wording, and no point in discussing it!

It is possible, however, that both contain accurate recollections. The apostles, in using only the name of 'Jesus', were either ignoring the 'letter' of the great commission or were convinced that they were fulfilling the 'spirit' of it. Could they have considered that the single name 'Jesus' was, in fact, tantamount to an explicit reference to the Trinity? After all, they now knew that God was the 'Father of Jesus' and that the Holy Spirit was the 'Spirit of Jesus' (Acts 16:7). Indeed, the 'Upper Room Discourse' (John 14–16) had so intermingled the three persons of the Godhead (see, for example, John 14:26) that to relate to one was to relate to all three. The single name 'Jesus' could then have been regarded as a kind of 'shorthand' term for the Trinity.

This suggestion is not as far-fetched as first impressions might indicate. The single name 'Jesus' may not be strictly consistent with Matthew's wording, but it is compatible with it, as the following considerations show.

1. The whole context is in the first person singular (I, me, my). Jesus is not here speaking on behalf of the Trinity (we, our). He does not say '. . . teaching them to observe all we have commanded'.

2. 'in the name of' is singular rather than plural, indicating that one name could cover all three. He does not tell them to baptise 'in the names of . . .'

3. Eusebius quotes this verse as saying 'make disciples of all nations, baptising them into my name, teaching them . . .' While this is unlikely to be a reliable testimony to the original version of Matthew's text (no one else quotes it in this way), nevertheless it does provide evidence of a general understanding of the application of the great commission which is entirely compatible with the record in Acts (even with the unusual use of the preposition in '*into* the name of the Lord Jesus' – Acts 19:5).

This last point is important. In Acts the baptism was not just 'in' (Greek: *en*) but 'into' (Greek: *eis*) the name of Jesus. This means much more than the 'delegated authority' of the *baptiser*. It signifies a personal identification with Jesus on the part of the *baptised*, an intimate union which leads to all that Paul later intends by the phrase '*in* Christ' (Gal 3:27). The meaning is not unrelated to the ancient practice of soldiers swearing themselves into the absolute possession and disposal of an Emperor (the original meaning of the word 'sacramentum' was an oath of allegiance to a 'Lord'). So the candidate in baptism is, in a sense, losing his own identity and therefore his own name; he is then being given a new name, that of the person whose identity is now his, namely, 'Jesus'. So baptism is a 'naming' ceremony (yet in the very opposite manner to the christening of a baby, which is given its own name; this practice is also quite different from giving a believer a new name at baptism, to indicate the new birth, as distinct from the 'old' one).

So whatever other words or names used in baptismal formulae, the name 'Jesus' should figure prominently, for the authority and power of the whole Godhead resides in this name (notice that in the book of Acts the 'name of Jesus' and the 'power of the Spirit' are nearly synonymous and occur with almost equal frequency in the early chapters).

However, it would be gross legalism of a dangerous and divisive kind to invalidate (or validate) any particular baptism on the sole ground of the verbal formula used, as if that is the one factor that makes baptism effective (or ineffective). To insist that the wording *must* be 'Jesus only' or 'fully trinitarian' to be Christian baptism would be sectarianism and lead to multiple rebaptisms. Perhaps the tension would be reduced by using a more flexible form of words, such as: 'In the name of Father, Son and Holy Spirit we baptise you into the Lord *Jesus*, into his death, his burial and his resurrection' (this was the wording I used for years, which kept everyone happy!), or: 'We baptise you into the name of the Lord *Jesus*, his Father and his Spirit.' And we have already reminded readers of the early church's practice of encouraging the candidates themselves to call on the name of the Lord as they approached baptism (Acts 22:16 – see chapter 3).

Finally, we note that 'baptising' is only the first step in

'discipling'. This moment of initiation leads to a lengthy period of instruction. The 'catechumenate' *begins* with baptism (whereas today it often ends there!). Having been buried and raised with Christ, the baptised then needs to be taught how to work this out in daily life (Col 2:20–3:17 provides an excellent syllabus!).

There is one stream of transatlantic Pentecostalism which drifted into unitarian doctrine based on the person of Jesus. Denying three persons in the Godhead, they regarded him as the *total* incarnation of the God of Israel. Refusing all trinitarian formulae, they baptised in the name of 'Jesus only' and became known as 'the oneness movement'. Since those who baptise in the single name of Jesus may or may not subscribe to this heresy, it is therefore necessary, when the practice is encountered, to enquire further about the theology behind it.

8   THE MARKAN POSTSCRIPT
(Mark 16:9–20)

[9]When Jesus rose early on the first day of the week, he appeared first to Mary Magdalene, out of whom he had driven seven demons. [10]She went and told those who had been with him and who were mourning and weeping. [11]When they heard that Jesus was alive and that she had seen him, they did not believe it.

[12]Afterwards Jesus appeared in a different form to two of them while they were walking in the country. [13]These returned and reported it to the rest; but they did not believe them either.

[14]Later Jesus appeared to the Eleven as they were eating; he rebuked them for their lack of faith and their stubborn refusal to believe those who had seen him after he had risen.

[15]He said to them, 'Go into all the world and preach the good news to all creation. [16]Whoever believes and is baptised will be saved, but whoever does not believe will be condemned. [17]And these signs will accompany those who believe: In my name they will drive out demons; they will speak in new tongues; they will pick up snakes with their hands; and when they drink deadly poison, it will not hurt them at all; they will place their hands on sick people, and they will get well.'

[19]After the Lord Jesus had spoken to them, he was taken up into heaven and he sat at the right hand of God. [20]Then the disciples went out and preached everywhere, and the Lord worked with them and confirmed his word by the signs that accompanied it. (Mark 16:9–20)

The original ending of Mark's gospel is irrevocably lost. The earliest Greek manuscripts break off in the middle of a sentence ('for they feared . . .'). Later copies have a variety of alternative 'endings', all of them different in style and vocabulary from the rest of the gospel and therefore presumed to be from other writers attempting to 'complete' the work. The 'longer' of these postscripts is the one usually included in our modern Bible versions.

The anonymous writer appears to have drawn his material from the other three gospels and Acts (which indicates a late date for his editorial work). There is little here that cannot be found elsewhere in scripture. Even the promised protection from reptiles and poison is mentioned in both the gospel (Luke 10:19) and Acts (28:3–6), though it is sensible to apply this to accidental risk rather than deliberate folly.

Though this passage may not have apostolic authorship, that does not mean it is totally devoid of apostolic authority. The words may be an accurate recollection of Jesus' own words during the six weeks of instruction between his resurrection and ascension. We have very little record of what he said, but what there is follows a consistent pattern, with which our passage is compatible. (But it has to be added that this would be the only mention of 'tongues' and the only use of the phrase 'the Lord Jesus' before Pentecost; but cf. John 20:28.)

However, even as a later editorial summary, there is still real value in having this testimony to the outlook of the early church at the end of the first century. In particular, we are given insights into its understanding of evangelism, which is the main theme of the passage.

On the one hand, baptism is seen as a necessary and integral element in being 'saved', which is totally consistent with apostolic teaching (see Tit 3:5 and 1 Pet 3:21, expounded more fully in chapters 26 and 29). Note, however, that a person is 'condemned' on the day of judgement for not believing, not for being unbaptised.

On the other hand, miraculous 'signs' are seen as a necessary confirmation of the truth of the gospel; again, this is consistent with apostolic experience (cf. Rom 15:18–19; 1 Thess 1:5; Heb 2:4). Note that the expectation here is that *all* believers will have such 'charismatic' powers, not just the apostles. The gospel was to be *seen* as well as *heard* (a point dealt with more fully in chapter 33). Evangelism would thus be a joint activity by the Lord and his followers working together – they would deliver the *message* and he would deliver the *miracles* (Acts 4:29–30; 6:8; 8:6; 11:20–21; 14:3). The very lateness of the 'longer ending' actually strengthens the point that the early church expected this combined mission to continue long after the apostles had left the earthly scene!

9 THE DYING THIEF (Luke 23:40–43)

⁴⁰But the other criminal rebuked him. 'Don't you fear God,' he said, 'since you are under the same sentence? ⁴¹We are punished justly, for we are getting what our deeds deserve. But this man has done nothing wrong.'

⁴²Then he said, 'Jesus, remember me when you come into your kingdom.'

⁴³Jesus answered him, 'I tell you the truth, today you will be with me in paradise.' (Luke 23:40–43)

Sooner or later, any discussion about Christian initiation turns to the question, 'What about the dying thief?' It is usually raised to support the view that conversion is a simple step rather than a complex process. In particular, it is taken as proof that salvation may be obtained without either water-baptism or Spirit-baptism. All that is required is faith, however naive.

If this is true, most of the content of this book is unnecessary and even misleading. There would be no need to study any biblical passages except this one! The truth is, however, that this simplistic view of initiation is not borne out by other key verses (Acts 2:38 – see chapter 15) or key passages (Acts 19:1–6 – see chapter 20).

There are a number of fairly obvious reasons why this event cannot be taken as the normal pattern for Christian 'conversion' today.

First, the thief's circumstances were unique. He was within hours of his own death; and this was judicial rather than natural. He was a young man suffering capital punishment. His case is therefore a good precedent for anyone facing imminent and deserved execution (it was thus used by John and Charles Wesley as they rode with condemned felons to Tyburn, now Marble Arch, where they were hanged; and by

Padre Gerecke with the Nazi war criminals at Nuremburg). At a stretch it might be applicable to challenge and comfort anyone facing imminent death of a natural or accidental nature. But to use the story to convince healthy people anticipating a normal span of life that this is 'all they need to do' seems quite unwarranted.

Second, the thief's complete initiation was impossible. There is very little anyone can do after being nailed to a cross. The mouth is still free – to curse or to pray (this thief chose the better alternative). But he had no opportunity to produce deeds of repentance, nor to be baptised in water. He did everything he could: he confessed his sins and confessed his faith in Jesus (see below). To use his case to reassure those who could do more that they *need not* do so is dangerous counsel.

Third, the thief was with Jesus in the flesh. This story is in one of the gospels, not the book of Acts. Relating to Jesus when he was on earth is quite different from relating to him after he returned to heaven and sat at the right hand of his Father. In the former, the encounter was through the physical senses – particularly seeing and hearing, as in the case of the dying thief. Furthermore, it was then possible to 'receive' Jesus by 'believing in his name' and regeneration accompanied this level of relationship (John 1:12–13). A change in the relationship took place at Jesus' ascension, when he was 'taken up into heaven' (Mark 16:19). From Pentecost onwards, one became a Christian by 'receiving the Holy Spirit', who had taken the place of Jesus on earth. The thief could not have received the Spirit; he was born and died too soon (John 7:39).

So the *whole* picture of Christian initiation today must be gleaned from the post-Pentecost apostolic preaching and practice. However, it is possible to illustrate the parts that make up that whole from incidents in the gospels, where they often occur in 'embryo'; therefore Zacchaeus is for us an excellent example of practical repentance, and the dying thief exemplifies the dimension of faith, in which he was quite outstanding.

The thief was the only person on that dreadful day who believed that the notice above Jesus' head was true. Only a week before, thousands had been convinced that Jesus was the 'King of the Jews', but now disillusion had set in and would lead to despair among his followers (Luke 24:21). Pilate's words, written out of stubborn resentment and judicial frustration, only produced general scepticism (Luke 23:37) – except in the dying thief, who with an almost incredible leap of faith declared his conviction that this dying man would one day have his kingdom, that he would exchange his cross for a throne, his thorns for a crown, his nakedness for royal robes and his nails for a sceptre and footstool!

We are in the realm of conjecture if we try to decide where and when he expected Jesus 'to come into his kingship'. But the fact that he asked to be 'remembered' indicates that he was thinking of an extended period during which Jesus' memory might lapse ('When you come into your kingdom, please cast your mind back to the day you died alongside the thief who believed in you . . .'). In much the same way as he brought Martha's faith in the future back to the present (John 11:25), Jesus told the thief that he would not have to wait long, so there was no risk of being forgotten! The emphatic 'Verily, verily' or 'Truly, truly' (Hebrew: *amen, amen*; perhaps in English it is something like 'Honestly') is an assurance that Jesus would never give false comfort to the dying (cf. John 14:2); it is also a recognition that what he has to say will seem utterly incredible. His prayer will be answered *today*! His dream will come true within hours! There is an element of foreknowledge in this prediction – death on a cross usually took between two and seven days. The thief only died the same day as Jesus because his legs were broken, which Jesus must have foreseen, whereas Jesus himself *chose* to die on that day, at the very moment the Passover lambs were killed, in total obedience to God and control of himself to the last breath (cf. Exod 12:6; Luke 23:46; John 10:18).

'Paradise' is not just a synonym for 'heaven'. Its original meaning was a 'garden', especially a royal garden where the king would entertain honoured guests (as Buckingham Palace garden parties do today): it is a special place for special people. This promised privilege may be more than a tribute to the outstanding faith of a discerning criminal; it could well indicate how much it meant to Jesus himself to have the moral support and understanding of just one solitary human being, who shared his physical agony but also dimly perceived the moral pressures being put upon him (Luke 23:41).

Jesus redirected the thief's thoughts about the future by focusing his attention on the person he would be with rather than the place he would be in. 'You will be with me' is a remarkable reassurance. This friendship formed in the last hours of life will not be interrupted by death! Just as soon as they've both got rid of their crosses, they'll go for a stroll in the palace garden – *together*! Though their bodies would be dead and 'asleep', their spirits would be alive and 'awake' (1 Pet 3:18). Jesus' words to the dying thief argue the case for full consciousness between death and resurrection, as against the concept of 'soul-sleep'. Furthermore, Paul would hardly have looked forward to an unconscious existence as 'gain' and 'better by far' compared with his exciting, if exhausting, life here (Phil 1:1–23).

The whole incident is shot through with the notion of mercy and is rightly cited as a signal demonstration of justification by faith. There was no way the criminal could earn favour or forgiveness, no ground on which he could appeal except his own need. The gates of heaven are flung wide open to those who recognise their own worthlessness. Those who earned their living from prostitution or protection rackets (which is what 'tax-collectors' really were) found it easier to 'storm' the kingdom than the religious and the respectable, precisely because they knew they were no good. The dying thief is simply the culminating example of many such 'trophies of grace'.

However, he missed out on a great deal his salvation might have brought him under other circumstances. His redemption was effective only in another world. His life in this world can only be regarded as wasted. Nor would he ever know the joy of living a good life here and now, free from criminal motives, habits and company. He could not express his gratitude in faithful service to the one he now called 'Lord' and therefore would not qualify for reward or responsibility in the new age to come. Forgiveness cannot restore lost time or opportunities.

This is why he must not be allowed to become a 'model' Christian. Regarding him as such can only produce 'minimum' Christians who reluctantly ask, 'How little do I need to be sure of getting to heaven?' The Lord is looking for 'maximum' Christians who eagerly ask, 'How much can I have to be sure of holiness here as well as happiness hereafter?' The latter will want more than the dying thief could ever have. They will seek water-baptism and Spirit-baptism until they get both, without secretly envying the dying thief who 'got by' without them. Rather pity the poor man for dying before he could have them!

10   THE SECOND BIRTH (John 3:3–8)

³In reply Jesus declared, 'I tell you the truth, no-one can see the kingdom of God unless he is born again.'

⁴"How can a man be born when he is old?" Nicodemus asked. 'Surely he cannot enter a second time into his mother's womb to be born!'

⁵Jesus answered, 'I tell you the truth, no-one can enter the kingdom of God unless he is born of water and the Spirit. ⁶Flesh gives birth to flesh, but the Spirit gives birth to spirit. ⁷ You should not be surprised at my saying, "You must be born again."⁸ The wind blows wherever it pleases. You hear its sound, but you cannot tell where it comes from or where it is going. So it is with everyone born of the Spirit.' (John 3:3–8)

Of all the sermons preached and tracts written on the text 'You must be born again', how many have explained how 'water' fits in – or even mentioned it? A phobia about the bogey of 'baptismal regeneration' has led to an evangelical conspiracy of silence on the subject, stripping the new birth of any connection with a physical act. Nicodemus was not the last to misunderstand Jesus' teaching, and many remain with him 'in the dark'!

The great majority of commentators (including the Church Fathers, Roman Catholics, Protestant Reformers, English Puritans and most modern scholars) accept that verse 5 is an expansion of verse 3, spelling out the second birth in greater detail.

There is some division over whether the Greek word *anothen* means 'again' or 'from above'. In favour of the latter is the 'heavenly' reference of the phrase 'born of God' (in John 1:13). That Jesus is referring to a divine rather than a human event is obvious; he is contrasting a supernatural birth with a natural one (v. 6). Nicodemus himself took it as 'again' (v. 4) and confused himself by thinking of it as a mere repetition of the first birth. Elsewhere in John's gospel the word clearly means 'above' (see 3:31; 19:11, 23); and it is worth bearing in mind that if Jesus was speaking Aramaic at the time, that language has no adverb 'again'. Some translators, like William Barclay, hedge their bets and translate the phrase 'Reborn from above'! Whichever way it is translated makes little difference to the main meaning of Jesus' statement in verse 5, which corrects Nicodemus' mistaken notion that the second birth would be the *same* as the first by specifying how *different* it would be. Unlike birth of the flesh, this one will be 'of [Greek: *ek* – lit. 'out of'] water and the Spirit'.

This is where the difficulties of interpretation begin! Broadly speaking there are three possible ways of understanding the phrase rendered by the NIV 'of water and the Spirit':

1. Two births, one physical and one spiritual;
2. One birth, purely spiritual;
3. One birth, with both physical and spiritual aspects.

We shall consider each of these in detail.

A PHYSICAL BIRTH AND A SPIRITUAL BIRTH

Briefly, on this interpretation the parallelism of verse 6 in terms of the contrast between 'flesh' and 'Spirit' is read back into verse 5 and the physical concept of birth in verse 4 is read forward into verse 5. Nicodemus was wrongly assuming that a man must have two physical births, and Jesus corrects him by saying that a man needs one physical birth ('of water') and one spiritual birth ('of the Spirit').

'Water' is therefore a synonym of 'flesh' and must in some way refer to physical birth. Some modern evangelicals would see this as a reference to the 'breaking of the waters' which precedes physical birth (see, for example, Kenneth Taylor's footnote in the Living Bible paraphrase). The following difficulties attend this view.

First, there is no evidence that 'born of water' was ever used in the ancient world of physical birth. There is an occasional reference to *semen* as 'water' (and as 'dew' or 'rain'), but this would refer to conception rather than birth; and there is no known link with the words 'born of'.

Second, it would have been much simpler for Jesus to say 'born of flesh and the Spirit', if this is what he actually meant. Why confuse Nicodemus further by introducing the word 'water' at this point?

Third, on this understanding the first part of the statement becomes a bit of a *non sequitur*! 'A man cannot enter the kingdom unless he is first born physically . . .' hardly seems a point worth making! 'A man', by definition, is already some-one who has been born. And the emphatic position of 'unless' qualifies the whole sentence by highlighting the vital criterion for entrance.

Fourth, 'water' may accompany physical birth, but it does not cause it to happen. The application of the *one* preposition (*ek* = 'out of') to *both* words (water and Spirit) means that this birth is in the same cause/effect, means/end relationship to both. It cannot be accompanied by one and caused by the other. There would then be no parallel between birth 'out of' water and birth 'out of' the Spirit.

Fifth, the grammar indicates one birth rather than two. Jesus does not say 'born of water and born of the Spirit', or even 'born of water and of the Spirit', but 'born of water and the Spirit' (which virtually makes the two a 'tandem' cause of the birth).

Sixth, it is highly unlikely that Nicodemus took 'water' as a reference to the first (physical) birth.

For these six reasons we must reject this interpretation.

A PURELY SPIRITUAL BIRTH

Whereas the first view treated 'water' and 'flesh' as synony-mous, this approach treats 'water' and 'spirit' as synonymous. The phrase 'gives birth to spirit' in verse 6 is taken as the total equivalent of 'water and the Spirit' in verse 5.

In support of this thesis, it is pointed out that John often uses 'water' as a metaphor for non-physical, spiritual realities, particularly for the Holy Spirit (e.g. John 4:14; 7:38). This follows Old Testament usage (e.g. in Ezek 36:25, where 'clean water' brings inner cleansing to the heart).

At first sight, the problem is in this way neatly resolved – but closer examination reveals it to be too simple a solution. It fails to explain the following points.

First the word 'water' seems a superfluous addition if it is a synonym for 'spirit'. Why make such a double statement, in an indirect and a direct word? 'Born of spirit [i.e. 'water'] and the Spirit' does not sound like a remark by the greatest teacher of all time!

Second, 'water' in John *always* means physical water (H_2O!). It means this throughout these early chapters and even later in this same chapter (1:26, 33; 2:7; 3:23). In the few later passages where it is used metaphorically of the Holy Spirit, it is invariably qualified by an additional adjective (e.g. 'living') or phrase (e.g. 'that I give him') or even by a noun (e.g. 'spring' or 'streams') – it is *never* simply 'water' by itself.

Third, it is extremely doubtful if Nicodemus, to whom the statement was directed, would see it as a metaphor for the Holy Spirit. He would be even more confused if Jesus almost immediately switched to the metaphor of 'wind' to help him understand! 'Unless a man be born of water and wind . . .'!

Therefore, on these three grounds this interpretation must also be ruled out.

ONE BIRTH WITH PHYSICAL AND SPIRITUAL ASPECTS

On this interpretation, Jesus is telling Nicodemus that he needs a transforming experience, mediated to him through both physical and spiritual channels – the second birth is therefore an event with both physical and spiritual dimensions. 'Water' refers to the physical act of being baptised, but this of itself and by itself cannot bring about the new birth if it is not accompanied by the divine activity of the Holy Spirit. In favour of this understanding, we may cite the following considerations.

First, there is a sound principle of biblical study which takes scripture in its plainest meaning, unless there are very good reasons for doing otherwise. In the present case, 'water' is taken to mean 'water' and 'spirit' is taken to mean 'spirit'!

Second, this does justice to the grammar, in which both nouns are controlled by the same verb and preposition. The juxtaposition of 'water-and-spirit' is taken as a double ground for a single event.

Third, Nicodemus would almost certainly understand 'water' in terms of ritual cleansing, being well-versed in both the prophetic promises and the Pharisaic practices. Furthermore, the background to the conversation is not only Jesus' miraculous ministry, but also John's ministry of a baptism into repentance (1:19–28; 3:22–26). We know that the Pharisees were refusing and being refused this baptism (Matt 3:7; Luke 7:30). There may even be a slighting reference to John in Nicodemus' opening remark in John 3:2, since John did no miracles (John 10:41). There may also be a mild rebuke for Nicodemus' flattery in the word 'water', since the Pharisees, of whom he was one, were fully aware that Jesus was also baptising at this time (John 4:1). Is Jesus not telling Nicodemus that he cannot have the secret of powerful ministry while refusing to submit to baptism, either John's or his own?

Fourth, the conjunction of 'water' and 'spirit' is already a familiar theme in all four gospels, in that John preached two baptisms, one in water and the other in Spirit (Matt 3:11; Mark 1:8; Luke 3:16; John 1:33). It is too much of a coincidence to believe that John 3 has no connection with this existing link between the two baptisms.

Fifth, this interpretation is entirely congruous with the instrumental language used by the New Testament writers about water baptism (see chapter 4). They obviously believed that baptism 'effected what it symbolised' and was as much an act of God as of man. John 3:5 is remarkably parallel to Titus

3:5 – 'born of water' and 'bath of regeneration' are not all that different.

Sixth, the vast majority of Bible scholars through the ages, both Catholic and Protestant, have taken 'water' to be a clear reference to baptism.

The usual reasons for rejecting this line of interpretation are not internal and textual ones; rather they are external and theological. On the one hand, there is the chronic separation of the physical and the spiritual in the Western world, which owes more to Platonic philosophy than to biblical teaching. On the other hand, there is an evangelical phobia about 'baptismal regeneration' which blinds many eyes to the plain meaning of our Lord's words. A 'Zwinglian' view of the sacraments (as mere symbols) is reluctant to attribute spiritual effects to physical acts – in spite of the disastrous results of eating the physical fruit of the tree of knowledge (Gen 2:17) or of taking the bread and wine of the Lord's Supper unworthily (1 Cor 11:29–30).

I too am concerned about the view that a person can be 'born again' of water only (provided the right person is using the right words!). This is especially offensive when predicated of babies, who are quite incapable of making any response of repentance or faith. But if 'water' refers to the baptism of the truly penitent and believing person, then that is quite a different matter, far removed from that superstitious or magical notion of what has been traditionally understood as 'baptismal regeneration'. Furthermore, the close connection made by Jesus between 'water' and 'spirit' ensures that no one can presume that it could ever be by water only. Without the Spirit's vital contribution there could be no new birth. That brings us to our final question: What exactly does the word 'spirit' mean in this connection?

Careful readers will have noticed that in closely following the NIV's rendering, 'Spirit' has been used when directly quoting the text of John 3:3–8, but that 'spirit' has been preferred when dealing with the disputed interpretations of 'water' and 'spirit'. My latter usage highlights the fact that verse 5 lacks the definite article. This means that 'born of . . .

spirit' (v. 5) therefore might not be the same thing as verse 6's '*the* Spirit gives birth to spirit' (though even here the article is missing in some early manuscripts); however, the NIV's rendering clearly indicates the translators' interpretative decision on this matter.

Where 'water' is taken as a reference to baptism, 'spirit' is usually assumed to refer to the Holy Spirit's activity during the administration of the sacrament itself. While a human agent applies the 'medium' of water, the divine agent (the Holy Spirit) is using the occasion to accomplish the inward and spiritual work. Certainly we can agree that without such activity by the Holy Spirit there could not be any spiritual effect of the physical event, for neither the human agent nor the material medium have the power to do that. But does this do full justice to the unusual grammatical features of Jesus' statement?

These features, as we have noted before, are the absence of the definite article and the striking fact that 'water' and 'spirit' are governed by the same preposition (*ek* = 'out of'), which implies they have the same relationship to the new birth (whereas the view we have just looked at makes 'water' the medium and 'Spirit' the agent).

The difficulties are completely resolved if 'water and spirit' is taken to refer to water-baptism and Spirit-baptism, the two being so closely related yet never totally identified in New Testament teaching. The following considerations point in this direction.

First, as we have noted, 'water' and 'Spirit' have already been linked in John's preaching, referring to these two 'baptisms' – one his work, the other the Messiah's work. Nicodemus would be fully aware of John's preaching; he was a keen observer of all unusual ministry!

Second, the common preposition, and its unusual meaning, now make complete sense. Even physical birth is a coming 'out of' a previous condition 'in the mother's womb' (this is the very point Nicodemus makes in v. 4 – that it is impossible to get back 'into' that state, in order to come 'out of' it again!). Jesus is saying that the second birth is not 'out of' a womb but out of 'water and spirit'. Those who are baptised 'in' water and 'in' Spirit come 'out of' the dual experience into new life. Both 'water' and 'Spirit' are the *medium* in which this birth takes place (see chapter 23 on 1 Cor 12:13).

Third, the absence of the definite article indicates a subjective experience of the power of the Holy Spirit; its presence focuses on the objective existence of the person of the Holy Spirit (see Appendix 2 for a fuller treatment of this neglected point). The phrase 'baptised in Holy Spirit' never includes the definite article; the emphasis is on what the receiver of this gift is evidently experiencing. In water-baptism the candidate is hardly aware of the Spirit's inward work in the sacrament, but in Spirit-baptism that awareness is the central feature, both for the candidate and for others present. In his conversation with Nicodemus, Jesus emphasises this consciousness of the Spirit's activity – as of feeling wind blowing in the face and *hearing* the sound of it, a statement impossible to dissociate from Pentecost, when they were all 'baptised in Holy Spirit'. When a person is 'born of Spirit' the event may be invisible, but it *will* not be inaudible!

Incidentally, Jesus was also answering his original question as to how a teacher can produce works as well as words. Jesus himself could not do so until after his baptism in water and reception of the Spirit. Such works are also signs of the kingdom of God (Matt 12:28).

The time has come to summarise our findings. To be born again is to be born of water and Spirit, which is to be 'baptised in water and in Spirit' and to come 'out of' both to live the new life in Christ by his Spirit. The same truth is stated in different words by the apostle Paul, when he says we are 'saved . . . through [again, one preposition for two things] the washing of rebirth and renewal by the Holy Spirit, whom he poured out on us generously' (Tit 3:5–6 – see chapter 26). Thus, water-baptism and Spirit-baptism are not just integral to initiation; they are fundamental to regeneration and salvation!

11   THE LIVING STREAMS (John 7:37–39)

³⁷On the last and greatest day of the Feast, Jesus stood and said in a loud voice, 'If anyone is thirsty, let him come to me and drink. ³⁸Whoever believes in me, as the Scripture has said, streams of living water will flow from within him.' ³⁹By this he meant the Spirit, whom those who believed in him were later to receive. Up to that time the Spirit had not been given, since Jesus had not yet been glorified. (John 7:37–39)

In the Middle East the Feast of Tabernacles comes after six months without rain and this 'Harvest Thanksgiving' climaxes in a ceremony of prayer that the 'early rains' may begin. In New Testament times water from the Pool of Siloam was poured over the altar on the eighth day, the 'great day', of the festival. Rain was always the major token of divine blessing on the land and people, just as its being withheld was a divine curse (Deut 28:12, 24).

On this very day, Jesus promised the abolition of the 'dry season'; henceforth there would be a perpetual abundance of liquid refreshment flowing from within each individual. There were, however, two important conditions which qualified his offer.

First, it depended on human activity. There are three imperative verbs: 'Come . . . drink . . . believe'. All of them centre on himself. Implicit in all this is an extraordinary claim – 'You are busy asking *God* for water; *I* will give it to you!'

John's comment (in v. 39) makes it clear that Jesus' language is figurative (as was his claim to rebuild the temple in three days). He was talking about a spiritual refreshment that would do far more than sustain physical life. This is what he meant by 'living water', or the 'water of life'.

Second, it was not immediately available. Jesus was not offering instant blessing!

Again, John's explanation is necessary. Since the reference is to the gift of the Holy Spirit, it would be a year or two before that could be received by anyone, since the gift could not be released until Jesus had returned to his former status in heaven. Only after the day of Pentecost could this promise be fulfilled.

There are some important points to notice in the text itself. The most puzzling is the reference to a promise to this effect in 'the Scripture', namely the Old Testament. There is no clear prophecy associated with the coming messianic age that can be cited in cross-reference to this particular claim of Jesus. Among the suggested candidates are the following:

Isaiah 12:3, drawing water from the wells of salvation;
Isaiah 58:11, a spring whose waters never fail;
Ezekiel 47:1–12, water flowing from the temple itself;
Zechariah 14:8, water flowing out from Jerusalem.

The last text has the merit of being part of a whole prophecy about the Messiah's appearance in Jerusalem at the Feast of Tabernacles. However, we have to confess that we cannot be really sure which scripture passage Jesus (or John, interpreting Jesus) had in mind. We are on surer ground when we look at some of the other features in the text itself.

It is interesting to notice that 'believe' and 'receive' were quite separate events for the followers of Jesus at that time. They had already believed in Jesus, but could not yet receive the Spirit. At least for that generation, believing in Jesus was not the same thing as receiving the Spirit. The word translated 'believed' in verse 39 is *pisteusantes*, an aorist participle for a single, decisive step already accomplished, whereas 'receive' is still clearly future.

Of course, all this was pre-Pentecost, when they could believe but couldn't receive, even if they had wanted to (because the Spirit was not yet 'given' – see below). The distinction between 'believing' and 'receiving' could only be maintained in the *post*-Pentecost world if two things could be established.

First, that there were *any* cases *after* Pentecost where people believed in Jesus without receiving the Spirit. In fact, there were a number, including Paul himself, but the clearest is the case of the Samaritans (see chapter 16 on Acts 8, where the aorist tense is again used: *episteusan*).

Second, that apostolic doctrine distinguished between the two. This Paul does implicitly with his question to the Ephesians: 'Did you receive the Holy Spirit when you believed?' (see chapter 20 on Acts 19, where again as with John 7:39, the aorist tense is used: *pisteusantes*).

We conclude that both before and after Pentecost, 'believing in Jesus' and 'receiving the Spirit' were neither synonymous nor necessarily simultaneous (see chapters 16 and 20 for further evidence of this conclusion).

The latter half of verse 39 also contains an unusual construction of considerable significance. Most versions of the Bible have here additional English words which do not correspond to the Greek; the extra words clarify rather than distort the meaning, but nevertheless disguise the import, and impact, of the original. Translated literally, it would read: 'For not yet was Spirit'. Two points emerge from this rendering which throw light on other scriptures.

First, this cannot mean that the Holy Spirit did not yet *exist*. He is one of the three persons of the eternal Godhead. The clear meaning is that his resources were not yet fully available to human beings. The usual addition of the word 'given' points to the future manifestation of his person and power. But in Acts 19:2 almost the same construction is used in the Ephesians' reply to Paul's question: 'We have not heard that Holy Spirit is' (Acts 19:2 – see chapter 20); again, the addition of the word 'given' makes sense of their statement. They had heard about the future baptism of the Spirit (they were, after all, John's disciples and he had told all his followers about this); what they had not heard was that this gift was now available. Most versions wrongly phrase their answer to suggest they were totally ignorant of the Spirit, which is very misleading.

Second, both here in John 7:39 and in Acts 19:2 the phrase lacks the definite article, which is very significant. Let Bishop Westcott's comment in his *Gospel of John* (John Murray,

1903), p. 123, illuminate this omission: 'When the term occurs in this form [without the article], it marks an operation, or manifestation, or gift of the Spirit, and not the personal Spirit.' Note that the beginning of the verse emphasises the person of the Spirit, by including the definite article (and see Appendix 2 for a detailed examination of this characteristic of New Testament references to the Holy Spirit).

Finally, we must note the progression in this passage from 'drinking in' to 'flowing out'. 'Drink' is equivalent to 'receive' and is used this way in 1 Corinthians 12:13 (see chapter 23), though there the verb is in the aorist tense (referring to the very first 'swallow'), whereas here it is the present imperative, which means to 'go on drinking'. The point here seems to be that intake and output will correspond. A man will be a channel, not a reservoir! Those who continue to imbibe the Spirit will continue to impart the Spirit. This emphasis on continuity is also to be found in the present participle of 'believe' in verse 38 (Greek: *ho pisteuon* = 'he who is believing' rather than 'he who has believed', in contrast to v. 39).

The two volumes of Luke and Acts were written primarily for unbelievers, hence the main emphasis is on the *initial* intake of the outpoured Spirit (also such phrases as 'fall upon, come upon, poured out upon', emphasising the Spirit outside a person). John, writing for believers ('that you may go on believing . . . and go on having eternal life' – John 20:31), emphasises the *continual* output of the indwelling Spirit (hence such phrases as the AV's 'out of his belly [inmost being]', emphasising the Spirit inside a person).

How important it is to take seriously the different viewpoints of all the New Testament writers, synthesising these into a whole and balanced theology. In no other doctrine is this quite so important as with the person and work of the Holy Spirit. Luke, John and Paul each have their own special contribution to make – and should probably be studied in that order to get a true understanding!

12 THE KNOWN STRANGER
(John 14:17)

'The world cannot accept him [the Spirit of truth], because it neither sees him nor knows him. But you know him, for he lives with you and will be in you.' (John 14:17)

On the night before he was to die in agony, Jesus had to comfort his disciples! Their sense of impending disaster sprang from his announced departure. The promise of a replacement 'Stand-by' (a better translation than 'Comforter') did little to help. How could a complete stranger ever take his place in their hearts and lives?

Now comes the astonishing announcement that they are already acquainted with the replacement! Jesus is not talking about the general influence of the Spirit in the world, since this has never been, and could never be, the basis of a personal relationship. The world has never set eyes upon him nor experienced intimacy with him. But the disciples had been aware of his personal presence, though they may not have been aware of his identity.

Their relationship with this 'Spirit of truth' ('truth' being the same word as 'reality' in Greek) can only be expressed in the form of a paradox. It has both continuity and discontinuity in it. The same person will be 'staying' on with them, yet he will be 'sent' to them. It is not a new relationship, yet it will be a new relationship. He has been with them, but he will be in them.

Some copyists of New Testament manuscripts found this ambiguity too much and amended the verb tenses so that they were either both present ('he is with you and is in you') or, more frequently, both future ('he will be with you and he will be in you'). But the most reliable readings undoubtedly contain both past and future tenses. Scripture should be taken as it stands, not changed to make 'sense' to us; that can turn truth into nonsense! The mixture of past and future tenses points to both continuity and discontinuity in the relationship.

CONTINUITY

'He [already] lives [or stays] with you'. There are two possible ways in which the Spirit could already be with (actually, the Greek word is *para* = 'beside') them.

First, *in the physical presence of Jesus*. Since he had received the Holy Spirit 'without limit' (John 3:34), they were already experiencing the presence of the Spirit in the character, conversation and conduct of Jesus. His message and his miracles were the work of the Holy Spirit (Matt 12:28).

Second, *in the physical absence of Jesus*. To their complete astonishment, they had discovered they themselves could cure diseases and cast out demons, even when Jesus sent them out from his company. This very real experience brought them great joy (Luke 10:17).

Strictly speaking, it was the second of these experiences which would continue into the future after Jesus' final departure (and was therefore the primary reference of Jesus' words). Yet since both experiences 'felt' so similar, the second would be as good as the first, and even better (John 16:7). Indeed, it is hard to distinguish between them in terms of existential experience (John 14:20, 23). This explains their incongruous joy when Jesus finally left them (Luke 24:52).

DISCONTINUITY

There is to be a radical shift in the relationship from an external ('beside') to an internal ('inside') knowledge of this person. Just what is the significance of this change, which most scholars rightly identify with the pre- and post-Pentecost phases of discipleship (see also chapter 13 on John 20:22)? The most significant changes Pentecost made may be listed as follows.

Unconscious to conscious. This full awareness of the Spirit's presence would lead them to talk as naturally about him as a person as they would have spoken about Jesus (the Spirit is directly mentioned about forty times in the first thirteen chapters of Acts).

Temporary to permanent. They had known his power on occasion, when sent on 'apostolic' tours; they had known the lack of it on other occasions (Mark 9:28). Now they would have a constant, as well as a conscious, ability to use his resources.

Hesitant to confident. They had known failure in ministry and their morale had been totally shattered at the cross. After Pentecost they were noted for their courage (Greek: *parrhesia* = 'boldness of speech'). Their opponents mistakenly attributed this to their past association with Jesus (Acts 4:13), whereas it was the result of their present association with his Spirit.

Delegated to direct. While they had effectively acted as the representatives of Jesus during his lifetime, they now used his name with an 'authority' they felt they 'possessed' themselves ('What I have I give you . . .' – Acts 3:6).

These and other contrasts constitute a change in degree rather than in kind – yet that change came suddenly rather than gradually.

Perhaps the most important thing to note is that the language of 'indwelling' only became appropriate for the disciples after the change that took place at Pentecost, after they had 'received power', after they had been 'baptised in the Holy Spirit', and after they had been 'filled' and 'anointed'. This usage persists in the rest of the New Testament (e.g. Paul writes: 'Do you not know that your body is a temple of Holy Spirit, who is in you, whom you have received from God?' – I Cor 6:19). This thinking is at variance with modern evangelical teaching that the Spirit 'indwells' from the moment one believes in Jesus (see chapter 21 on Rom 8:9).

There is a similar change in relationship to the Spirit in the life of Jesus himself. Conceived by the Holy Spirit (Luke 1:35), it is difficult to believe that during his childhood and early manhood he had less of the Spirit's presence than his cousin John, who was 'filled with the Holy Spirit even from birth [or from his mother's womb]' (Luke 1:15). Yet at the age of thirty and, significantly, immediately after his water-baptism, as he prayed (Matt 3:16; Luke 3:21), he was 'anointed with the Holy Spirit and power' (Acts 10:38) and proceeded to perform the miracles which John, who had not been baptised in water (Matt 3:14) nor anointed by the Spirit in the same way, had never been able to do. This may explain why Jesus, while holding John in the highest respect, regarded him as less significant than the 'least in the kingdom' (Matt 11:11).

In other words, there is a definite correspondence between Jesus' experience at the Jordan river and the disciples' experience at Pentecost (in both cases, the Spirit came 'down upon' them, i.e. from outside them). Both were an anointing with Holy Spirit power for ministry. The first was upon Jesus' physical body for the initiation of his messianic mission; the second was upon his mystical body (the church) for the continuation of that same ministry (see Acts 1:1).

Is there a similar change in the experience of subsequent believers, right up to today? It may be quite wrong to dismiss John 14:17 as no more than a historical statement, as only true of a fleeting phase in the story of salvation. There is a real sense in which all believers can have the same paradoxical shift in their relationship with the Holy Spirit.

From the very first touches of their spiritual awakening, through an earnest search for God to full surrender to his will, the Holy Spirit has been 'with' them. Without his presence there could be no conviction of sin, righteousness or judgement. It is the Spirit who prepares them for the new birth and brings them through it. It is the Spirit who conveys the divine 'grant' of repentance and the divine 'gift' of faith. It is the Spirit who leads them to the water of baptism and uses that event to accomplish their burial and resurrection. In all this the Holy Spirit is obviously 'with' them and they 'know' his presence, in the sense of experiencing his activity.

But a radical change in the relationship occurs when they are 'baptised in the Holy Spirit'. They now 'receive' him in manifest power (i.e. with outward evidence). What happened to Jesus at the Jordan and to the disciples at Pentecost has now happened to them – producing the same conscious confidence and miraculous ministry. So the shift in prepositions, from 'with' to 'in', may be legitimately and appropriately applied to them also.

The important point is that the language of 'receiving' and 'indwelling' is only used in the New Testament of those who have had this personal experience of Pentecostal power. Such terms are never used in the New Testament of the Spirit's activity in repentance, faith and water-baptism (though, as we shall see, in chapter 36, the word 'disciple' is applied to these early stages of initiation). It is possible, therefore, to be a penitent, believing, baptised 'disciple' – without having received the indwelling Holy Spirit (the Samaritans are the classic case of this anomaly – see chapter 16). Up to this point the Holy Spirit is 'with' the disciple in a way he cannot be with the world of unbelievers; but he is not yet 'in' the believer as he will be when initiation is complete.

This understanding cannot, of course, be based solely on this one verse in John's gospel; it simply cannot carry the weight of such a far-reaching conclusion. But as we continue to look at other passages, particularly in the Acts and in the epistles, we shall find ample confirmation of this position. The practical implications of this conclusion will be dealt with in the final section of the book, and particularly in chapter 35.

13 THE FIRST ELEVEN (John 20:22)

> And with that he breathed on them and said, 'Receive the Holy Spirit.' (John 20:22)

What is the connection between this occasion in the 'Upper Room' on the first Easter Sunday and the event of Pentecost in the temple court two months later? Why did the disciples make no apparent response to Jesus' action and command or, at least according to the record, experience no change in themselves? Why, after this, did they still have to 'wait' for the promise of the Father (Luke 24:49)? And why were they still cowering behind locked doors a week later?

The most common solution to these problems is the 'liberal' charge that John has distorted history for his own literary purposes. Since he never intended to duplicate Luke's work by writing a second volume on the early church, but nevertheless aimed at providing a complete coverage of the decisive events of our salvation-history, he has therefore altered the dating of Pentecost to be able to include it in his gospel. Having already mentioned that the Holy Spirit would be given after Jesus was glorified (7:39), he felt the need to complete the story and juggled the facts to do so!

Even in general terms, this interpretation is unacceptable. Apart from the slur on John's integrity (and his historical accuracy is increasingly recognised by scholars, some of whom are now claiming that in this regard he is superior to the synoptic authors), this manipulation of truth hardly fits a belief in the divine inspiration of scripture.

This explanation is to be rejected because such a conjectured transposition in time significantly alters the event itself: it becomes a private rather than a public happening; a much smaller group is involved (one twelfth the size!); and there are no recorded results, either in the people concerned or through them on others. It is very difficult to accept that John is talking about the same event as Pentecost.

For these and other reasons, it seems right to accept that John is historically sensitive. In the same context it is stated that the ascension is still in the future (20:17), as is Jesus' return to the earth (21:22). So we may take it that John is accurately reporting what Jesus said and did on the day he rose from the dead. But what exactly happened? There are at least three possible answers to that question: they received the Holy Spirit; they were regenerated; or they were 'rehearsed' for Pentecost. Let us examine each in turn.

THEY RECEIVED THE HOLY SPIRIT

This answer assumes that we have here the fulfilment of the promise made at the Feast of Tabernacles (7:38–39 – see chapter 11): those who had already believed in Jesus now received the Holy Spirit. They were told they were 'going to receive'; now they did. The necessary precondition (that Jesus be 'glorified' first – 7:39) was fulfilled in his crucifixion (12:23–33) and his resurrection. This event was therefore their full introduction to the third person of the Trinity.

At first sight this seems to be the only possible interpretation, but further meditation raises a number of doubts.

First, if we accept this understanding of the incident, then there are great difficulties in relating this to what came later on the day of Pentecost, which would then acquire a quite secondary significance. An event not even mentioned in Matthew, Mark or Luke, and in only one verse in John, becomes the crucial event in the lives of the apostles, beside which Pentecost becomes merely a release of power. If they had already 'received' the Spirit and he was now 'indwelling' them, what are we to make of the imagery of 'coming upon' and 'poured out upon' used to describe Pentecost – language which, to say the least, seems rather inappropriate?

Second, it is equally difficult to relate this 'Upper Room' incident to what was already true for them before this. If the Spirit was already 'with' them and they already 'knew' him (John 14:17 – see chapter 12), it is not easy to see what decisive change took place at this point. There is a complete absence of any evidence that there was a radical change in the demeanour or activity of the disciples between this event and Pentecost – other than the joy which can be totally explained by their reunion with the risen Jesus.

Third, if it were true this view would directly contradict Jesus' earlier insistence that the coming of the Spirit was contingent on his own departure, which had not yet taken place (16:7).

Fourth, does 'glorified' for John not also include his ascension to heaven, regaining his original glory there (e.g. 17:5)?

Fifth, Peter, who was present on this occasion and at Pentecost, always referred to the latter as the time when he 'received' the Spirit (see Acts 10:47; 11:17; 15:9 – all dealt with in chapter 18). If the apostles themselves did not think they 'received' the Spirit until Pentecost, we are hardly at liberty to imply that they had missed the significance of the 'Upper Room' event which we in our wisdom understand better than they did!

In the light of these objections of an identification of this event with the receiving of the Holy Spirit, we must look for another explanation.

THEY WERE REGENERATED

This view identifies the event as the moment when the disciples were 'born again' and brought into 'eternal life'. In this way they were 'prepared' for Pentecost, since 'only those who have been born of the Spirit can be baptised in the Spirit'.

The last-quoted remark reveals the theological presuppositions of those who favour this interpretation. It is the 'Pentecostal' two-stage, 'second blessing' view of salvation.

Separating Spirit-baptism from regeneration, its exponents teach that there is a double 'reception' of the Spirit for each believer. The Spirit is received first for salvation and pardon (on repentance and faith) and is subsequently received a second time for service and power. John 20:22 is almost the sole 'proof-text' for this theory (perhaps because it is the only verse in the New Testament where the Spirit is said to be 'received' apart from the experience of being 'baptised in Spirit'); the event is taken to be a standard precedent for all subsequent conversions. The gap of seven weeks between the apostles being 'born' of the Spirit and being 'baptised' in the Spirit, together with the 'waiting' in prayer, is used as a 'norm' for Christian initiation today.

This view has the advantage of being neat, but maybe it is too neat! There are in fact at least two clear indications that this was not the moment of the disciples' 'regeneration'.

First, scripture uses the vocabulary of 'rebirth' about the disciples prior to this event: John 13:10 says they were already 'clean'; John 1:12–13 says that all were 'born of God' who received Jesus and believed in his name (and this certainly included the disciples, if it included anybody!); Matthew 13:11 says that the revelation of the kingdom was already theirs; they could 'see' it (cf. John 3:3).

Second, not all the apostles were present at the 'Upper Room' event. This point is so terribly obvious, but it is nearly always overlooked! Only ten of the 'Twelve' were present. When was Thomas 'regenerated'? And Matthias? And, for that matter, when were the rest of the 120 disciples who were 'baptised in the Spirit' on the day of Pentecost 'born again'? If Pentecost is regarded as the second reception of the Spirit, when did all these get the first?

It seems that this second interpretation is also unsatisfactory. Perhaps, therefore, we should now consider the third and final view, to see whether it provides a more convincing explanation of the 'Upper Room' event.

THEY WERE 'REHEARSED' FOR PENTECOST

Instead of asking what happened on this occasion, we need to ask a more radical question: Did *anything* happen? That is, did anything happen other than what Jesus did and said? We can only answer this in terms of what John actually records – and the answer is quite simple: nothing happened!

If this is true, what was the incident all about? Why does John record it and what did it achieve?

Jesus was preparing his disciples for the totally unprecedented experience they would undergo in a few weeks time. It was a 'dummy-run' to familiarise them with some aspects of the coming event, so that when it came they would both recognise what was happening and respond to it in an appropriate way.

To prepare them Jesus gave the disciples both a sign (or signal) and a command (or order). It was a classic example of excellent training preparation of the 'When this happens . . . do this . . .' kind.

The sign

The text says (literally) that 'Jesus blew'. The additional words 'on them' are an attempt to translate the unusual Greek verb *emphusao*, which literally means to 'blow into' or 'inflate'. Such blowing would be both heard and felt by the disciples (cf. 3:8). The sound in their ears would resemble that of a wind. When they heard this seven weeks later (Acts 2:2), they would immediately know that Jesus was blowing on them again, breathing his Spirit into them. Incidentally, in Greek the same word – *pneuma* – is used for the three words 'breath', 'wind' and 'spirit'. Likewise in the Old Testament *ruach*, an onomatopoeic Hebrew word (that is one where the sound and the meaning are the same, and where in this case the *ch* is pronounced as in the Scottish word 'loch') is used for these three words.

The command

'Receive' is here an imperative; it is an order. It is also in the aorist tense, indicating one single act of receiving. Receiving the Spirit is an active rather than a passive response. It implies reaching out and taking hold rather than just 'letting it happen'. Co-operation is required; as Jesus breathes out, they must breathe in! The aorist imperative does not necessarily imply that Jesus was ordering the disciples to do this immediately on that particular occasion. Nor is there any hint in John 20 that they did respond to the command at that time. But when the day of Pentecost came, they certainly did. When the wind/breath of Jesus blew on them, the disciples 'began to speak in other tongues . . .' (Acts 2:4). They 'yielded their members' to his moving. This was a volitional act of co-operation, freely receiving his gift of the Spirit.

Additional considerations

As soon as we see this 'Upper Room' event on the first Easter Sunday solely in terms of what is actually recorded and read nothing more into it, the difficulties disappear, since these arise because of our speculation about what might have been happening. Seen as a preparatory rehearsal or, in more biblical terms, as a 'prophetic action' prefiguring a future event, John 20:22 fits more comfortably into its wider context. Such prophetic actions are familiar in both the Old and the New Testament (e.g. Ezek 4; Acts 21:10–11). The following additional considerations provide cumulative evidence for this interpretation.

First, the text itself is more easily explained on this hypothesis. We have already noted that the word 'them' is not in the original Greek; simply that 'Jesus blew into'. Even more striking is the fact that the command to 'receive' comes *after* the blowing, not before; had the blowing imparted the Spirit to them, Jesus would have said, 'You have received' (i.e. in the indicative, not the imperative mood).

Second, the whole context has a future rather than a present reference. In John 20:21 Jesus is sending the disciples out – but not yet! Though the verb is in the present tense, they are not to go immediately. This 'sending' will only become effective after Pentecost. In John 20:23 the disciples are (in the ol.!-

fashioned terminology) to 'loose and retain sins'. Yet this will not happen immediately; it will be undertaken only after Pentecost. The first recorded loosing is in Acts 2 and the first recorded retaining is in Acts 5. If John 20:21 and 20:23 obviously have such a future reference, in spite of their use of present tense verbs, the odds are that John 20:22 is similar.

Third, they have already had an example of such 'proleptic' (i.e. anticipatory of the future) action by Jesus in this very 'Upper Room'. He had taken bread and wine, told them to eat and drink them as his very body and blood – on the day before his actual death, before his body was broken and his blood shed. We do not have to believe that on that very first occasion of the 'Lord's Supper' the bread and wine were in reality the 'communion' of his body and blood they subsequently became (1 Cor 10:16). On that unforgettable night, when his blood was still in his body and his body was still with them, he was literally rehearsing what was to become their central act of worship. On that occasion also he had limited himself to giving a sign (bread and wine) and a command ('Do this in remembrance of me'); and on that occasion also, there is no record of the disciples receiving anything more than the sign. The act became a sacrament only after the event to which it looked forward; indeed, it looks as if it was not repeated until after Pentecost!

Fourth, the fact that nothing whatever is said to have happened to the disciples after Jesus' words and actions now seems highly significant. John is being totally accurate in his reporting. Jesus was certainly delegating his *authority* to the disciples, but he was not yet communicating his *power* to them.

So Jesus has, in this simple word and deed, associated Pentecost indelibly and intimately with himself. No wonder that when the event itself took place – following such a prophetic 'pre-enactment' – Peter could so confidently assert that 'he [Jesus himself] . . . has poured out what you now see and hear' (Acts 2:33). It was the final proof that 'God has made this Jesus, whom you crucified, both Lord and Christ' (Acts 2:36).

14 THE FIFTIETH DAY
(Acts 1:4–5; 2:1–4)

⁴On one occasion, while he was eating with them, he gave them this command: 'Do not leave Jerusalem, but wait for the gift my Father promised, which you have heard me speak about. ⁵For John baptised with water, but in a few days you will be baptised with the Holy Spirit.' (Acts 1:4–5)

¹When the day of Pentecost came, they were all together in one place. ²Suddenly a sound like the blowing of a violent wind came from heaven and filled the whole house where they were sitting. ³They saw what seemed to be tongues of fire that separated and came to rest on each of them. ⁴All of them were filled with the Holy Spirit and began to speak in other tongues as the Spirit enabled them. (Acts 2:1–4)

Because the Bible is a 'self-interpreting' book, it is necessary to study the whole in order to understand any part. The significance of any single event can only be fully appreciated when it is seen as a link in the chain of sacred history. Some happenings are so crucial that without them the whole story would fall apart. Pentecost is one such event.

The day of Pentecost is rooted in the Old Testament, which is, above all, a library of *prophets* (from the five books of Moses to the one booklet of Malachi). The patriarchs themselves were prophets (Gen 20:7; Ps 105:15). Moses expressed the hope that one day all the Lord's people, not just his elders, would 'prophesy' (Num 11:25–29). Joel went further and predicted that 'in the last days' they all would (Joel 2:28–29).

Prophets prophesied because the 'Spirit of the Lord' had 'come upon', 'fallen on', 'filled' or been 'given' to them.

Therefore, when the day came in which all the people would prophesy, it would be because there had been an 'outpouring' of the Spirit on a wider scale than ever before. This would be the very essence of the 'new covenant' which God would establish, in place of the 'old' one made at Sinai (Isa 32:15; Jer 31:31–34; Ezek 36:26–27).

This 'promise' is confirmed and amplified in the gospels. All four record John the Baptist's prediction. As the last representative of 'old covenant' prophecy, he outlined the two-fold ministry of the coming Messiah-king as taking away sins and replacing them with the Spirit. But John introduces a new term for this prophetic anointing, made possible by his own introduction of the practice of water-baptism, which was a vivid analogy for what was to happen. The Christ would himself be anointed by the Spirit and would then '*baptise*' others in the Holy Spirit. This would not be a new thing, but it is a new name for an old experience, which is why it is virtually synonymous with the Old Testament terms mentioned above (see chapter 5). The new word emphasises the enveloping, overwhelming nature of the anointing; the recipient will be immersed, soaked, drenched, submerged, drowned in the Spirit – total permeation and penetration!

On the last night before he died, Jesus enlarged his disciples' understanding of the 'promise', emphasising that the Spirit is a *person* and not just a *power*, his function being to continue the convicting and teaching ministry of Jesus himself, filling the gap left by his departure (John 14–16). On the day of his resurrection, he took them through a 'rehearsal' of the fulfilment of the promise (see chapter 13). Luke records his ascension command to wait in Jerusalem until the 'clothing with power' has taken place (another Old Testament term – Judg 6:14; 1 Chron 12:18).

The stage for the drama of Pentecost had thus been set over many centuries, and we now need to address the significance of the day itself. As one of the three annual Jewish feasts, this particular one celebrated the giving of the law at Sinai, which occurred exactly fifty days after the 'Passover' lamb's blood had been shed in Egypt, hence the name 'Fiftieth' or '*Pente*cost'.

The giving of the law had resulted in the judicial death of three thousand Hebrews who broke the law (Exod 32:28)! Since entering the promised land, the day had acquired agricultural overtones, though this had been foreseen in the law (where it is referred to as the Feast of Weeks in Exod 34:22; the Feast of Harvest in Exod 23:16; and, most significant for the New Testament, the Day of First-fruits in Num 28:26). It was, indeed, to be a day of 'first-fruits' centuries later – when three thousand were brought from death to life (the letter kills, but the Spirit gives life – 2 Cor 3:6).

There was a human as well as a divine 'preparation' for the event. The one hundred and twenty people involved (this number is presumed from Acts 1:15) were followers of Jesus and were all 'northerners' from Galilee (Acts 2:7; cf. 1:11); the only one of the Twelve from the 'south', Judas of Kerioth, had already been replaced. They had witnessed the death and resurrection of Jesus and had already shared the profound feelings of despairing sorrow and delirious joy. They would be corporately free of emotional inhibition (so common a barrier today, especially in England!) and ready to respond in unembarrassed abandon to the outpoured Spirit. They were also engaged in regular prayer together; the Lord Jesus had made it quite clear that the Father gives the Holy Spirit to those who 'go on asking' (Luke 11:13; note the continuous present tense). So they all wanted to be 'baptised with the Holy Spirit' and 'receive power' (Acts 1:5, 8). But what did they expect to happen when their prayers were answered, and did they have any idea when it would happen? Or was Pentecost totally unexpected, both in timing and content?

As to what they expected, we can only guess. It seems likely that they anticipated hearing the sound of their ascended Lord 'breathing heavily' on them again (see chapter 13), though few would imagine it would sound like a howling gale this time! And they would almost certainly assume the result of receiving the promised Spirit would be an outpouring from their own mouths (they would be familiar with such examples as Saul in 1 Sam 10:10, to say nothing of the prophets), though they would probably not have guessed they would do so fluently in languages they had never learned and probably never even recognise themselves.

As to when they expected the Spirit to 'come upon' them, it is more than probable that they had already focused on the Feast of Pentecost. They could hardly ignore the fact that Jesus had 'arranged' his own death to coincide with the slaughter of Passover lambs (to the minute, at 3 p.m. on the eve of Passover – see Exod 12:6, 'mid-afternoon'). It would be the most natural thing in the world to expect the next great momentous event at the following Feast of Pentecost, when once again the Jewish people from far and wide would be gathered together in Jerusalem. In any case, one of the last things Jesus had told them was that they would be baptised in the Holy Spirit 'in a few days' (Acts 1:5). That they had already guessed the right day is indicated by the time and place they chose to meet together.

There is no hint in Acts 1 that 9 a.m. was a regular time for their own prayer-meetings. It was, however, the hour of public prayer in the *temple*, and it was here that they gathered together 'for one purpose' on the first day of the Feast. That it was the temple rather than the Upper Room may be deduced from the fact that later some thousands of people came to where they were gathered (and not vice versa); the only movement by the disciples was that twelve of them stood up, while the rest remained seated where they were (Acts 2:14). It is probably the word 'house' that has misled readers, who take it to mean a 'home'; but the word was also used of the temple as God's residence (2 Sam 7:5–6; Isa 6:4; 56:7; Luke 19:46; Acts 7:47; etc.). We also know that it was the regular meeting-place for the early disciples after Pentecost (Acts 3:1; the unusual phrase '*the* prayers' in Acts 2:42 may also refer to the temple liturgy). More than likely, it was in the area of Solomon's Porch that they met, where both sexes could mix (in which case, the spot is marked by the Mosque El-Aksa today).

'Objective' phenomena 'outside' themselves formed the overture. Wind and fire are a highly volatile combination. Notice too the combination of sight and sound; the eye and the ear are the two main gateways of communication to the soul which Peter was later to offer as proof of the truth of his claims 'that which you see and hear' (Acts 2:33). The meaning of the wind would be self-evident to any Jew, who used the same word (*ruach*) for breath, wind and spirit. Air in motion is a symbol of life and power; wind is a metaphor for God's invisible might (Ezek 37:9–10). The fire is not so obvious, though it is a frequent sign of the presence of God, as at the burning bush before Moses (Exod 3:2). Usually it points to his destroying judgement, for God is a consuming fire (Deut 4:24; 9:3; Ps 97:3; Heb 12:29); and this is probably what John the Baptist was referring to when he said the Messiah would baptise with the Spirit and with fire (cf. Mal 4:1 with Matt 3:11–12). In Acts 2 the 'fire' is far more likely to symbolise God's presence than his purging. We are not to imagine each head with a single flame burning upwards (the distinctive shape of a bishop's mitre owes much to this popular misconception); the language suggests a huge blaze burning downwards, dividing into branching flames whose tips touched each head, though without singeing a single hair.

It was the divine equivalent of the laying-on of hands! Since 'each' was touched at the same time, they 'all' received the Spirit at the same time. Thus, it was only a collective experience because it was an individual experience. This is a vital point – a group cannot be filled with the Spirit unless each member of it is filled. The Spirit is not given to the 'church' as a corporate entity, though this is commonly preached on Whit Sunday in many congregations. He is given to each member individually, and through them to the whole body. The church, therefore, cannot continue to possess the Spirit if its members have not received him; nor can church officials pass the Spirit to its members through a liturgical rite if they have not themselves been baptised in the Spirit. The day of Pentecost is wrongly celebrated when it is thought of as the unique occasion on which the church as a whole received the Spirit; it is more truly seen as the first occasion, though far from the last, when church members received the Spirit, even though they were met as a group and received the Spirit

simultaneously. On the later recorded occasions when a group
received the Spirit at the same time, it was not usually
simultaneous; the Greek text makes it clear that they received
'one by one' as hands were laid on them (see chapters 16 and 20
on Acts 8 and 19).

Notice that what was predicted as being 'baptised with the
Holy Spirit' in Acts 1:5 is now reported as being 'filled with
Holy Spirit', showing that the two terms are interchangeable,
except that 'filled' could be used more than once of the same
individuals (as in Acts 4:31), whereas 'baptised' was reserved
for the initial filling. The same experience would later be
described as 'poured out upon', 'given', 'received', 'fallen
upon', etc. when it happened to others (see chapter 5 for a
complete list of the various terms used).

At this point, the 'objective' phenomena (coming from
outside) gave place to 'subjective' phenomena (coming from
inside). They were 'filled to overflowing'! As we have already
said, the mouth is the normal overflow of the heart – humour
spills out in laughter, anger in shouting, sorrow in howling,
fear in a cry. A person filled with the Holy Spirit bursts into
'prophesying' of some kind (one of the meanings of *nabhi*, the
Hebrew word for 'prophet', is 'one who bubbles forth').
Spontaneous speech is the sign which accompanied this and all
later receptions of the Spirit. The tongues, formerly 'set on fire
by hell' (Jas 3:6), now speak only the words inspired by the
Spirit.

At Pentecost the words were all in languages unknown to
the speakers themselves, though all would be known to God.
Indeed, this is the second time in history that God 'came down'
and caused men who knew only one language to speak out in
many. However, Pentecost is a reversal rather than a repetition of Babel (Gen 11:7). There, it was an act of divine
judgement; the intended purpose was to confuse, separate and
exclude. (In a different sense, 'strange tongues' would figure in
a later judgement on Israel itself – cf. Deut 28:49 with Isa
28:11–12; these scriptures lie behind Paul's argument against
corporate tongues in worship, in 1 Cor 14:21–23.) Here, at
Pentecost, the same ability is given to comfort, unite and

include. Instead of driving people apart, they would be drawn together (2:6).

That the 'tongues' were real languages (or, at the very least, different dialects), with grammar and syntax, was recognised by the fascinated observers. (The word 'tongues' – the usual word used in English Bible translations – is quite misleading, conveying as it does an impression of incoherent babbling. The New English Bible, to its credit, translates the Greek word used here (*glossai*) more accurately as 'other languages' – but then quite inconsistently translates it as 'ecstatic utterance' elsewhere in the New Testament, which is unwarranted. The only 'ecstasy' recorded in Acts 2 is the description of the bystanders' amazement when they realised that their own languages were being spoken by semi-literate northerners!)

Notice that this speech was the result of human co-operation with the divine initiative. '*They*' began to speak, which involves the conscious act of vibrating the vocal chords. The Spirit only 'gave them utterance' – that is, he controlled the tongue and lips, turning the sound into coherent language. He did not 'make them speak' but 'gave expression' to the thoughts and feelings overflowing from their mouths. The disciples did the speaking, the Spirit told them what to say. All gifts of the Spirit have this dual character; no one is ever forced to use them. They may be given, but they must be received actively, not passively.

It was only after all this had happened that a large crowd of onlookers gathered. As it was the Feast of Pentecost, Jerusalem in general and the temple in particular would be crowded with pilgrims. They had not witnessed the objective phenomena of the wind and the fire (they would have been even more 'astonished' had they done so!), but were attracted by the unusual outburst of uninhibited behaviour, normally associated with inebriation! When near enough to make out what was being said, they encountered a feature which did not fit this explanation. Evidence of an extraordinary happening was both audible (they heard their own languages) and visible (they saw that these were Galileans, probably from their dress). Peter later appealed to this audio-visual evidence (Acts 2:33).

Seizing the opportunity of an interested crowd, the twelve apostles 'got up' and Peter, on their behalf and in one language, preached his first, and maybe greatest, sermon. The rest, as they say, is history.

In pursuit of our purpose in this book – to discern the New Testament teaching on Christian initiation – we must ask a crucial but simple question: Was this event unique and unrepeatable, or does it provide a precedent for later initiations?

Those who believe that Pentecost was unique and must in no way be regarded as a norm for later experience usually emphasise the collective aspect of the event. The day is regarded as 'the birthday of the church'. The promise that Jesus would 'baptise with the Holy Spirit' is regarded as entirely fulfilled with the first group of 120 believers. The whole church throughout all ages was then 'baptised' in the Holy Spirit and retains this experience as a permanent possession. There is therefore no need for an individual disciple to seek a 'Pentecostal experience' of baptism in the Spirit; all he needs is to join the church – by faith, according to the evangelical; by baptism or confirmation according to the Catholic – and he has automatically entered into this 'Spirit-baptism' of the true church, whether that body is defined invisibly or institutionally. However, we have already seen that this approach does not do justice to the clear emphasis on the individual aspect of Pentecost; nor does it adequately explain what happened to others after Pentecost.

To be sure, there were some unique features of the original event which were never repeated. The sound of the wind and the sight of the fire do not reappear within the New Testament, though there are scattered references to such phenomena in later church history. Nor is there any other recorded occasion when the 'tongues' were recognised as known languages – though, again, later church history contains some examples. Thus, the 'objective' phenomena, as we have called them, cannot be paralleled elsewhere in the New Testament.

But the 'subjective' phenomena can! The book of Acts contains at least another three accounts of similar events, using the same descriptive language and exhibiting the same practical results. In one case, the apostle Peter specifically identified what was happening with the original event (see chapter 18 on Acts 10:47; 11:15 and 15:8, all referring to Cornelius' household at Caesarea). So how do exponents of the solitary uniqueness of Pentecost explain these 'irregular' happenings at Samaria, Caesarea and Ephesus? The answer they give is to apply the same 'collective' concept to these also, seeing them, not as groups of individuals being 'baptised in the Holy Spirit' together, but as fresh ethnic categories of the human race, representing the ever-widening circle of the church. Thus, Samaria becomes the Pentecost of the Samaritan half-caste; Caesarea becomes the Pentecost of the Gentile outcast. Ephesus does not quite fit into the series, so it is treated as something of a historical anachronism, the Pentecost of the former disciples of John. Believing that these four subsidiary Pentecosts cover the entire human race, exponents of this view do not expect any further (collective) initiations of this kind. Presumably the Chinese, Russians and Americans were all 'baptised in Spirit' at Caesarea with Cornelius.

Such views have been used to 'comfort' myriads of professing Christians. Treating these four events as foundational, and therefore abnormal, excuses them from seeking such a Spirit-baptism for themselves.

But is this the right interpretation? Is it true to the scriptures themselves? A careful examination of five New Testament teachers reveals a unanimous expectation that 'Pentecost' would be repeated in the experience of every individual believer!

John the Baptist. John's prediction of the future ministry of the Messiah 'baptising in Spirit' was at least as wide in application as his own ministry of 'baptising in water'. In saying 'he will baptise you in the Holy Spirit', he was potentially referring to every one of the thousands who had come to him for the water-baptism of repentance. He was describing a continuing and far-reaching ministry to follow his own. He would have been astonished to be told that his prediction would be over in one day (or at most, three or four)! He was confidently forecasting a 'Spirit-baptism' that would be universally available.

John the apostle. The fourth gospel shares this universal expectation, recording Jesus' open invitation to *anyone* who was thirsty to come and drink (John 7:37–39), to which the author added his own comment identifying this offer with Pentecost. He, too, would have been astonished to be told the offer would be limited to a hundred and twenty people who happened to be at the right time and place!

Peter. At the end of his first sermon, Peter confidently invited his hearers to share in the experience they had just observed, in the firm conviction that 'the promise' just fulfilled in the hundred and twenty was now universally available through all time ('and your children') and all space ('all who are far off').

Luke. Luke's record of the events at Samaria and Caesarea shows that the only unusual feature in each case was in the timing. In every other way, as we shall see, these occasions conformed to the normal pattern of initiation which all other believers had received, particularly the 'Pentecostal' phenomena that accompanied their 'reception' of the Spirit. Even the incident at Ephesus is an alignment to this norm.

Paul. 'Pentecostal' language is applied to the initiation experienced by all Paul's readers. They have been 'baptised by one Spirit' (1 Cor 12:13 – see chapter 23), had the Spirit 'poured out' upon them copiously (Tit 3:6 – see chapter 26) and in this way 'received the Spirit' (Gal 3:2).

In the light of this evidence, there is therefore little or no ground in the New Testament for regarding the event of Pentecost as a collective event, unique and unrepeatable, and containing the total fulfilment of John's prophecy of a coming Spirit-baptism. All the descriptive language used of the disciples' 'subjective' experience on that day is applied freely to later believers who were not present at the time. There may have been some unique 'objective' phenomena to mark this first occasion, but in essence it was the first of many such 'outpourings' of the Spirit.

We conclude that the day of Pentecost 'inaugurated' the

final element in Christian initiation, enabling Spirit-baptism to complete the fourfold pattern, together with repentance, faith and water-baptism. The experience of those present is therefore a paradigm, establishing the norm for subsequent believers.

15   THE THREE THOUSAND
(Acts 2:38–41)

³⁸Peter replied, 'Repent and be baptised, every one of you, in the name of Jesus Christ for the forgiveness of your sins. And you will receive the gift of the Holy Spirit. ³⁹The promise is for you and your children and for all who are far off – for all whom the Lord our God will call.'

⁴⁰With many other words he warned them; and he pleaded with them, 'Save yourselves from this corrupt generation.' ⁴¹Those who accepted his message were baptised, and about three thousand were added to their number that day. (Acts 2:38–41)

Why did Peter not tell his hearers to believe in the Lord Jesus? Does the phrase 'and your children' sanction infant baptism? Why is there no mention of manifestations of the Spirit among the new converts? This short passage has raised many such questions and stimulated much controversy!

We could call this the first example of 'post-Pentecost' evangelism! We may therefore expect it to yield some clues about Christian initiation for the rest of the church age. The genuine enquiry by Peter's hearers, who wanted some very practical instruction about how to respond to his message, makes his answer very significant. Here is the very first situation in which enquirers were counselled for salvation. Peter's teaching and technique repay careful analysis.

The surprising feature is the absence of the verb 'believe', or even the noun 'faith'. The nearest equivalent would be the later comment that they 'accepted his message' (2:41). We may presume that Peter either deduced from their enquiry or intuitively concluded that they already believed his claim that

'Jesus [is] . . . both Lord and Christ' (2:36). Certainly they revealed no desire whatever to challenge Peter's preaching or even discuss it. They were now as convinced about the reality of Jesus' resurrection and ascension as they had been of his crucifixion and burial. Their question acknowledges that they were perfectly aware that intellectual acceptance of these facts was not enough; the facts must lead to action ('Brothers, what shall we *do*?' – 2:37). It would, therefore, be superfluous to tell them to 'believe', having reached this stage of wanting to respond in a practical way.

But their question has a moral overtone. Peter accused them of being parties to the crucifixion ('whom you crucified' – 2:36). They accepted his charge without question or excuse. They were guilty of the most heinous crime they could ever have committed – as Jews they have murdered their own long-awaited Messiah! Their question is then to be seen as a cry from the heart rather than as a query from the head. It is a mixture of despair and hope. We might paraphrase their plea: 'Is there anything we can possibly do to right such a terrible wrong?' The stress of the question seems to be 'What *shall* we do?'

Even though they may have wondered if the situation could ever be put right, Peter's reply is full of hope. Their sin can be dealt with. They can 'get themselves saved' (the significance of the passive voice verb in v. 40), if they follow his careful instructions.

His first counsel is the imperative command to 'Repent' – the very same word used when both John the Baptist and Jesus announced that the kingdom was 'at hand' (i.e. within reach – see Matt 3:2; 4:17). For Peter's audience it would mean the same radical change in thought, word and deed. Realising how wrong their judgement of Jesus had been, they must now openly admit it and come over to his 'side' with the disciples, whatever that might cost them. Public acknowledgement that Jesus was indeed both Lord and Christ would prove their repentance.

'Get yourself baptised' (v. 38) shows that from the very first the apostles understood that the practice of water-baptism, originated by John and continued by Jesus, was to be continued after and alongside the Spirit-baptism of the messianic age. Both baptisms would characterise the 'last days'. Only a clear command of Jesus himself, such as Matthew records (Matt 28:19), can explain why Peter and the other apostles never considered that Spirit-baptism had made water-baptism obsolete or superfluous (Acts 10:47 illustrates the exact opposite – that Spirit-baptism made water-baptism urgently necessary). Furthermore, Peter gave exactly the same reason for water-baptism as John had, namely: the 'remission' or 'forgiveness' of sins (cf. Acts 2:38 with Mark 1:4). The language is clearly *instrumental* – Peter believes that water-baptism will *effect* the cleansing. For him, as for the other apostles, the washing of the body and the cleansing of the conscience were the outside and the inside of the same event, the external act causing the internal change. Their understanding was 'sacramental' rather than 'symbolic'. To put it quite starkly, Peter would have been surprised if someone had asked if they could have forgiveness of sins without being baptised; he would probably have questioned the sincerity of their profession of repentance and faith.

The two imperatives ('Repent and be baptised') are addressed to the individual, *not* the family or the nation. There can be no vicarious repentance and no vicarious baptisms on someone else's behalf. '*Every one* of you' must take full responsibility for '*your* sins' which need forgiveness. Peter's demands are only made of those who are morally responsible for their own wrong attitudes and actions (many of his hearers would no doubt recall with appalling guilt having joined in the cries of the mob to 'Crucify him'). Such a baptism would be totally irrelevant to babies, who had no part whatever in the actual sins of their parents. Baptism is a moral act for immoral persons and must be a voluntary choice of the individual, even though another will do the baptising.

Having outlined this double demand, Peter then declared the offer: 'And you will receive the gift of the Holy Spirit.' Many have assumed that this statement, with the verb in the indicative rather than the imperative, together with the confidence with which Peter speaks, must have the following two corollaries.

First, that absolutely nothing more than repenting and believing need be done in order to have this gift. Once these requirements are fulfilled, 'receiving' is entirely passive. In other words, it is *automatic*.

Second, that on the basis of this assurance, we can be quite sure that every believer has received the gift of the Spirit, even *without any outward evidence* at the time. Faith in Peter's promise is enough ground for confidence.

But Peter himself would be astonished at these modern deductions from his preaching! Apart from the fact that he made baptism rather than believing the necessary precondition for receiving the gift – indicating that baptism normally preceded reception of the Spirit (Cornelius being the only New Testament exception) – Peter's subsequent behaviour at Samaria shows that he neither accepted nor acted upon either of the above propositions.

Where penitent, baptised believers showed no clear outward evidence of having 'received', Peter did not assume, as so many would today, that they must have received the Spirit automatically and unconsciously; rather, he concluded that they had not received and took active steps – such as further prayer with laying-on of hands – to rectify their incomplete initiation.

Nevertheless, Peter was confident that every person truly responding in repentance and baptism could and would receive this gift, whether immediately or ultimately. When he prayed, with John, for the Samaritans, he did so with the same confidence. It is one thing to state that every person responding to the gospel in repentance, faith and baptism will receive the Spirit (as in 2:38). It is quite a different thing to state that every person responding in this way *has* received the Spirit – an understanding that is wrongly read into this verse.

THE PROMISE

Peter's certainty that they *would* receive the Spirit was firmly grounded in the very terms of the Father's promise, which were unlimited in scope. What had already happened that day to one hundred and twenty people was of universal application and clearly extended to three other groupings:

'*You*'. This is not just the three thousand, but everybody else listening at the time and others of that same 'corrupt generation' who would hear about it. The personal pronoun covers all Peter's contemporaries in Israel at that time.

'*And your children*'. The Greek word rendered 'children' is not that for a tiny baby (*brephos* or *nepios*) or even a small infant (*teknion* or *paidion* or *paidarion*), but a general term for 'descendants' (*teknon*). It refers not just to the next generation but to all succeeding generations. The promise is not limited to Peter's contemporaries but will extend through time to the end of history.

'*All who are far off*'. The promise is unlimited in space as well as in time; it is as wide as the ascending Jesus' mandate to be witnesses 'to the ends of the earth' (Acts 1:8). At the time Peter himself probably did not realise that this would include all *peoples* as well as all countries. Maybe he was thinking of the dispersed Jews, who were 'far' from home. However, when Cornelius received the promise, Peter quickly recovered his equilibrium after his initial surprise! Perhaps his experience with the half-caste Samaritans had prepared him, though it took a spectacular vision to complete his education! Peter was not the last preacher to find himself speaking beyond his own experience, only to realise later the full implication of his own words.

There are a number of other important points to note in this verse. The first thing to underline is that the 'promise' is solely concerned with the gift of the Spirit (2:33), not with the more general matter of salvation. If 'to your children' is taken out of its context and is assumed to refer to the much more limited concept of family unity, then it needs to be pointed out that Peter is here offering Spirit-baptism, not water-baptism, to the children – he is offering 'confirmation' rather than 'christening'!

It is also important to realise that the scope of the promise was wider than its fulfilment would be. The gift was available to all persons in all three groups, but it would not be automatically theirs. Not all would avail themselves of the offer. There are two qualifying conditions necessary to receiving the promise (both come from Joel 2:32):

A divine call: the phrase 'all whom the Lord our God will call' qualifies all three groups – this electing invitation must first be heard.

A human call: this must answer the divine call and a fitting response be made by 'repenting and being baptised' – this phrase also qualifies all three groups ('you', 'your children', 'all who are far off').

So, just as with Christ's atoning work on the cross, while the 'promise' is universally sufficient, it will only be individually efficient. It will only work for 'as many as' hear the call of the Lord, for 'every one' who calls on his name, for 'each one' who repents and is baptised. It should be obvious that there is no ground here for a vicarious response by a head on behalf of his household or by parents on behalf of their family. To baptise children on the basis of this verse would logically involve the baptism of all that are far off, with or without their repentance! Peter's offer and demand are made exclusively to persons who are themselves able to respond.

The offer and demand are followed up by an extended appeal which is summarised by Luke in one sentence. 'Save yourselves' is an inadequate rendering of an aorist, passive, imperative verb. The passive means 'be saved', rather than 'save yourselves' (DIY salvation is unknown in the New Testament!). The aorist means to take a decisive, once-for-all, step. The imperative means that Peter is telling rather than asking them – insisting rather than inviting; the tone is that of a life-guard ordering a drowning man to seize the life-belt thrown to him. (This exhortation compares with Ananias' words in Acts 22:16 to Paul: 'wash your sins away' – another aorist imperative, but this time in the middle voice, as is the preceding command to 'be baptised'; the nearest English equivalent would be: 'Get yourself baptised and have your sins washed away'.)

Of the group addressed by Peter as 'you', we know that three thousand claimed the promise by submitting to baptism. Advocates of baptism by affusion claim that insuperable logistical problems would have made the immersion of three thousand people on one day in Jerusalem impossible; but the pools of Siloam and Bethesda would have sufficed (to say nothing of the recently discovered ritual baths at the temple entrance). Since 'Pentecost' occurred in the morning, they would have had the rest of the day for the baptisms.

The only logistical problem lay in the discipling after such a successful mission. Each church member, only just baptised in the Spirit themselves, had to look after an average of twenty-five new converts – and that was just the first day! Acts 2:42–47 shows that the follow-up was totally successful. Baptism led right on to teaching, fellowship, worship, service and further evangelism. That they coped so well was almost certainly due to Jesus having given three years' training to the men who would lead the community.

An interesting question is raised by the large number of baptisms on this occasion. It is more than probable that many among them, perhaps even most, had already been baptised by John – and therefore that this was a 're-baptism'. However, Peter made nothing of this. All who received his message were baptised, whether for the first or second time. Clearly, this baptism was different from the former one. Christian baptism involved an identification with the Lord Jesus Christ, particularly by the use of his name. So Peter did not hesitate to 're-baptise' those who responded to the full Christian gospel, for the same reason that Paul did at Ephesus (see chapter 20).

One further question remains, concerning a surprising omission from the whole account: there is no mention of any outward manifestation of the Spirit in the experience of the three thousand. If Luke's report is comprehensive, all they apparently got was wet! Those who would like to believe that the Spirit is received automatically, and more often than not without any outward evidence at the time, seize on this omission to support their case. But this is an 'argument from silence', and such provide a notoriously slippery foundation since they can be immediately countered by making the opposite deduction. Furthermore, the silence is not total, as we shall see.

Let us indulge in a little speculation for a moment. When Peter promised his hearers that they were included in the promise that had already been visibly and audibly fulfilled in himself and those standing or seated around him, what expectations would he raise in his hearers? Certainly not the rushing wind, which they had not heard; nor the flaming fire, which they had not seen. But the people would expect to share in that verbal release of praise and prophecy in many languages which they had at first mistaken for symptoms of intoxication. And Peter himself would surely expect this to happen to them. At the very least there would be considerable disappointment, if not frustrated resentment, if all they 'received' was a soaking! That situation would have caused more bewilderment than the original manifestation! It is almost impossible to imagine Peter resorting to the rationalisation of much modern counselling and telling his hearers 'Don't worry if you don't feel anything' or 'Don't expect anything to happen.'

However, since the silence is far from total, we do not need to indulge in such imaginative speculation. Peter's later actions and speeches are clearly based on the premise that the three thousand did 'receive the Spirit' in the same manner as the one hundred and twenty (Acts 10:47; 11:17; 15:8–9). Both the absence of outward phenomena in the Samaritans and the presence of them in Cornelius are evaluated by Peter in the light of the experience of all the Jerusalem believers, whose initiation he takes as the norm. Only if all previous believers had received the Spirit with such outward accompaniments could Peter possibly have known that the Samaritans had not so 'received' or that Cornelius had (this vital point is fully developed in chapters 16 and 18); in both cases, the timing of their reception was unusual, if not unique; but the manner of their reception was exactly the same as everybody else's.

The omission of any mention of this in the present context is of literary rather than theological significance. Luke was not given to unnecessary repetition. For this reason, they are not described as having repented or believed. Both are implied. That they 'accepted the message' may be taken as synonymous with faith. And their submission to baptism may be taken as proof of their repentance. If Luke mentioned all four 'spiritual doors' every time he mentioned a conversion, his style would be quite tedious. On each occasion he singles out that element which is most striking or significant on that particular occasion. The sight of three thousand baptisms at one time would be sufficiently striking to remain in the memory, but there is a deeper reason why baptism should be singled out on this occasion. Here were accessories to the murder of Jesus publicly repudiating their action and totally identifying themselves with his death and resurrection, taking upon themselves his name as Lord (of the universe) and Christ (the Jewish Messiah-king). That so many should do this the very first time the gospel was proclaimed was what struck Luke as the most significant aspect.

That their subsequent lives revealed long-term evidence of having received the Spirit is indisputable. Faithfulness in worship, fellowship, teaching and prayer; supernatural awe; spontaneous sharing of material resources; joyful praise; continual growth – all these are the results of Spirit-baptism, not water-baptism. But it was not from these later by-products that the apostles knew they had received the Spirit. Evidence for this was a matter of observation at the time, rather than by later deduction; from immediate behaviour rather than ultimate bearing. This is particularly clear in the Samaritan episode . . .

16 THE SAMARITAN CONVERTS
(Acts 8:4–25)

[4]Those who had been scattered preached the word wherever they went. [5]Philip went down to a city in Samaria and proclaimed the Christ there. [6]When the crowds heard Philip and saw the miraculous signs he did, they all paid close attention to what he said. [7]With shrieks, evil spirits came out of many, and many paralytics and cripples were healed. [8]So there was great joy in that city.

[9]Now for some time a man named Simon had practised sorcery in the city and amazed all the people of Samaria. He boasted that he was someone great, [10]and all the people, both high and low, gave him their attention and exclaimed, 'This man is the divine power known as the Great Power.' [11]They followed him because he had amazed them for a long time with his magic. [12]But when they believed Philip as he preached the good news of the kingdom of God and the name of Jesus Christ, they were baptised, both men and women. [13]Simon himself believed and was baptised. And he followed Philip everywhere, astonished by the great signs and miracles he saw.

[14]When the apostles in Jerusalem heard that Samaria had accepted the word of God, they sent Peter and John to them. [15]When they arrived, they prayed for them that they might receive the Holy Spirit, [16]because the Holy Spirit had not yet come upon any of them; they had simply been baptised into the name of the Lord Jesus. [17]Then Peter and John placed their hands on them, and they received the Holy Spirit.

[18]When Simon saw that the Spirit was given at the laying on of the apostles' hands, he offered them money [19]and said, 'Give me also this ability so that everyone on whom I lay my hands may receive the Holy Spirit.'

[20]Peter answered: 'May your money perish with you, because you thought you could buy the gift of God with money!' [21]You have no part or share in this ministry, because your heart is not right before God. [22]Repent of this wickedness and pray to the Lord. Perhaps he will forgive you for having such a thought in your heart. [23]For I see that you are full of bitterness and captive to sin.'

[24]Then Simon answered, 'Pray to the Lord for me so that nothing you have said may happen to me.'

[25]When they had testified and proclaimed the word of the Lord, Peter and John returned to Jerusalem, preaching the gospel in many Samaritan villages. (Acts 8:4–25)

The crucial question for the purpose of our study is a simple one: Was the Samaritan experience of 'conversion' normal, as Pentecostals claim, or abnormal, as evangelicals claim? The theological issue behind this may be put differently: Does the delay between the Samaritans 'believing in Jesus' and 'receiving Holy Spirit' indicate a distinction between the two (even when they happen together) which means that it is possible for believers to have one without the other? Most Bible scholars accept that there was a 'delay' between believing and receiving in their particular case, but explain this in different ways.

Evangelical commentators have concentrated on the question why there was a delay. Samaritans were half-caste descendants of the mixed marriages between the Jews left behind in the land when the nation was taken into exile and the 'native' inhabitants of Canaan. Considering these ethnic factors such commentators rightly see this whole episode as a quantum leap for the church, beyond its hitherto exclusively Jewish boundaries. Though this radical step had been taken spontaneously rather than deliberately (Acts 8:4), it was totally in line with their missionary mandate (Acts 1:8).

However, the profound antipathy between Jews and Samaritans – which was so strong that a Jew would take the long way round via Jericho to avoid meeting a Samaritan (Luke 10:33) and would not even use the same drinking vessel as a

Samaritan (John 4:9) – introduced the first threat of schism to the new people of God, the church. The outcome might have been two 'national' churches, which would rapidly have become three (Jewish, Samaritan and Gentile). To avoid this danger, it is postulated that God himself withheld his 'seal of approval' from this new category of believers until he could mediate it through representatives of the Jewish believers, thus preserving the church's unity through interdependence and preventing the ethnic groups from becoming independent of each other. Disintegration of the body of Christ was thus averted by this act of divine wisdom in delaying the 'gift' until Peter and John, two key apostles, were present.

To digress for a moment, some have found here the beginnings of an 'Apostolic succession', later developed by a 'monarchical episcopate' into the rites of confirmation and ordination. That this is highly improbable is shown by the fact that the apostles did not have a monopoly on imparting the Spirit, even in those days (in the very next chapter Ananias renders this service to Paul – Acts 9:17). And Philip himself could have claimed to have such 'delegated authority', having had the apostles' hands on himself (Acts 6:5–6).

On the other hand, it is unlikely that Peter and John simply represented the Jewish believers in Jerusalem (as Philip himself could have done). They represented the highest 'authority' in the church (the 'Twelve' and, in this case, the inner circle of three, which comprised Peter, James and John) and were totally identifying with this extension of the church's boundary. What had been started almost casually by an enthusiastic 'deacon' must be seen to be totally consistent with the apostolic strategy of the whole church.

Having said this, it must be pointed out that all of the foregoing 'explanation' for the delay in the Samaritan 'reception' of the Spirit is pure speculation, going well beyond the statements of scripture. The reasoning may be perfectly valid, but Luke does not draw such a conclusion. He simply gives the facts, without any interpretation. He tells us what happened, but makes no attempt to say why he thought it happened that way. There is a description, but no explanation. It is simply part of his 'accurate account' of how they brought the good news from Jerusalem to Rome . . . via Samaria.

Even if the theory is correct, it cannot be the main point of the story. Indeed, such speculation can be a distraction and in this case it has successfully diverted attention from the important implications of those details which Luke has taken the trouble to record. Discussing why God delayed 'giving' is one way to avoid debating how the Samaritans 'received'; yet it is the latter which is essential to understanding Luke's theology of initiation.

Two questions will open up the passage for us. First, how did anyone know that the Samaritans had *not* received the Spirit? Second, when they did, how did anyone know that they *had* received the Spirit? The answer is really the same for both questions: *every reception of the Spirit, up to and including them, was always accompanied by clear, outward evidence*.

The point needs to be emphasised, for its implications are far-reaching. We can only conclude that every other conversion prior to Samaria had included a self-evident 'Pentecostal' outpouring of the Spirit, from the three thousand on the day of Pentecost onwards, and that this was the only known way of 'receiving the Spirit'. Furthermore, this 'reception' is therefore distinct from repentance, faith and baptism in water (and even 'great joy', v. 8) – all of which can take place without it.

To avoid such conclusions, attempts have been made to cast doubts on the adequacy of their faith before Peter and John arrived, as if it were not full 'saving' faith. That this is a doctrinal rationalisation is confirmed by the complete absence of further instruction by the apostles, who obviously accepted the validity of their repentance, faith and baptism without question. The Samaritans had believed the good news of the kingdom of God, been baptised into the name of the Lord Jesus and witnessed miracles of healing and deliverance (so they were a long way ahead of the 'disciples' encountered by Paul in Ephesus – see chapter 20). To claim that all this was in some way 'sub-Christian' is to fly in the face of plain language. The Samaritans' deficient experience was not due to any lack of understanding or commitment on their part. The delay was due to God's response to them (for whatever reason, arguably that outlined above), not to their response to him. Peter and John must have thought them fully eligible to receive the Spirit, for when they came they addressed God in prayer, not the Samaritans with preaching!

It cannot be too strongly stated that for the apostles, the absence of outward manifestation at the time of initiation was taken as evidence that the Holy Spirit had *not* been received. The modern view, that they must have received but needed to be 'released' in the Spirit, is quite foreign to New Testament terminology, never mind New Testament theology. The apostles did not lay hands on them to 'release' what was already in them, but that they might 'receive' what was yet to 'come upon' them (v. 16; cf. 1:8; 10:44; 11:15; 19:6).

By the same token, the presence of outward manifestation was taken as evidence that the Holy Spirit *had* been received. While this passage does not specify the exact nature of the evidence on this occasion, it was clear enough to convince others present that they had received: the imperfect tense of the verb, 'were receiving', indicates that it was happening 'one-by-one' as Peter or John laid hands on each, rather than all together as a group, which seems to have been true on the day of Pentecost. It was when Simon 'saw' this happening that he coveted the power to make this happen to whoever he laid his hands on. It is clear that the evidence was immediate, and not a later deduction from the outworking 'fruit' in character or conduct.

There is more to be said about Simon, whose exhibitionist habits as a magician made him more interested in the ability to give this power to others than the opportunity to receive it for himself. He was not the last to want supernatural power to elevate himself rather than to serve others, nor the last to think that gifts of grace may be purchased. In trenchant language (the equivalent of 'To hell with you and your money!') Peter excluded him from any 'share in this ministry' (was he referring to imbibing or imparting the Spirit?) and questioned both the reality of his repentance and the possibility of his forgiveness. Simon is still the magician – in both his frame of mind and his state of heart. He ignored Peter's counsel to confess his base motives directly to the Lord and instead begged for Peter's intercession on his behalf (the Bezan text adds that he 'did not stop weeping copiously'). There is no hint that Peter accepted this sacerdotal suggestion or that Simon found forgiveness, much less received the Spirit. He is a reminder that faith and baptism do not guarantee salvation, especially where there has been no true repentance. Some would dismiss his 'faith' as superficial, but neither Peter at the time nor Luke later felt the need to say this. The one useful service that he rendered was to confirm for us that reception of the Spirit was accompanied by immediate outward evidence as the 'gift' was individually given.

The incident also underlines the link between the reception of the Spirit and the laying-on of hands. This is the first record of it being done for this purpose and constitutes the appropriate action to take when the Spirit has not been received 'spontaneously' (i.e. without human help, as at Pentecost itself). Expressing as it does a combination of identification and intercession, there should be no surprise at the apostles' action. Laying-on of hands had already been used in a blend of appointing and anointing for particular responsibility (which had included Philip himself – Acts 6:5–6).

Incidentally, the Samaritan incident bears witness to the changed attitudes of the apostles themselves. The last time they had been in Samaria, they had wanted to call down fire from heaven on the people for their insulting behaviour towards Jesus for not breaking his journey to Jerusalem (Luke 9:51–56)! Now they were praying for something rather different to descend on them from on high.

To sum up, the Samaritan experience was neither so unique nor so special as some make out. It was not the 'second Pentecost' to mark the accession of the Samaritans, as so many expositors have called it. In essence and content their reception of the Spirit was perfectly normal and identical to that experienced by every other believer before them. 'Pentecost' had already been repeated as many times as there were new disciples!

There were, however, two variations from the norm in the

Samaritan case. First, there was the long delay between their water-baptism and their Spirit-baptism, which were normally very much closer to each other, though never simultaneous. Second, there was the human act of laying-on of hands, which is mentioned in subsequent accounts in Acts, though never previously. An adequate explanation has been given above for both of these features, which are unusual if not exceptional.

But these differences in no way affect our basic conclusion that an experiential reception of the Spirit is an essential element in normal Christian initiation which can and must be differentiated, in content if not in chronology, from repentance, faith and water-baptism. When this does not happen as it should, the appropriate action to take is prayer with the laying-on of hands.

Above all, this incident proves that it was possible, even after Pentecost, to repent, believe and be baptised without having received Holy Spirit. Only one such case is needed to prove that it is a *possibility*, but the *probability* of this situation recurring cannot be directly deduced from – or ruled out by – this passage. However, the apostolic understanding that absence of immediate outward evidence must be interpreted as meaning the Spirit has not yet been received remains valid as a permanent criterion. Applied to the churches today, we may conclude that the incomplete experience of initiation of the Samaritans is far from unique!

To ask about the Samaritans' spiritual status or state between their water-baptism and Spirit-baptism (e.g. 'Would they have gone to heaven if they had died before the apostles arrived?') is to import modern evangelical notions into the New Testament. Contemporary definitions of 'saved' and 'Christian' do not sit comfortably with apostolic categories. The apostles were clearly concerned with where the Samaritans should be rather than with where they were! To be a 'disciple' then was seen more in terms of being on 'the Way' (Acts 18:25, 26; 19:9, 23) than of having crossed a line; of setting out on a journey rather than having arrived at a destination. But these questions do arise today, even if Luke ignored them, so they are dealt with more fully in chapter 36.

17 THE ETHIOPIAN EUNUCH
(Acts 8:36–39)

> 36As they travelled along the road, they came to some water and the eunuch said, 'Look, here is water. Why shouldn't I be baptised?' 38And he gave orders to stop the chariot. Then both Philip and the eunuch went down into the water and Philip baptised him. 39When they came up out of the water, the Spirit of the Lord suddenly took Philip away, and the eunuch did not see him again, but went on his way rejoicing. (Acts 8:36–39)

The first thing to say about this passage is that it is an extremely condensed account. For example, we know little about Philip's discourse except its theme: Jesus. He was given the best conversational opening that a personal evangelist could possibly wish for! If ever an enquirer asked the right question, this one did; but then, he was reading the scriptures already! However, the answer must have occupied a considerable amount of time, in spite of the grounding in Jewish knowledge of God that could be assumed.

Nor should it surprise us that the eunuch himself raised the topic of baptism. Philip had probably mentioned it, since the gospel began with the ministry of John the Baptist (Mark 1:1–4). But as a Gentile 'God-fearer', an adherent of the Jewish religion, if not a proselyte, the eunuch would be quite familiar with the need of such a ritual bath to 'join' the people of God and count their Messiah as his. It is possible, however, that his castrated condition might have been a handicap in being fully accepted by the Jewish priests (depending on whether they went by Deut 23:1 or Isa 56:4–5).

What catches our attention is that baptism is apparently the only response he makes to Philip's 'preaching'. If this was all he did, we might here have a genuine case of 'baptismal regeneration'! His repentance might be deduced from his sincere pilgrimage to Jerusalem, putting him in a similar spiritual condition to Cornelius before Peter's visit; but there is no specific mention of faith or reception of the Spirit.

It is obvious that some scripture 'copiers' in the early church were uneasy about his inadequate initiation (at least as far as the record of it went) and its adverse influence on later 'catechumens'. Extra verses have been added to later manuscripts, compensating for the more important omissions.

Some manuscripts add a verse (v. 37 in some Bibles): 'Philip said, "If you believe with all your heart, you may." The eunuch answered, "I believe that Jesus Christ is the Son of God."' There is more than a trace of later notions of faith as credal assent in this additional exchange, but it does indicate that the early church wanted to make it quite clear that the eunuch was a true believer before his baptism.

One manuscript (commonly known as the 'Western Text') has a rather different version of verse 39: 'The Holy Spirit fell upon the eunuch, and an angel of the Lord snatched away Philip.' The New Testament scholar Henry Alford suggested that the variant reading arose 'from a desire to conform the results of the eunuch's baptism to the usual method of the divine procedure'. If this addition is a genuine tradition dating back to the event itself, it would mean that Philip's ministry was quite sufficient to complete the initiation in this case, where it had apparently not been in Samaria. Even if it is not historical, the amendment shows us that the early church did not consider that 'apostolic' hands were necessary.

Both additions are clear evidence for the outlook of the early church, even if they are not original to Luke; they reveal a persistent conviction about the complete complex of Christian initiation.

On a minor point, the language of 'going *down* into' and 'coming *up* out of' the water indicates immersion rather than affusion; clearly the person is taken to the water, not water to the person! It would be somewhat incongruous to immerse the bottom half in order to sprinkle the top half (though so much

Christian art depicts this rather ludicrous combination, possibly portraying a transitional stage between the two modes!)

Some have raised the topographical objection that the Gaza strip is desert and would not contain a stretch of water adequate for total immersion. Apart from its slur on Luke's historical or geographical accuracy, this criticism may be met in either of two ways. First, there is a 'wadi', referred to in scripture as the 'river of Egypt', which occasionally floods after infrequent 'flash' rainstorms in the hills; this might explain the eunuch's tone of surprise when he saw it. Alternatively, the encounter may have taken place much further back on 'Desert Road', which went all the way from Jerusalem to Gaza.

This palace official from the Sudan (which was the biblical 'Ethiopia') was apparently the first 'Gentile' to be baptised. Why was this not mentioned when Peter was questioned for baptising Cornelius? It could simply be that the eunuch would have been regarded as Jewish by religion, if not by birth. It would be totally consistent with Luke's overall theme if this incident is recorded primarily in order to demonstrate the Spirit's prompting to spread the gospel to the ends of the earth – in this case, to the continent of Africa.

18 THE ROMAN CENTURION
(Acts 10:44–48; 11:11–18; 15:7–11)

[44]While Peter was still speaking these words, the Holy Spirit came on all who heard the message. [45]The circumcised believers who had come with Peter were astonished that the gift of the Holy Spirit had been poured out even on the Gentiles. [46]For they heard them speaking in tongues and praising God.

Then Peter said, [47]'Can anyone keep these people from being baptised with water? They have received the Holy Spirit just as we have.' [48]So he ordered that they be baptised in the name of Jesus Christ. Then they asked Peter to stay with them for a few days. (Acts 10:44–48)

[11]'Right then three men who had been sent to me from Caesarea stopped at the house where I was staying. [12]The Spirit told me to have no hesitation about going with them. These six brothers also went with me, and we entered the man's house. [13]He told us how he had seen an angel appear in his house and say, "Send to Joppa for Simon who is called Peter. [14]He will bring you a message through which you and all your household will be saved."

[15]'As I began to speak, the Holy Spirit came on them as he had come on us at the beginning. [16]Then I remembered what the Lord had said: "John baptised with water, but you will be baptised with the Holy Spirit." [17]So if God gave them the same gift as he gave us, who believed in the Lord Jesus Christ, who was I to think that I could oppose God?'

[18]When they heard this, they had no further objections and praised God, saying, 'So then, God has granted even the Gentiles repentance unto life.' (Acts 11:11–18)

[7]After much discussion, Peter got up and addressed them: 'Brothers, you know that some time ago God made a choice among you that the Gentiles might hear from my lips the message of the gospel and believe. [8]God, who knows the heart, showed that he accepted them by giving the Holy Spirit to them, just as he did to us. [9]He made no distinction between us and them, for he purified their hearts by faith. [10]Now then, why do you try to test God by putting on the necks of the disciples a yoke that neither we nor our fathers have been able to bear? [11]No! We believe it is through the grace of our Lord Jesus that we are saved, just as they are.' (Acts 15:7–11)

The events at Caesarea are often referred to as 'the Gentile Pentecost'. Those using this term usually assume that this was only the *third* such 'initial' outpouring of the Holy Spirit in the early church (Acts 4:31 being in the nature of a 'refill'). The very special circumstances surrounding the occasion are taken to rule out any relevance these events might have for a doctrine of normal initiation today.

That there were some unusual, if not unique, features cannot be denied. The happenings which brought Peter and Cornelius together were hardly commonplace – involving as they did angels, visions and a trance! The nub of this supernatural matrix was Peter's release from his racial and religious prejudices against Gentiles and his realisation of the full implications of his own preaching at Pentecost – that 'all who are far off' meant just that!

But the Gentile angle can be over-stated. Though this was Peter's first such encounter, Philip had actually beaten him to it (see the previous chapter). And it must be noted that this Roman, like the Ethiopian, was already in the outer circle of Judaism's adherents, who were called 'God-fearers' (Acts 10:2). It is not without significance that Peter, who was to be the apostle to the Jews (Gal 2:7), should be divinely guided into this Gentile situation, just as Paul, the apostle to the Gentiles, would be led into Jewish situations – spheres of missionary endeavour were never exclusive.

However, our main concern is to analyse Cornelius' (and his household's – see next chapter) experience of initiation, the most unusual aspect of which was the sudden and unexpected outpouring of the Spirit upon all of them simultaneously, *before* they had professed faith and been baptised, and even before Peter had finished preaching. Peter's only mention of the Spirit had been in connection with Jesus' own ministry (10:38) and the only gospel offer Peter had made was the forgiveness of sins. He had certainly not reached the 'appeal' or told them what to do to respond to his message.

It seems valid to assume that their 'God-fearing' attitude had already included repentance ('do what is right' in 10:35 may be taken to refer to 'fruits worthy of repentance'). God, who looks inside the heart, obviously discerned their faith in the preacher's message, and Peter himself came to the same conclusion (see Acts 15:7–9). But this is the only recorded instance where the Spirit was received before water-baptism. In 'normal' patterns of initiation, God's part in the proceedings followed the completion of man's part. No wonder Peter and his companions were so astonished, though their surprise was perhaps even more due to the subjects than to the sequence! Up to that moment, they had not even imagined that Gentiles could, never mind would, inherit the 'promise' made to their forefathers.

The exegetical question usually asked about Cornelius is the same as that asked about the Samaritans: Why did God depart from his normal timetable and procedure? In Samaria the Spirit was given later than usual; and a rational explanation can be postulated why this happened (see chapter 16). At Caesarea the Spirit was given earlier than usual; but this time there are clear hints as to the reason in the text itself.

Peter's deep-seated prejudice against Gentiles could only be corrected in stages. It was a major step for him to enter a Gentile home, let alone share the gospel there. It is therefore highly unlikely that even a profession of repentance and faith would have persuaded Peter that Gentiles were eligible for Christian baptism. The Lord had to remove this final reservation himself, by acting unilaterally and giving Peter convincing proof that the Lord had accepted Gentiles as full members of his Spirit-filled body on earth. Had the Lord not taken this initiative, the baptisms would never have taken place. However, Peter is to be credited for accepting the situation immediately and daring anyone to disagree with his completion of the Gentiles' initiation as brothers in Christ.

Three things are noticeable about the baptisms. First, Peter did not conduct the rite himself, but left it to his colleagues (as did Jesus before him and Paul after him – John 4:2; 1 Cor 1:14), probably to avoid invidious comparisons among the baptised about the baptiser. Second, all the baptisms were voluntary acts of responsible 'adults'. Since only those who had 'received the Spirit' were baptised in water, and only those who had 'heard the message' received the Spirit, it is obvious that no babies were involved (see the next chapter for further examination of 'households' in this connection). Third, and most important, the reception of the Spirit did not make water-baptism superfluous; it made it all the more necessary. When the two baptisms are wrongly merged, the 'inner reality' of Spirit-baptism devalues the 'outer rite' of water-baptism. The two baptisms are never so closely identified in the New Testament that either 'mediates' the other. Though they often happen very close together, there is no recorded case of them happening simultaneously.

Nothing has so far been said about the Gentiles' experience of receiving the Spirit, its content, as distinct from its timing. Was this also highly unusual, even abnormal – and therefore of purely historical interest (as many commentators imply)? Or was this aspect perfectly 'normal', and therefore 'normative', for Christians today?

How did Peter know that the Holy Spirit had been 'poured out' on these Gentiles? The evidence was audible and consisted of a spontaneous overflow of inspired speech. Two forms of this are mentioned – 'speaking in tongues' (other languages, not babbling) and 'praising' (presumably in their own language). The 'and' forbids us to roll them together into 'praising God in tongues' and discourages the assumption that all did both; the natural sense is that some did one and some did the other. If this is so, then it would be going beyond the New Testament evidence to insist that 'tongues' are the only and indispensable sign of having received Spirit-baptism.

The combination of tongues and praise is clearly reminiscent of the day of Pentecost (Acts 2:11). And because this is the first mention of 'tongues' since that event (always allowing, as many scholars do, that it may have occurred in Samaria), it has been widely assumed, and even dogmatically asserted, that this 'infrequent' phenomenon was an extraordinary sign to mark the accession of the Gentiles. This interpretation, and its doctrinal application, must be directly challenged in the light of Peter's own comments on the event.

Both at the time and during subsequent debates, Peter was at pains to emphasise that he had only acted as he did because these Gentiles' experience had been exactly the same as everybody else's! The outward manifestations had been perfectly normal, not uniquely special. In making this vital point, Peter effectively silenced his critics.

The first group he had to convince were the 'brothers from Joppa' who had come to Caesarea with him. Peter persuaded them to do the baptisms precisely because 'They have received the Holy Spirit just as *we* have.' The most natural interpretation of his word 'we' is that Peter was appealing to the experience of his travelling companions. But there is no hint that they had been among the hundred and twenty at Pentecost; for both geographical and statistical reasons, the likelihood is that they had not been present. What can be stated is that these believers from Joppa had received the Spirit in exactly the same way as had Cornelius' household.

We can pursue this line of enquiry into the next discussion Peter had, after he returned to Jerusalem (Acts 11:1–18). This time he faced the 'circumcised' (i.e. Jewish) believers, who numbered many thousands by now, of whom the vast majority were not part of the original group at Pentecost. Ironically, they seemed more worried that Peter had eaten with Gentiles than that he had baptised them! Peter uses the same argument again: 'the Holy Spirit came on them as he had come on *us*'.

Again, the plain sense of his words is an appeal to his hearers' experience, inviting them to identify with what had happened. Cornelius' initiation had been normal, not exceptional.

This understanding could be challenged by drawing attention to the additional phrase Peter used on this occasion: 'at the beginning'. This appears at first glance to be a reference back to the original Pentecost and therefore limits the comparison to the minority who had been there; 'us' thus becomes almost a royal 'we' and refers to an élite group in Jerusalem. However, this impression may be the result of our English translations, which have usually added to the phrase 'at the beginning' the definite article 'the', though it is not in the Greek text. This has the misleading effect of turning a general reference into a specific one. Without the article, the word 'beginning' (Greek: *arche*) is used of Christian initiation generally, the commencement of discipleship (1 John 2:24 is an example); whereas with the article, it is used of a definite historical event (Acts 26:4 is an example). If Peter's words are translated literally, they would read 'as he had come on us in beginning', or, in better English 'as he came on us when we began'. The reference would then be a general one to all Peter's hearers, rather than a particular one to the privileged few who had been present at 'the' beginning (i.e. Pentecost). This approach finds confirmation in the expanded remark concluding Peter's defence: 'God gave them the same gift as he gave us, who believed in the Lord Jesus Christ . . .' (the aorist tense means 'having believed'). It is an incongruous choice of words if Peter was referring exclusively to the hundred and twenty on the day of Pentecost itself; it is a description that applies to the whole church. Further evidence is to be found in Peter's quotation of Jesus' own promise just before his ascension: 'John baptised with water, but . . . you will be baptised with the Holy Spirit' (Acts 1:5; 11:16); the quotation is word-accurate, except for the significant omission of the phrase 'in a few days', the inclusion of which would have limited this promise to the day of Pentecost.

Exactly the same point recurs at the Jerusalem Council. Peter did not mind repeating himself when he discovered an unanswerable argument! 'God . . . showed that he accepted them by giving the Holy Spirit to them, just as he did to *us*' (15:8). There is some ambiguity as to whether Peter was addressing the 'apostles and elders' (15:6) or the 'whole assembly' (15:12) at this point; but he made no direct reference to the day of Pentecost and no distinction between those who were present on that day and those who were not. The whole thrust of his speech was that Cornelius' experience was identical to that of all Peter's audience.

This appeal carried the day and silenced Paul's and Peter's critics, even causing some of them to explode in praise (11:18). Would the response have been so unanimous had Peter been arguing that the Gentiles had experienced a very special manifestation not given to most believers in Jerusalem or Joppa? That would have set the Gentile believers above the Jewish believers, a claim more likely to stimulate controversy and jealousy rather than contentment and joy! No, the strength of Peter's case lay precisely in the fact that God had 'made no distinction between us and them' (15:9). There is no warrant for taking 'us' to mean 'some of us' or 'those of us who were privileged to experience the first outpouring at Pentecost'.

To conclude, the only abnormal aspect of the Gentile reception of the Spirit was its timing, in coming before water-baptism. In every other respect it was normal rather than special, an example rather than an exception. Though Luke has included the event in his account primarily for its ethnic significance, this does not evacuate it of all evangelistic relevance. Luke and Peter shared a common understanding of what was needed to enter the kingdom of God on earth.

19 THE WHOLE HOUSEHOLDS
(Acts 11:14; 16:15, 31; 18:8)

'He will bring you a message through which you and all your household will be saved.' (Acts 11:14)

When she and the members of her household were baptised, she invited us to her home. 'If you consider me a believer in the Lord,' she said, 'come and stay at my house.' And she persuaded us. (Acts 16:15)

They replied, 'Believe in the Lord Jesus, and you will be saved – you and your household.' (Acts 16:31)

Crispus, the synagogue ruler, and his entire household believed in the Lord; and many of the Corinthians who heard him believed and were baptised. (Acts 18:8)

I am considering all these passages together (1 Cor 1:16 may be included also) in the light of the basic thesis that Christian initiation is a fourfold process (repenting, believing, being baptised and receiving). The question naturally arises whether the *order* in which the process occurs is important or whether the sequence is of little or no significance, provided the elements are all ultimately present.

For example, it is clear that the Spirit can be received before water-baptism, though there is only one such case recorded in the New Testament (Acts 10:47).

However, the big issue is whether water-baptism may come before all the other three components. It is freely granted that repentance and faith are both ongoing characteristics of the Christian life and will continue to develop after water-baptism as a single event. But can water-baptism be valid and effective if it is administered before either repentance or faith have

begun as far as the baptised person is concerned? The importance of this question lies in the widespread practice of baptising 'infants', usually babies who are only a few weeks old and
are quite incapable of conscious repentance or faith.

Defendants of baby baptism frequently claim biblical support for their position by appealing to the recorded 'household' baptisms during the ministries of Peter and Paul –
associated with the names of Cornelius, Lydia, the Philippian
jailer, Crispus and Stephanas. Two kinds of argument are
based on these incidents. At the practical level, it is held that
such households must have included babies, who in turn must
have been included in the baptisms. (This can be stated less
dogmatically by saying that babies were not necessarily excluded.) At the theological level, it is held that the baptism of
whole families confirms the continuity of the Old Testament
concept of covenant as including a man's descendants as well
as himself – as, for example, in the covenant God made with
Abraham. Babies may therefore be baptised as a sign that they
belong to this covenant of grace by virtue of their physical
ancestry, their baptism being the equivalent in the New
Testament to circumcision in the Old.

There is a great deal to unpack in all this and some of it will
be dealt with later (see Appendix 1). Technically, only practical implications can be read *out of* the texts before us; theological assumptions can only be read *into* them. However, we shall
look at both aspects, the practical from particular texts and the
theological from general truths.

The word 'household' is itself a good place to begin. Its
modern application to the 'nuclear' family (parents plus children) is seriously misleading. The biblical meaning was even
wider than the concept of an 'extended' family, though it
could certainly include aged parents and grandparents (1 Tim
5:4). Normal use of the term included all servants, slaves and
employees directly associated with a family – and these could
far outnumber the physical relatives. Such was the situation of
Abraham, when he circumcised his son first, then all the male
members of his 'household' (Gen 17:23–27), of whom there
were at one time three hundred and eighteen! In this context

there is almost a distinction between 'family' and 'household', as there certainly is with Rahab later (Josh 6:25). This semi-distinction can be traced right through biblical history and into early church history (one of the early Church Fathers mentions a 'bishop's wife, her household and her children' – note the order!). There is no real equivalent in our Western egalitarian society, where 'servanthood' is out of fashion, but the Victorians would have understood it better, though they would have used such terms as 'staff' or 'retinue'. Perhaps 'personnel' is the nearest we could get to the idea today!

All this hardly proves that babies were not included in the New Testament concept of 'household', but it does demonstrate that it included far more than the 'family', than a man's physical descendants (cf. John 4:53). Indeed, it could be used where there was no family at all; a single person could still have a 'household' of slaves – which may, or may not, have been the case with any of the New Testament examples we are considering, since in no case is the marital status of the household 'head' mentioned. Therefore these texts prove far too much for the advocates of baby baptism! If it is held that a 'head' automatically brings his whole 'household' within the covenant of grace, then that must apply to his parents and grandparents, his domestic servants and employees in the family business. This may be salvation by grace, but it is salvation without faith! It is no use claiming that babies would be exempt from faith whereas adults would not; no such distinction can be found in the records. The promise that 'you will be saved – you and your household' (Acts 16:31) either requires the faith of the household's head alone (i.e. the jailer) or requires the faith of every member of the household; the grammar might carry either implication but cannot possibly mean the faith of all the adults but none of the children!

Actually, the context confirms that Paul's statement is to be interpreted as an extended invitation to the whole household to 'Believe in the Lord Jesus, and . . . be saved'. The jailer's question has revealed an exclusive concern for his own future, but Paul seizes the opportunity to include his frightened staff, giving them the chance to have a share in his salvation, by sharing his faith. That this is the correct understanding is clear from Luke's careful account of their response. The gospel was preached not only to the jailer but to *all* the others in his household; they were *all* baptised, and they were *all* filled with joy because they had *all* believed!

The same point may be made in relation to the other situations. 'All' of Cornelius' household heard the message, received the Spirit, spoke in tongues and prophesied. The group is described as 'his relatives and close friends' (Acts 10:24). They had all been devout and God-fearing, and were all expecting a message that would lead to the salvation of the 'entire' household. The 'entire household' of Crispus became believers first and were then baptised (Acts 18:8). The whole household of Stephanas 'devoted' themselves to the service of the saints (1 Cor 16:15 – the first converts in Achaia). Whatever else may be said, all these households consisted *entirely* of those capable of making an active response to the gospel (I have myself been involved in such 'household baptisms', where everyone 'under one roof' has repented and believed around the same time, though today this obviously involves a smaller number of individuals).

Though the case for excluding passive babies from the household baptisms in the New Testament is not watertight (!), the onus of proof would seem to rest on those who include them (and, by implication, would exclude adult members of the 'household' who could believe, but didn't). So far we have only considered the textual material, but the deeper issue of the theological background to these texts must also be considered, since this is the real reason why they are interpreted as they are.

There are some weighty theological objections to the practice of baptising babies before they have repented or believed for themselves. The most obvious is the difficulty of applying the New Testament meaning and significance of baptism (see chapter 4) to a passive recipient who is incapable of making a response. The concept of bringing repentance and faith to full expression and effectiveness in the act of baptism is altogether lost. The instrumental language, which sees the act as bringing about what it represents – an actual burial and resurrection with Christ – gives way to one or other of two distortions. With some, an extreme sacramental view takes over, believing the water and the words will be enough to bring salvation to the baby (an outlook rightly termed 'baptismal regeneration'). With others, an extreme symbolic view takes over; baptism itself does little or nothing, but is a 'sign' pointing back to something that has already happened (entry into the covenant by physical birth) or forward to something that hopefully will later happen (entry into the kingdom by spiritual birth). One of these views makes too much of the rite, the other makes too little! Both see baptism as incomplete, requiring the addition of some form of 'confirmation' when years of responsibility are reached. A few would say that water-baptism must be completed later with Spirit-baptism (though Catholic theology identifies the two and believes the Spirit is received by the baby at baptism).

The most consistent 'paedobaptist' position is that which builds on the notion of covenant. Usually based on the premise that there is only one 'covenant of grace' in the whole Bible, and that it is revealed in various stages and modes, it is argued that God's dealings with people are more collective than individual and his grace is physically inherited as well as spiritually imparted. He makes his covenant with a 'people' rather than with persons. The family is the unit of salvation, and a person is born into the spiritual 'status' of the parents. Thus, 'household' baptisms are totally consistent with God's ways, when understood as 'family' baptisms.

The basic assumption behind this thinking, that there is only a single 'covenant of grace' running throughout the Bible, must be challenged. The phrase itself never occurs. Neither does the concept. The Bible speaks of various covenants (plural), distinguishing between them according to their recipients, promises and conditions. Even in the Old Testament there are the very different covenants made with Noah (the first mentioned), Abraham, Moses and David. The last three were very much interrelated, and all three involved physical descendants or relatives – so the 'collective' concept of 'covenant' is certainly relevant to God's relationship with Israel.

But the New Testament speaks of a 'new' covenant, predicted in the Old Testament by Jeremiah, who said this would not be like the covenant made with Moses (Jer 31:32). It would render the old covenant obsolete (Heb 8:13). We must examine the ways in which this new covenant was to be different from the old covenant.

One major contrast is that it would be made with each individual person rather than a collective people. This had been foreseen by the prophets (Jer 31:29–30, 34; Ezek 18:2; Joel 2:32) but comes out very clearly in the preaching of John the Baptist and Jesus, who were at pains to say that ancestry had become irrelevant (John 3:9; 8:39). Flesh can only produce flesh; a second birth of the Spirit is now needed (John 3:5–6). There is therefore a new emphasis on personal responsibility (which implies the ability to respond!). The language of the new covenant is intensely personal – 'everyone', 'each one' and 'whoever'. The stress is on the need for each individual to make their own response to God ('if anyone' in Luke 14:26–27; 'whoever' in John 3:16; 'every one of you' in Acts 2:38). The coming judgement will be on an individual basis (Rom 2:6), as is the redemption from the wrath to come.

There cannot be two ways into the kingdom – some entering by being born of the flesh and others by being born of the Spirit! Baptism belongs to the latter, not the former.

One corollary of this is that the family is no longer the unit of God's saving activity. Sure enough, the New Testament indicates that a 'household' and even the family itself may be divided by the gospel. Jesus said that he did not come to bring peace, but a sword – that would divide parent from child, brother from sister. For example, a family of five might be split into two and three (Luke 12:51–53) – the only intimate relationship Jesus did not envisage being broken was that between husband and wife in 'holy' matrimony (see chapter 22).

We conclude that the 'new' covenant is established on quite a different basis from the 'old', and that its rites of recognition are to be differently applied. But which is the 'old' covenant? All New Testament references use this adjective of the covenant made with Israel through Moses, never of that made with Abraham. Indeed, in the New Testament Gentile believers are said to be 'Abraham's offspring' (Rom 4:16), inheriting the blessings promised to him. Since the covenant made with Abraham was also inherited by his 'descendants', does this not also apply to the descendants of Christians today? Is not 'household' baptism the direct substitute for Abrahamic circumcision?

It is important to note that the New Testament never actually uses the word covenant when linking Christian believers to Abraham. Their link with him is spiritual and not physical, of faith and not flesh. They are his 'offspring' or 'sons' in that they bear his likeness by sharing his faith; he is the 'father' of many nationalities of believers (Rom 4:16–17). Christians have not inherited all the things promised to Abraham – for example, they have not received the land of Canaan – but they have received the promised Spirit (Gal 3:14). We need also to remember that circumcision for Abraham came *after* his faith and could only be a 'seal' of his own faith; it could not be a 'seal' on the faith of any of his descendants (Rom 4:10–11). He is the Father of all those who believe first and are sealed afterwards. Water-baptism is never called a 'seal' at all; that term is reserved for Spirit-baptism in the New Testament. And the only New Testament passage in which water-baptism and circumcision are mentioned together in the same context makes it quite clear that the physical rite of circumcision is not in mind at all (Col 2:9–12 – see chapter 25).

The link between the Abrahamic and the 'new' covenant is the Lord Jesus Christ himself. The 'old' covenant ended with him. His circumcision at eight days was the last required by God, Jesus being the single 'seed' inheriting the Abrahamic blessing (Gal 3:16). The 'new' covenant began with him. Jesus' baptism in water at thirty and his suffering and death at thirty-three were both required to inaugurate a new way of inheriting the Abrahamic blessing (Luke 12:50; 22:20). He did not choose to be circumcised, but he did choose to be baptised.

Therein lies the key. The contrast is between the life of the flesh and the life of the Spirit. Genealogy, so vital to the people of God under the 'old' covenant, reaches its climax and conclusion in the family tree of Jesus (Matt 1; Luke 3); from that point heredity is an irrelevance. The new covenant forms a new people on a new basis. Having inherited the blessing of Abraham through his flesh, Jesus now dispenses it to others through their faith alone (cf. Acts 1:33 and 11:17 with Gal 3:2–14).

After this major digression, we can return to the passages about 'household' baptism and state with some confidence that neither the internal (textual) evidence nor the external (theological) evidence allow them to be used to support the practice of infant baptism. Even allowing for a margin of ambiguity, we must insist that the case for this practice should be established without these texts (if it can be!).

Let me close this chapter with a quotation from the *Apology of Aristides*. (Aristides was a Christian contemporary of the Emperor Hadrian, who ruled from 117 AD to 138 AD.) The *Apology* reveals the attitude of Christian 'householders' in the period immediately following the New Testament writings: 'As for their servants or handmaids, or their children, if any of them have such, they persuade them to become Christians for the love that they have towards them; and when they have become Christians they call them without distinction "Brothers".' Thus both servants and children in a Christian 'household' were regarded as objects of evangelism; and the key to their conversion was the love they received from Christian members of the household.

20 THE EPHESIAN DISCIPLES
(Acts 19:1–6)

¹While Apollos was at Corinth, Paul took the road through the interior and arrived at Ephesus. There he found some disciples ²and asked them, 'Did you receive the Holy Spirit when you believed?'

They answered, 'No, we have not even heard that there is a Holy Spirit.'

³So Paul asked, 'Then what baptism did you receive?'

'John's baptism,' they replied.

⁴Paul said, 'John's baptism was a baptism of repentance. He told the people to believe in the one coming after him, that is, in Jesus.' ⁵On hearing this, they were baptised into the name of the Lord Jesus. ⁶When Paul placed his hands on them, the Holy Spirit came on them, and they spoke in tongues and prophesied. (Acts 19:1–6)

This passage is a classic case of the damage done by the uninspired division of God's word into chapters, never mind verses! The story of the mission to Ephesus begins in Acts 18. Paul was not ploughing virgin soil, but reaping where others – namely, his friends Priscilla and Aquila and, particularly, the Egyptian Jew Apollos – had sown. It surely cannot be a coincidence that both Apollos and the disciples whom Paul discovered 'knew only the baptism of John' (18:25; cf. 19:3).

If, as seems highly probable, the group encountered by Paul owed their spiritual knowledge to Apollos, it would go a long way towards explaining why Luke called them 'disciples' without any qualification and why Paul assumed they were 'believers'. For Apollos knew enough about Jesus to be able to prove from the Jewish scriptures (i.e. the Old Testament) that he was the expected Messiah (Greek: *christos*), presumably by matching the prophetic predictions with what he knew of the life, death and resurrection of Jesus (in much the same way as Jesus himself had done on the road to Emmaus – Luke 24:25–27).

This connection would also explain Paul's cautious, even suspicious, questioning of their spiritual experience. For Apollos' ministry had been deficient. His teaching about Jesus was accurate, as far as it went, but it was not adequate to foster full Christian experience. He appears to have been ignorant of the fact that baptism was now administered by command of the risen Jesus and carried a fuller significance 'into' his name; and he was almost certainly unaware of the subsequent out-pouring of the Holy Spirit by the ascended Jesus. Without these insights, 'faith' would be seen by Apollos as primarily a mental acceptance of self-evident truths (believing *that* Jesus was the Christ) rather than an existential relationship (believing *in* Jesus as personal Saviour and Lord), inaugurated through baptism in water and Spirit.

A couple who had already been colleagues of Paul recognised Apollos' shortcomings. Instead of having roast preacher for dinner, they wisely took the preacher for a roast dinner! Privately and informally, they enlightened him about the full gospel. They also seem to have introduced him to another group of 'brothers' (not those he had been teaching), who encouraged him to preach his deeper understanding else-where, in Achaia.

It looks as if Apollos had thus been related to two groups in Ephesus. The first, associated with the synagogue, consisted of those Jews who had accepted his case that Jesus was the Messiah promised in their scriptures. The second, to which he was introduced by Aquila and Priscilla, was a group of Christians, probably meeting in their home. The two groups do not seem to have been directly related to one another; and the couple who corrected Apollos seem not to have extended their concern to those he had been teaching.

However, since Paul's initial contacts in a city were usually through the synagogue, they would be the first group he came across. His conversation with them, the subject of so much debate and even controversy, becomes entirely explicable against the background explained above. Their replies to his 'cross-examination' exactly reflect the earlier phase of Apollos' teaching. They had obviously not had the benefit of conversation with Priscilla and Aquila.

Luke has no hesitation in describing them as 'disciples', the most common title for Christians in the book of Acts. The word is used of one believer (9:10, 36), of some believers (9:19, 25) and of all believers (6:1, 7). Had they simply been 'disciples of John', Luke would surely have said so, in his desire to be accurate (cf. Luke 1:3). The lack of the definite article ('the') is not significant here (cf. 9:10, 36). He accepted them as 'disciples' because they were already on 'the Way' (note how often this 'denomination' for Christianity is used in the Ephesus saga – 18:25, 26; 19:9, 23). However, the key question is how far they had gone along 'the Way'; Paul wanted an answer to that before he ministered to them.

To understand the passage properly, the right starting-point is not the spiritual state or status of the 'disciples' but the mental outlook of the apostle. This passage contains clearer clues to Paul's theology of initiation than any of his epistles, largely because they were written to those who had already been fully initiated and contain only occasional references to their beginnings, whereas here in Acts he is counselling the beginners themselves. We witness him directly involved in evangelism. Painstaking analysis of his conversation and conduct on this occasion yields invaluable insights and challenging principles.

Paul's first question to these 'disciples' needs careful unpacking; both too much and too little can be read into it. He is not querying their doctrine, but their experience; yet he is doing so on the basis of his theology.

From the wording of the question, we can take it that he found their spiritual condition less than satisfactory. We must take Paul's words at their face value as a genuine summary of his first impressions, even if his further investigation was to modify his initial opinion. In brief, he was at first sure that they had 'believed' in Jesus, but not at all sure that they had 'received' the Spirit (only later did he have doubts about their faith also).

What had led to this double impression? There must have been some signs that they had 'believed' – as Apollos' pupils, they would know the 'Christian' interpretation of Old Testament scriptures and be able to talk freely about Jesus being 'the Christ', all of which would give Paul the impression that they had heard and received the gospel. But some other signs must have been absent – signs that they had 'received'. There was probably no manifestation of gifts of the Spirit. To use another of Paul's expressions, they did not appear to 'be having the Spirit' (Rom 8:9 – see chapter 21). This deficiency could be due to one of two causes: either they had already 'received' but had since 'quenched' or 'resisted' his influence, or they had never actually 'received' the Spirit. Paul's question is carefully designed to discover which is the real reason, and therefore what ministry would be appropriate to meet the situation.

The wording is very significant. Literally translated, Paul's question reads 'Having believed, did you receive Holy Spirit?' The verb 'believe' is in the aorist tense, referring to that single step of faith that begins the life of faith for the believer (the same tense is used in conjunction with the verb 'receive' in John 7:39 and Acts 11:17, and both contexts are almost identical to the present one). There has been a lot of argument whether an English translation should read '*when* you believed' (favoured by those who think 'believing' and 'receiving' are synonymous and therefore simultaneous) or 'since you believed' (favoured by those who teach a two-stage 'second blessing' which must be subsequent). Actually, either translation is perfectly valid! Paul is really asking: 'Having believed in Jesus, did you, either then or since, receive the Holy Spirit?' (in Acts 10:44 it was simultaneous; in Acts 8:17 it was subsequent!). He is not the slightest concerned about when they 'received', but is very concerned to know whether they have received. In asking whether both had taken place, one conclusion is absolutely clear: *for Paul, believing in Jesus and receiving the Holy Spirit were not one and the same thing*. It was perfectly possible, to his way of thinking, for them to have had one without the other, as had been the case with the Samaritan converts and in his own experience for three days in Damascus. This state may be 'sub-normal', but it is not 'abnormal'.

The next thing to emphasise is that Paul expected the disciples to know whether they had 'received' or not. They were not in a position to deduce this 'knowledge' from New Testament scriptures, as so many try to do today, since these were not yet written! They could only reply in terms of an experience that was so definite they could have no doubts about its occurrence. Further confirmation that Paul is appealing to their experience is the absence of the definite article – 'Did you receive Holy Spirit . . . ?' This usually has the effect of emphasising the subjective power rather than the objective person; it is a characteristic omission when the Spirit is viewed as part of human experience (see Appendix 2).

The disciples' answer to Paul's first question must also be very carefully handled. A superficial reading (as in too many translations) take it as a confession of abysmal ignorance about the third person of the Trinity, admitting to having never heard anything about him! Such total lack of knowledge is highly improbable, since Apollos' teaching almost certainly included the promise that the Messiah would fulfil his mission by the powerful anointing of the Holy Spirit (Isa 61:1), which was fulfilled for Jesus at his baptism by John in the Jordan. They must also have heard about John's teaching that his baptism in water was not to be compared with the Messiah's baptism in Holy Spirit, which was to come later.

When we look again at the actual wording of the reply, we find it betrays knowledge rather than ignorance – but mental rather than experiential knowledge. What they really said (translated literally) was 'But we have not heard that Holy Spirit is.' Noting again the absence of the definite article (pointing to the power rather than the person), we must explore the strangely 'unfinished' sentence (Holy Spirit 'is' what?). Some assume 'is' means 'exists', but this involves turning the sentence right round and making the Holy Spirit the object rather than the subject of the verb ('We have not heard that there is a Holy Spirit'). To be sure, a literal translation of the Greek into English cries out for an additional word to complete the sense. Happily, there is an exact parallel elsewhere in scripture (how often this provides the solution to an exegetical problem!). John 7:39 literally reads: 'For not yet was Spirit, because not yet was Jesus glorified.' What 'was' Spirit not yet? To take it to mean that the Spirit did not yet exist would be a heretical denial of the eternal Trinity! To avoid this error, English translations invariably add an extra word (not in the Greek): 'for not yet was Spirit *given*' (i.e. manifested in men). This makes sense, and it clarifies the reference to Pentecost (which could only take place after the death, resurrection and ascension of Jesus – his 'glorification'). As soon as this valid additional word is inserted into the same grammatical construction in Acts 19:2, the disciples' reply is altogether different: 'We have not heard that Holy Spirit is given' (the Western text makes this even clearer with its variant reading *Lambanousin tines*: translating this, their reply reads: 'We have not heard that any have received the Holy Spirit'). In other words, they knew that the anointing on the Messiah would be available to his followers, but they had not been informed that this had already happened. Their ignorance was not of theHoly Spirit as such, but about the event of Pentecost and its significance for all subsequent believers.

This told Paul what he needed to know, so he pursued his enquiry further back into their initiation by asking about their baptism. Note that he assumes they have all been baptised, though he wonders whether it was properly administered: they are still at this stage 'believing disciples' in Paul's mind. If they are so unaware of Pentecost, he begins to ask himself how much 'Christian' content there had been in their baptism, and what had they understood about the purpose of the rite, hence the use of the preposition 'into' (see chapter 23 for the full significance of this in connection with baptism). For every baptism there is an 'in' (the medium – here, water) and an 'into' (the meaning or intended purpose achieved by the act). In simple English, Paul is asking: 'What did your baptism do for you or mean to you?'

Before considering the disciples' reply, we need to pause

and ask what the question reveals about Paul's thinking. Clearly, there is some connection in his mind between baptism in water and receiving the Spirit. Though Paul never actually identifies these two things, he obviously associates them very closely, almost, though not quite, linking them together in terms of cause and effect. Water-baptism is both a prelude to and a condition for Spirit-baptism; in practice, the one normally led to the other. A faulty baptism is therefore one possible cause for a delay in receiving the Spirit. Putting this another way, the Lord usually responds to a proper baptism by demonstrating his acceptance of the penitent believer with the gift of the outpoured Spirit. So it is not just what the baptism has meant to the candidate that facilitates or delays the reception of the Spirit; a delay could well mean that the Lord himself is declaring the baptism inadequate for some reason.

The answer these 'disciples' gave to Paul's second question finally revealed their true position and told Paul all he needed to know. Their baptism had been a genuine expression of repentance towards God, but it had not been a personal act of faith in the Lord Jesus. Because it had not been explained as such, it had not been seen by them as an identification with Jesus in his death, burial and resurrection (Rom 6:3–4), expressed in giving them a new identity by baptising them 'into' his name. It had not been 'Christian' baptism.

This revealed that their faith had not been all it should be. Only now did Paul realise that he had been mistaken in assuming that they had 'believed', at least in his own understanding of that term. In fact, of the four elements of Christian initiation, they only really had one – repentance! Paul sought to take them on from this by pointing out that their ultimate mentor, John the Baptist, had fully realised the limitations of his own ministry and baptism, directing his followers to redirect their dependence to 'the One' for whom he was only a forerunner. His own baptism of repentance was intended to 'prepare the way' for faith in the coming King, who turned out to be his own cousin, Jesus.

It is important to notice that Paul's introduction of Jesus at this point caused neither surprise not protestations of ignorance ('We have never heard that Jesus is'!). There is a puzzle here: the name of 'Jesus' must have been both familiar to them and used among them when Paul 'found' them (or why would Luke call them 'disciples' and Paul assume they had 'believed'?), yet Paul now tells them to 'believe in' Jesus. The explanation may again be found in the ministry of Apollos. He had taught them 'about' (Greek: *peri* – 18:26) Jesus and shared his belief that Jesus was the Christ, which was accurate but not adequate. But this was not the full saving faith that consists of believing *in* Jesus (actually, Paul uses the Greek preposition *eis* = 'into'). Saving faith is personal rather than propositional – hence the use of the name 'Jesus' with such prominence, both to be called upon in direct address and used as authority by those who became his 'relations' and 'representatives'.

All this and more must then have been fully explained by Paul. The disciples' response to Paul's further enlightenment was a wholehearted desire to enter into this more personal relationship with Jesus Christ. Incidentally, an eagerness to go further is usually a sign that someone is already on 'the Way'; it is not a good sign when someone thinks they've already got all they need! So the Ephesian 'disciples' readily submitted to baptism in water into the name of the Lord Jesus. Paul did not perform the rite himself, but left it to his helpers, Timothy and Erastus (19:22), presumably to avoid the disciples associating his own name with the rite (1 Cor 1:15).

Before going any further, we must realise that this act was what many today would call a 're-baptism' (To avoid the uncomfortable implications of this, Calvin, in his *Institutes* 4.15.18, denied that water-baptism was administered in Ephesus and insisted that Paul only laid hands on these 'disciples'!). Paul had no hesitation in putting these disciples into water for the second time, neither had Peter on the day of Pentecost (see chapter 15). Even though their first baptism had been accompanied by genuine repentance, the absence of personal faith in Jesus meant that it had not been 'Christian' baptism. It had not been accepted by the Lord as fulfilling his command. Paul did not attempt to 'add' the dimension of faith retrospectively to that first baptism by some devised ceremony of 'confirmation'; that would have reduced baptism to a mere anticipatory symbol, which it was never meant to be. The use of water with a form of words that included the name of Jesus would hardly have satisfied the apostle that a Christian baptism had taken place. It is not the formula – the use of Jesus' name by itself – that makes the sacrament effective, but the faith in his name, the calling upon his name by baptiser and baptised alike (Acts 2:21; 3:16; 22:16). Nor is there any evidence that Paul would have accepted vicarious repentance or faith as a substitute for the baptised person's own response to the gospel (see the previous chapter).

Whatever the original state of their faith, there could be no doubt that the Ephesian disciples were now true believers – having repented of their sins, put their faith in the Lord Jesus and brought both to fruition in water-baptism. It is therefore somewhat irrelevant to argue about their spiritual status when Paul first met them. It is a simple fact that when they came up out of the water they were *still* in the condition of having believed but not yet received! This vital point is completely overlooked by most modern evangelicals (who yet maintain they must have received when they believed, in spite of there being no outward sign of this) and by most modern sacramentalists (who yet maintain they must have received when they were baptised, in spite of there being no outward sign of this); were these two outlooks correct, there would have been no need whatever for *further* ministry from Paul. The apostle, however, did not think in either of these two ways. He showed no surprise that so far nothing had actually 'happened' to indicate that the Spirit had been given. He seems to have proceeded on the simple assumption that these 'disciples' were now fully eligible to 'receive', so the next appropriate step was to ask that the gift would be given – using that intensive and expressive form of prayer known as 'the laying-on of hands'. This had already been practised by other apostles (Acts 8:15–17) and was, in fact, the very way Paul himself had received the Holy Spirit after he had repented and believed (Acts 9:17). Unlike the water-baptisms, Paul now did this himself – not because it needed an apostle (Ananias had sufficed in his own case) or because he had raised the subject in the first place, but because his prayer request would make it quite clear that this time it was no human being doing the baptising, but Jesus himself (the words used being directed to him rather than the candidate). That is, *every* believer, without distinction, will be baptised in the Holy Spirit by Jesus himself, whereas they will be baptised in water by different disciples of Jesus (when distinctions could be made).

At last, having fulfilled all the conditions and dealt with the obstacles, the Ephesian disciples received the Holy Spirit and could now have answered Paul's original question with a resounding affirmative (they did not need to, because reception of the Spirit was always perfectly obvious to others present at the time; Paul only asked because he had not been present at their beginnings). Their initiation was now *complete*. It was also now *normal*. They had repented and believed before baptism and received Holy Spirit after baptism, the exact sequence usually experienced by all who responded to the gospel in those days. The *timing* was a little unusual, in that their faith took some time to reach its saving effectiveness. The time-lag between attaining full faith and receiving the Spirit was brief, but real (baptism came between the two). Whether it is measured in minutes (as here) or days (as at Samaria), the 'gap' is sufficient to show that 'believing' and 'receiving' are clearly not the same thing.

The clinching argument is that in Ephesus, as everywhere else and for everyone else, receiving the Holy Spirit was accompanied by audio-visual evidence of a 'Pentecostal' nature. On this occasion there were 'tongues and prophesying'. Both are forms of *spontaneous* speech; the first would be in unlearned and probably unrecognised languages, while the second would be in their own language. The content of both would come from their spirits rather than their minds, the Holy Spirit telling them what to say. It is probably significant that whenever 'signs' of receiving the Spirit are listed, the gift of 'tongues' is *always* included. On the other hand, when other 'signs' are also listed, there is no clear claim that *all* spoke in tongues as well as using other gifts (such a 'blanket' statement is only made about the day of Pentecost itself, when tongues were the only manifestation – Acts 2:4; see chapter 14). Here at Ephesus it appears that some spoke in tongues and some prophesied (this is the most natural sense of the wording). Pentecost itself excepted, there is neither any record of every person speaking in tongues when the Spirit was received nor any apostolic teaching that they must. That this may well be the outward sign can be well supported from scripture, but to state dogmatically that it is the only valid evidence is to go beyond scripture itself.

One or two final observations complete our study. The fact that there were twelve 'men' to whom this happened probably has little significance, other than to underline Luke's meticulous accuracy in recording events. Nor does it necessarily exclude their wives or believing members of their families. Note that they did not receive the Holy Spirit simultaneously as a collective group – the main time that happened in the New Testament was at Pentecost – but individually, one by one, as the apostle's hands were laid on them (as had happened at Samaria – Acts 8:17). The claim that the New Testament only records corporate Spirit-baptisms is simply not true.

Detailed attention has been given to this passage because of its unique significance in providing a direct link between the Lukan and Pauline theologies of the Spirit. It is fashionable in some circles to emphasise the difference between them and then to choose one as a criterion for the other! Evangelicals tend to choose the Pauline, using it to neutralise the charismatic dimension of Luke, while Pentecostals tend to choose Luke, using it to neutralise the integrated doctrine of Paul. Acts 19 demonstrates that Paul's understanding of Christian initiation was the same as that of the other apostles – namely, the pattern consistently reported throughout Luke's interpretative history of the early church. The essential features of this common theology may be listed as follows:

1. Complete initiation consists of four elements – repenting towards God, believing in Jesus, being baptised in water and receiving the Holy Spirit.

2. Christian baptism requires repentance of sin and personal faith in Jesus as necessary preconditions.

3. Believing in Jesus and receiving the Holy Spirit are not the same thing, and they may be separated in time.

4. Receiving the Holy Spirit is a definite experience with demonstrable evidence.

5. When any of the four elements is lacking, steps need to be taken to supply the deficiency.

Of course, Acts 19:1–6 is not the only passage from which these conclusions can be drawn (e.g. see chapters 16 and 27); but it is one of the clearest examples of apostolic practice, from which apostolic doctrine may be deduced. (The pastoral application of these principles will be discussed later in the book, in chapters 32 to 35.)

The challenge to rethink our modern assumptions is superbly expressed by Bishop Lesslie Newbigin in his *The Household of God* (London: SCM Press, 1953) – one of the most prophetic writings on the church in our day, by a missionary statesman akin to Roland Allen:

The apostle asked the converts of Apollos one question: 'Did ye receive the Holy Spirit when you believed?' and got a plain answer. His modern successors are more inclined to ask either 'Did you believe exactly what we teach?' or 'Were the hands that were laid on you our hands?', and – if the answer is satisfactory – to assure the converts that they have received the Holy Spirit even if they don't know it. There is a world of difference between these two attitudes. (p. 95)

21 THE ACID TEST (Romans 8:9)

> You, however, are controlled not by the sinful nature but by the Spirit, if the Spirit of God lives in you. And if anyone does not have the Spirit of Christ, he does not belong to Christ. (Rom 8:9; the last phrase in Greek is 'of him'.)

This is one of the favourite 'proof-texts' of those who hold that the Holy Spirit is 'received' automatically, and usually unconsciously, at the moment a person 'believes', thus making it unnecessary and even misleading to expect any further evidence or experience to confirm that the 'gift' has indeed been given.

However, those who use this verse for that purpose handle it in a quite extraordinary manner. Paul's statement is not taken as it stands, but reversed twice – first from negative to positive, then from back to front! Furthermore, the word 'Christian' is introduced, though it is not in the original. The result is that some exegetical 'sleight-of-hand' is successfully disguised. The argument proceeds as follows:

anyone not having the Spirit is not a 'Christian', therefore
anyone having the Spirit is a 'Christian', therefore
anyone who is a 'Christian' must have the Spirit.

The third statement is then taken as the meaning of the text, and to the untrained ear it sounds like a perfectly legitimate deduction. But there is a fatal flaw in the logic, which is easier to spot in a single reversal:

every dog has four legs, therefore
everything that has four legs must be a dog.

Having understood the basic fallacy, we can now give an example of a double reversal:

anyone not born of British parents is not 'British', therefore
anyone born of British parents is 'British', therefore

anyone who is 'British' must have been born of British parents.

This could be taken as an impressive argument until it is realised that the meaning of 'British' may not be the same all the way through; in the third statement it may include those who have been through a legal process of adoption or naturalisation. In exactly the same way, 'Christian' in the third statement may be quite different from its meaning in the first statement. In its modern usage, 'Christian' would be used of the Samaritans before they had received the Spirit, in which case Romans 8:9 could be used to prove they had received the Spirit! If 'Christian' is used for anyone who has 'believed' in Jesus, then this understanding of Romans 8:9 makes utter nonsense of Paul's question to the Ephesian 'disciples', which could now be read as 'Did you receive the Holy Spirit when you became Christians?'

Having cleared this widely accepted misinterpretation out of the way, we can proceed to a fresh understanding by considering the wider context and the actual wording of the text itself and then examining its bearing on Paul's doctrine of initiation.

Paul writes to Rome because it is his ambition to minister among them (as the hub of the Roman Empire) and beyond them (as a 'field base' from which to reach westwards into Spain). Since their church was not planted by him and they have never been on the receiving end of his ministry, he writes his own 'letter of commendation' (cf. 2 Cor 3:1–3). This explains both the minor feature of so many personal greetings (in Rom 16) and the major feature of so extensive a statement of the gospel he preaches (the nearest he ever came to setting down a 'systematic' theology!). They need to know as much about him as possible before he arrives, so that he may be speedily accepted and sent on (Rom 15:24).

It is also important to realise that he does not know them any better than they know him. Though he has heard excellent reports of their corporate faith (Rom 1:8), he is not taking anything for granted. Not having evangelised them himself, he does not assume that they are all they should be. At times he addresses them as if they are still sinners, even though they are 'called saints' (Rom 2:5; cf. 1:7). He may even at one point be hinting that they are not all baptised yet (Rom 6:3). He assumes they could do with more spiritual gifts than they have (Rom 1:11; cf. 1 Cor 1:7). He expects, quite reasonably, that they need considerable help and counsel in godly living, both together in the church and separately in the world (Rom 12–15). The verse we are considering (Rom 8:9) fits this whole 'atmosphere' very well, since it contains the gentle reminder that behind his teaching lies the basic premise that they all 'have' the Spirit; unless that can be assumed, his conclusions are inapplicable.

The first eight chapters of Romans set out Paul's gospel preaching, his 'theology' of salvation; the next three chapters deal with the relationship between Jews and Gentiles, an urgent issue in the church at Rome; and the concluding chapters spell out the ethics of salvation. Within the first section (Rom 1–8), there are three clear divisions:

the need for salvation (the wrath of God and the sin of man);
the beginning of salvation (justification);
the continuing of salvation (sanctification).

Romans 8:9 is invariably interpreted as if it belongs to the second, but it is part of the third. It is not so much a reference to the believer's *status* before God, which is the issue of justification, as a reference to the believers *state* in God, which is an issue of sanctification. It is therefore quite wrong to read into the verse a definition of how anyone 'becomes' a 'Christian' (this is another illustration of the maxim 'A text out of context becomes a pretext').

Romans 7 and 8 belong together. They provide the immediate background of the verse by contrasting life in the 'flesh' (both before conversion, in 7:7–13, and after conversion, in 7:14–25) with life in the 'Spirit'. One way of living leads to defeat, despair and death; the other to victory, hope and life. Drawing out the difference is one of Paul's favourite ways of stimulating believers to seek holiness (Gal 5:16–23 is a classic example of such a contrast). It is Paul's understanding that the believer has a choice which the unbeliever has not. An unbeliever can only live in the flesh. A believer, on the other hand, can live in the flesh and be 'carnal' – in which case his life will be as confused and depressing as it was in his pre-Christian days – or he can live in the Spirit and be 'spiritual'.

It is therefore perfectly natural, in the light of his theme and his relationship to the Romans, that Paul should slip in a remark to the effect that he is taking for granted that his readers all 'have' the Spirit. Unless this is so, the peace, the sonship, the help in prayer, the providential over-ruling of circumstances, the triumph over all adversity – all of these will be beyond their reach. They spring directly from walking in the Spirit, being led by the Spirit, witnessed to by the Spirit and helped by the Spirit. By the power of the Spirit, the flesh is made to 'stand down'. For it is impossible to live by the flesh and by the Spirit at the same time. The believer may be 'free' to walk in either the flesh or the Spirit, but never in both (cf. Rom 8:5 with Gal 5:17).

With all this in mind – and wearing the right context lenses! – we turn to Romans 8:9 itself, starting with a literal translation of the Greek: 'If any is not having Spirit of Christ, this one is not of him.'

The most striking thing about this statement is the tense of the verb 'have'. In Greek the present tense means either prolonged action (to 'go on' having something) or present condition (to 'be' having something). Common to both meanings is the element of continuity; it is often referred to as the 'present continuous' tense.

It cannot be too strongly emphasised that Paul is referring to his readers' present condition and not to their past conversion. He is talking about their present experience of sanctification rather than their past entrance into justification. When he wants to refer to a believer's initial reception of the Spirit, he uses the past tense, or more particularly, the aorist tense (which refers to a single event). This is the case earlier in the letter, in the section on justification, when he refers to 'the Holy Spirit, whom he has given us' (Rom 5:5). Notice that in Romans 5 Paul expresses complete confidence that his readers have all 'received', whereas here in Romans 8 he introduces a note of doubt as to whether they all 'have'. This points to a fundamental distinction in Paul's thinking and teaching. 'Receiving' and 'having' are not synonymous, though the former should lead to the latter. Where disciples do not appear to be 'having' the Spirit, the first thing to find out is whether they did 'receive'; this was the exact situation at Ephesus which prompted Paul's question (see chapter 20). Though at Ephesus he discovered they had never 'received', the form of his question shows that he was open to the alternative possibility that they had 'received' but had not gone on 'having'.

Confirmation of this understanding of 'having' and 'receiving' comes from the Septuagint, the Greek translation of the Old Testament scriptures. This version is the one Paul quotes most frequently, and through it he would have become familiar with this very phrase: 'having Holy Spirit'. It is there used, in the present tense, of such men as Joseph and Joshua, to describe their continued state of spiritual maturity (Gen 41:38; Num 27:18). Paul uses it about himself (1 Cor 7:40).

In other words, 'having' must be understood in continual and experimental terms relating to sanctification, instead of in doctrinal and judicial terms relating to justification. There may be an additional pointer to this understanding if the definite article is intentionally omitted; this would emphasise the 'subjective' experience of Holy Spirit power in a believer, as against the 'objective' existence of the person of the Holy Spirit in the believer (see Appendix 2). This is entirely congruous with the first half of Romans 8:9, which reads literally: 'You are not in flesh, but in Spirit, if indeed Holy Spirit goes on inhabiting you'. Here are the same grammatical features: the present continuous tense of the verb, the absence of the definite article, etc. In fact, the two halves of the statement read like a couplet of Hebrew poetry (based as it is on 'parallelism', the repetition of the same thought in different words); such couplets are not unlikely from the pen of a 'Hebrew of Hebrews' (Phil 3:5).

Most noticeable of all, both statements are prefixed by the crucial 'if', the first strengthened with the participle 'indeed'. This clearly expresses a conditional situation, as there is nothing automatic about either 'having' or 'indwelling'. It is possible to begin by 'receiving' and not to continue 'having' the Spirit.

What, then, is lost by those who do not continue to 'have'? Since this statement is in Romans 8 and not Romans 5, the first answer is: their sanctification, though not necessarily their justification. None of the blessings of 'life' in the Spirit can be theirs. They will find themselves 'in flesh' again, living 'carnal' lives (1 Cor 3:1). The law of sin, operating in their members, will prevail over the law of God in their minds. In a word, they will get stuck in Romans 7! That can only produce spiritual deadness.

But could that end in eternal death? Can justification be lost as well as sanctification? What is the meaning of the last phrase, 'this one is not of him'?

The first thing to decide is who 'him' refers to. All three persons of the Trinity (God, Christ, Spirit) are mentioned in this verse. It is, however, unlikely that 'him' refers collectively to all three. Normally it has been taken to refer to Christ, since he is the last person named before the pronoun. This view is particularly favoured by those who interpret the whole verse in terms of justification rather than sanctification. The phrase is then taken to mean 'he is not a Christian at all' (Living Bible paraphrase), usually with the additional implication 'and never has been'!

This interpretation, however widely it may be accepted, breaks the continuity of Paul's forceful argument, turning Romans 8:9 into an 'aside' (which therefore ought to be in brackets, like this aside!). It then becomes a kind of 'throw-back' to a much earlier part of his exposition and would more comfortably fit immediately after Romans 5:5, the section on justification where he talks of receiving the gift of the Spirit when 'becoming a Christian'. But in Romans 8, rightly seen as the climax rather than the commencement of the Christian experience, it seems strange that Paul should suddenly interrupt his flow with an abrupt remark like 'Of course, none of this applies if you're not even a Christian yet'!

The difficulty is resolved if we stick to our contextual approach. Not only is the theme of Romans 8 exclusively concerned with sanctification; the person primarily in view is the *Holy Spirit*. There has been a progressive emphasis through the epistle – from the wrath of God, through the redemption of Christ, to life in the Spirit. Here in Romans 8:9 the Spirit is central to the exposition, being variously described as 'the Spirit of God' and 'the Spirit of Christ', thus identifying him closely with the other persons in the Godhead, a piece of sound theology. The two titles are complementary and highlight more vividly the poetic parallelism of the two statements. The order of phrases varies, as it does in Hebrew Psalms, but a rearrangement of them will make the parallel clear:

Spirit of God + dwelling = in Spirit
Spirit of Christ + having = of him.

Since the 'of him' in the second line is synonymous with 'in Spirit' in the first, both phrases refer to the Holy Spirit and the final 'him' is not Christ, but the Spirit of Christ. There is a further parallel internal to each statement, which may be brought out thus:

When the Spirit dwells in you, you are in him;
when you don't have the Spirit, he doesn't have you.

Paul is making a profound point, first positively, then negatively – and all poetically!

He is talking about the ongoing rather than the incoming of the Holy Spirit in the believer. The whole verse is experiential rather than doctrinal, concerned with our 'salvation' in this world rather than the next, with sanctification rather than justification. He is not discussing who is 'of Christ' (his normal definition of a Christian is someone who is 'in Christ'); he is discussing who is 'of Spirit'.

There is no need, therefore, to discuss the bearing of this verse on the 'once saved, always saved' issue (see chapter 36). To lose one's sanctification existentially is quite a different thing from losing one's justification eternally. The former is Paul's concern in Romans 8.

The tone of Romans 8:9 is one of realism, with a fine balance between a strong dose of optimism in the positive line of the stanza and a slight tinge of pessimism in the negative line. It is the delicate combination of a necessary warning, impersonally postulated about 'anyone' failing to 'go on having' Holy Spirit, and a confident assurance, personally addressed to 'you', that the warning is hardly necessary in Rome, since they are not in the flesh but in the Spirit (and can therefore apply the whole of Romans 8 to themselves). This same blend of general warning and particular encouragement can be found in other apostolic writings (Heb 6:9 is a good example – see chapter 27).

To sum up, 'Holy Spirit' for Paul was not so much a sound doctrine as a spiritual dynamic. He was concerned that his converts, having first 'received' the Spirit (Gal 3:2 – aorist 'once' tense), should 'go on' being 'supplied' with the Spirit (Gal 3:5 – present 'continuous' tense). Complete salvation will only be experienced by those who '*still* have' the Spirit; it is not enough to have '*once* had' him.

The challenge of this distinction is needed perhaps more in our day than ever before. Baptism in the Holy Spirit is only a beginning. To have been filled is one thing; to remain full quite another. To 'receive' the Spirit is a vital step; to 'have' the Spirit is a victorious walk. That is the message of Romans 8, of which verse 9 is the acid test.

22 THE HOLY FAMILY
(1 Corinthians 7:14)

> For the unbelieving husband has been sanctified through his wife, and the unbelieving wife has been sanctified through her believing husband. Otherwise your children would be unclean, but as it is, they are holy. (1 Cor 7:14)

This is another favourite 'proof-text' for the baptism of babies without their consent or co-operation. It is often linked with the 'household' baptisms (see chapter 19), though in those cases it was the 'head' (i.e. *husband*) of the house whose faith was supposed to save his whole household, whereas here it is claimed to be achieved equally well by a believing *wife*.

Actually, this verse has nothing whatever to do with initiation, or even salvation as such. The context is a discussion about marriage and the problems that arise between two believers; and even more between a believer and an unbeliever. Can a believer escape from the pressures of such an 'unequal yoke'? Of course, a believer should never have got into such a situation (2 Cor 6:14) – so Paul is almost certainly considering the case where one partner has become a believer *after* the marriage.

Paul cannot quote detailed words of Christ to fit every such circumstance, but nevertheless considers that his 'apostolic' counsel has the authority of a 'command' (1 Cor 7:10). But the basic principle behind his counsel does have the Lord's precedent: divorce is not an option. If separation is the only solution to an impossible domestic situation, the believer must remain single or be reconciled to their former partner (but not marry another for the first marriage is not dissolved, simply held in abeyance).

Reading between the lines, it is obvious that some believers were trying to justify divorce, or even just separation, on the sole ground that the partner was an unbeliever. Such an unequal yoke was being claimed as an immoral relationship which ought to be severed; to be married to a 'sinner' was regarded as spiritual corruption of the 'saint'. More likely, it was simply an excuse to be rid of an irksome companion!

Actually, the influence is the other way round, according to Paul. Far from the believer being tainted, the unbeliever is 'sanctified'. But what exactly does this mean? It certainly cannot refer to that moral and spiritual refinement that follows justification, since Paul later states that the unbelieving partner is still not 'saved' (1 Cor 7:16). He must be using the term in a technical, legal and almost ritual sense as 'set apart for God' (its original connotation in the Old Testament). 'Holy' matrimony has put such unbelievers in a different category, rendering it inappropriate to 'come out from them and be separate' (2 Cor 6:17). The relationship is one that carries God's approval and blessing; what has God's endorsement must have the believer's also.

Paul clinches his argument by pointing out that if an unbelieving partner is regarded as too 'unclean' to live with (i.e. because of their unbelief rather than sins), the same principle would have to be applied to the children, and the believer would also have to desert them (either because they are the children of an unbeliever and therefore 'contaminated' or because they are not yet believers themselves). But this is not necessary, because the 'sanctity' of the family as a unit puts the children also in the category of 'holy' things which the believer may safely handle. Again, it is clear that Paul is using the word 'holy' in an objective and 'legal' sense (as 'undefiling') rather than in a subjective 'moral' sense (as 'undefiled'); only an idealist who has had no personal contact with children could believe that having one converted parent secures 'saintly' behaviour and character in the offspring!

To use this application of 'holy' to children as a justification for the baptism of babies is, to say the least, precarious. It could equally well be argued that such 'holy' infants do not need *any* cleansing rite (in the same way as Jewish proselyte baptism included the existing children of 'converting' parents, but regarded all subsequent offspring as already 'holy' and in no need of ritual cleansing). And it could further be claimed that a 'sanctified' but unbelieving husband was as eligible for baptism as his 'holy' children!

It would be sensible if all agreed to a moratorium on the use of this passage in all discussions on Christian initiation. It is a difficult enough passage to apply to its stated theme of divorce and marriage without dragging it into the quite alien context of baptism! It is only dealt with here because it has been so frequently appealed to in support of the wide separation in time of baptism and the other elements of Christian initiation.

Children of one believing parent are already 'holy' by birth into that family. Baptism cannot make them any more holy than they already are, and to use it simply as a recognition of what they already are grossly distorts the New Testament meaning of the act.

23   THE DISJOINTED BODY
(1 Corinthians 12:13)

> For we were all baptised by one Spirit into one body –
> whether Jews or Greeks, slave or free – and we were all
> given the one Spirit to drink. (1 Cor 12:13)

As with the majority of his letters, Paul is here dealing with
problems in a church he has planted. Some of these are
doctrinal (they were somewhat shaky in their understanding
of the resurrection), some moral (involving incest among the
members and drunkenness at the Lord's Supper) and some
social (concerning cliques gathered around different
preachers). Two of his basic concerns were the Corinthians'
immaturity (they were more 'carnal' than 'spiritual') and their
disunity (they were more interested in spiritual 'gifts' than
'fruit').

The immediate context of the verse we are considering is
a three-chapter section 'concerning spiritual gifts' (Greek:
charismata). 1 Corinthians 12 deals with the varied gifts
experienced in the body; 1 Corinthians 13 demonstrates that
the gifts when exercised *without love* can damage the body; 1
Corinthians 14 outlines the 'more excellent way' of using the
gifts *with love* to build up the body. It is a great pity that the
uninspired chapter divisions have interrupted the 'flow' of
Paul's treatment, allowing readers to lick the jam of love out of
its 'charismatic' sandwich!

Paul is responding to the Corinthian situation, either in
reply to direct questions from them about the use of spiritual
gifts or, more probably, to reports of their abuse in the
assembly. His underlying (or over-riding) concern, however,
is the unity of the body, without which the gifts are at best
useless toys or at worst dangerous weapons. Hence his

emphasis on 'love' (Greek: *agape*, which is 'caring' rather than 'liking'.) Such an attitude seeks to edify others rather than to express or exhibit one's self.

The theme of 1 Corinthians 12 is 'variety in unity', and the basic appeal throughout is to the Corinthians' experience of the Spirit moving them when they assemble together. Paul begins by reminding them that not every spontaneous utterance is from the Holy Spirit; there can still be pagan influence at work from their past. The content of such exclamations will indicate their source. Maybe Paul begins with this point because the majority of the spiritual gifts listed later take the form of supernaturally inspired speech.

The Corinthian church was experiencing the full range of charismata, for which Paul had already expressed gratitude to God (1 Cor 1:7). But the very variety of these was now a problem. Some were more impressive than others, enhancing the reputation of those who exercised them. The need for some gifts was being played up and the need for others played down. Envy, pride, anger, impatience, malice and rudeness had been lurking within these immature Christians, but the advent of the charismata brought such vices to the surface. The selfish use of gifts was dividing the body.

Paul therefore puts the emphasis on the unity of the gifts underlying this variety. Behind all the different kinds of gift, service and operation is the same God – Father, Son and Holy Spirit, all three of whom are directly involved in charismatic activity. Indeed, the Trinity is the perfect and original example of variety working in unity, and this is reflected in all divine activity in the church on earth.

From the 'all' of 1 Corinthians 12:4–6, Paul turns to the 'each' of verses 7–11. The same Spirit makes each person different in gifting, making the choice of gift himself. So there is only one person behind it all, and it is all for one purpose – 'for the common good'. The gifts are *from* unity and *for* unity.

The remainder of 1 Corinthians 12, beginning with verse 12, revolves around the metaphor of a physical body. Just as the Creator is an example of variety in unity, so is the creature made in his image. Spiritual gifts are to the church what limbs, organs and faculties are to the body. Health in both cases is the result of full *participation* and good *co-ordination* of all the parts. Note that Paul does not say this is how it *should* be 'for' Christians, but how it *is* 'with' Christ. The church is *his* body, not ours!

1 Corinthians 12:13 must be carefully examined in this context. Not surprisingly, the key word is 'one'; it is used three times, with the words 'all' and 'Spirit', both used twice, as runners-up. 'All-one-Spirit' sums up the verse and perfectly fits the overall argument.

Bear in mind that the whole appeal of this chapter is to the Corinthians' *experience*, not their theology, of the Spirit. They may have very different experiences of the varied gifts he gave to 'each'; but they have 'all' had exactly the same experience of introduction to the exercise of gifts within the body. This common 'starting-point' to their charismatic experience provides a basic unity behind the variety of gifts which followed. They all shared the same memory of a definite and datable initiatory experience of 'life in the Spirit'. It was also a 'dual' experience, best described by the two verbs 'baptised' and 'drink'. We shall consider the two halves of 1 Corinthians 12:13 separately.

'. . . BAPTISED IN ONE SPIRIT INTO ONE BODY . . .'

Apart from the changed adjective, from 'holy' to 'one' (which is entirely explicable in terms of the context and purpose of this passage, as explained above), this phrase is exactly the same as used elsewhere in the New Testament: 'baptised in Spirit' (Matt 3:11; Mark 1:8; Luke 3:16; John 1:33; Acts 1:5; 11:16). The verb (Greek: *baptizein*) is followed by a preposition (Greek: *en*) and the dative case (Greek: *pneumati*). Therefore the phrase in Paul must surely carry the same meaning as everywhere else. The preposition should therefore be translated by its usual 'in' (rather than the 'by' of many English translations, including the NIV). The Spirit is not the agent 'by' whom the baptism is administered, but the medium 'in' whom the baptism takes place. If it is taken as 'by', this would be the only verse in the entire New Testament attributing the role of 'baptist' (i.e. baptiser) to the third person of the Trinity!

Just as the Corinthian believers have all been baptised 'in water' (Greek: *en hudati*), so they have all also been baptised 'in Spirit' (Greek: *en pneumati*). The aorist tense of the verb 'baptised' points to a single, one-off event which happened to them all, though obviously not simultaneously, it being extremely unlikely that they all joined the church on the same day.

But did they all *experience* this 'baptism' in Spirit? Had they been conscious of it happening at the time? Was it an actual memory? Did they know what Paul was talking about, or was it a fresh 'revelation' to them that they had, in fact, been baptised in the Spirit without realising it? Such questions, so common today, would probably have astonished both Paul and the Corinthians. However, they must be faced, in view of the general evangelical interpretation of this verse, which treats it as Paul's doctrinal explanation rather than the Corinthians' dynamic experience. A great deal is at stake: do the words 'we were all' include all Christians today or not? In other words, have all contemporary believers been 'baptised in one Spirit', even without any conscious awareness of it having happened? The pastoral implications are enormous!

The clue to this deep difference of opinion lies in the interpretation of the phrase 'into one body'. At first sight, this appears to refer to a believer's initial entry into the church of Christ. The sacramental view understands water-baptism to mark the moment of entry, hence the Catholic claim that Spirit-baptism is the inward reality of the outward rite. The Spirit is received through that sacrament, even when applied to babies, and any later experience of him is said, quite unscripturally, to be the 'release' of the Spirit from within. The evangelical view understands faith to be the moment of entry, hence the claim that Spirit-baptism is the same as justification or regeneration. The Spirit is 'received' the moment a person believes, and any later experience of him is related to the 'fullness' (another unscriptural word) of the Spirit. Neither view is at all comfortable with the term 'baptised in Spirit' and rarely, if ever, uses it, the one preferring to talk of being baptised in water and the other to speak of being 'born again' of Spirit. This neglect is surprising, considering John the Baptist's prediction that this would be the outstanding feature of the messianic ministry of Jesus. The evangelical, in particular, seems strangely ignorant of the fact that 'baptised in Spirit' and 'born again' occur with almost exactly the same frequency – or, rather, infrequency – in the New Testament! To complete the record, the Pentecostal view, while quite uninhibited in using the phrase, does not believe it occurs in 1 Corinthians 12:13! The 'baptism' referred to here is taken to be an act of incorporating rather than one of empowering; though performed by the Spirit, it has no reference to the baptism in or of the Spirit or to baptism in water. In practice this is very close to the evangelical approach, though it allows for belief in a baptism in the Spirit as a 'second blessing' at a later stage. The liberal view seems shy of using either 'born again' or 'baptised in Spirit', and tends to believe that the Spirit is already at work in all men who are in the 'body' of mankind.

The Catholic, evangelical and Pentecostal approaches all assume that the word 'into' carries the same meaning in Greek as in English. It is understood to refer to the very first introduction to a new situation. When its meaning in English is extended to other stages of a journey, qualifying words are added, hence 'just into', 'further into' and 'right into'. The Greek word (*eis*) can carry any or all of these meanings, without any qualifying addition. It can refer to the beginning, middle or end of a journey – a departure or an arrival. Context alone indicates which aspect is uppermost.

When used with the verb 'baptised', it invariably means 'right into' rather than 'just into', indicating the completion rather than the commencement – bringing something to full expression, practical function or fitting climax. For example, the phrase 'baptised into Moses' (1 Cor 10:2) does not mean that he had not been leading the Hebrew slaves before they crossed the Red Sea, but that this event brought their dependence on him and trust in him to a total commitment, marking as it did the final break with Pharaoh's authority; from that 'baptism' there could be no going back, for it was final. The phrase 'baptised into Christ' (Gal 3:27 – assuming this refers to water-baptism, which seems likely with its reference to 'putting on' the new 'clothes' of Christ) carries much the same significance; it does not imply that there had been no faith in or relationship with Christ before their baptism, but that these are now brought to their proper consummation. The clearest example of this usage is John's statement: 'I baptise you in [Greek: *en*] water into [Greek: *eis*] repentance' (Matt 3:11) – yet he had already demanded fruit of repentance before their baptism (Matt 3:8)! They had to prove they were already *in* repentance before he would baptise them *into* repentance. This is the very opposite of normal English usage, where 'into' leads to 'in'. But if the meaning of 'into' (Greek: *eis*) with 'baptised' means 'right into', everything falls into place. Thus, a swimmer might put a foot in the water to test the temperature before plunging into the water. Another example from scripture would be Peter's announcement on the day of Pentecost that baptism is 'into' forgiveness of sins (Acts 2:38); it brings this freedom from the past to its climax and consummation, in much the same way as crossing the Red Sea brought the Hebrew freedom from Egyptian slavery to its conclusion, even though they had actually left their bondage some days earlier.

Applying this understanding to 1 Corinthians 12:13, we learn that being 'baptised in one Spirit' brings a person 'right into' the body, by anointing them with power to serve the body through a variety of gifts. Paul's understanding of 'membership' of the body is thoroughly functional – it is not so much getting on to the roll as getting into a role! It is 'baptism in Spirit' which brings about the effective functioning of each part of the body.

However, it is vital to note that this interpretation of the verse prevents the negative deduction, that those not 'baptised in Spirit' must therefore be 'right out' of the body. They may well be on their way *in*, while not having reached the point of being right *into* their God-ordained place and function. In much the same way, penitent believers who have not been baptised in water are well on the way, but have not yet fulfilled the basic requirement of discipleship (Matt 28:19). They are certainly not to be regarded as 'right out', but neither must they be thought of as 'right in' (their spiritual status is fully discussed in chapter 36).

This understanding also allows 'baptised in (one) Spirit' to have the full subjective and experiential meaning which it clearly has elsewhere in the New Testament, even though it is neither defined nor described in this particular verse (Paul assumes the Corinthians know perfectly well what he is talking about). It is always a conscious *experience*, accompanied by audio-visual *evidence*. All this would be ruled out if Spirit-baptism were to be identified with justification on the one hand or with water-baptism on the other – which only raises further doubt about either view. The 'drenching' in the Spirit (for that is what 'baptise' means) was surely the same as the 'outpouring' of the Spirit, which every New Testament believer had experienced (see chapters 16, 18 and 26). This subjective emphasis is underlined in the second half of the verse, to which we now turn.

'. . . GIVEN ONE SPIRIT TO DRINK . . .'

Sacramentalists, who have already identified the first half of the verse with water-baptism, apply the second half to Holy Communion! Evangelicals, who have already identified the first half of the verse with justification, tend to see here a reference to the ongoing appropriation of the Spirit that leads to sanctification. Both interpretations seem logical until the tense of the verb is examined – 'drink' is in the aorist, referring to one, single, unrepeated event! It cannot, therefore, refer to continued imbibing, whether sacramental or spiritual in nature. It is a reference to that one drink which starts a flowing stream from within (see chapter 11).

So what is this 'drink', and how do the two events in this verse relate to one another? Very few scholars have suggested they are entirely unrelated; this is partly because of the 'and' linking them, but primarily because the verse smacks of 'Hebrew parallelism', of which the Psalms are full and which would come naturally in the writings of a former Jewish rabbi! But opinion is divided over the 'type' of parallelism used here – whether it is *synonymous* (saying the same thing two different ways) or *synthetic* (supplementing the first line with additional information in the second).

Some see the couplet as synonymous, even though to be 'drenched' and to 'drink' are hardly the same thing! In order to maintain this view, resort is had to an alternative meaning of the second verb – namely, to 'irrigate' or 'saturate'. The two verbs would then be alternative ways of saying 'we were all inundated by Spirit'. This is just possible, but it is not really borne out by the rest of scripture – not least by Jesus' own offer of a 'drink' to the Samaritan woman and at the Feast of Tabernacles (see chapter 11).

To take the couplet as synthetic makes most sense. One single event or experience is being described from two different angles. It would be convenient to say that the first phrase denotes the objective aspect and the second the subjective. Yet this modern distinction might have seemed rather strange to the New Testament writers, in spite of their constant exhortation to 'become what you are', i.e. let your subjective state reflect your objective status, your sanctification express your justification. We have already seen that 'baptised' contains a strong subjective element. It seems more appropriate to see the first statement as the external aspect and the second as the internal. 'Drenched' implies something poured on us and therefore coming from outside us; 'drink' implies something poured into us, getting right inside us. Confirmation of this distinction may be found in the voices of the verbs – 'drenched' is *passive*, implying activity by the baptiser only, whereas 'drink' is *middle*, implying co-operation between the baptiser and the baptised.

Both words originated with Jesus (John 4:13; 7:37–39; Acts

1:5, 8). They were unusually linked at Pentecost – when the disciples were 'baptised' in Spirit, the onlookers wondered what they had been 'drinking' (Acts 2:13–15). Paul exhorts believers not to 'drink' wine, but be filled with Spirit (Eph 5:18). The two thoughts occur together in the context of nature – when it rains, the land is 'drenched' by 'drinking' (Heb 6:7).

So the experience to which Paul is referring combines being passively 'drenched' in, and actively 'drinking' in, the Spirit (note the implications for the use of the mouth at the co-operative stage). Together, they constitute what the apostles called 'receiving' the Spirit. In the early church, to say that a person could be 'drenched' and 'made to drink' without them or anyone else knowing anything about it would have seemed preposterous! It was this conscious experience which released a believer into the exercise of the spiritual gifts listed immediately prior to this statement (tongues and prophecy usually being among the first), thus becoming a fully functional 'member' of the body.

We may add a word about the general application of this verse today (though this will be more fully dealt with in chapter 35). The phrase 'we were all' was legitimately used of the Corinthian believers. Having been 'planted' by Paul, who always insisted that his converts 'received' the Spirit as well as 'believed' in Jesus, he could correctly assume that this experience had been included in their initiation – and base his argument for unity on their shared memory of that event. But this cannot be assumed of *all* 'Christians' or 'churches' today, any more than it can be assumed that *all* believers today have been 'buried with Christ' in water-baptism (Rom 6:4; 1 Cor 1:13; Gal 3:27; Col 2:12 – all assume this). There are, alas, many believers today lacking either or both baptisms.

This latter fact is almost certainly the explanation for the scarcity, and in many cases total absence, of the 'spiritual gifts' listed in 1 Corinthians 12. The church is then dependent on dedicated 'natural' gifts (i.e. those possessed *before* becoming a Christian and used after as well); since such gifts are very unevenly distributed, ministry divides the people of God into an active minority and a passive majority! When 1 Corinthians 12:13 is not part of our experience, verses 7–11 are not likely to be either! Even evangelical writers, who dislike and do not use the language of being 'baptised in Spirit', have frankly admitted that only where this phraseology is confidently preached do the spiritual gifts appear with any regularity and frequency. (See, for example, Michael Cassidy's quotation from Michael Green in his *Bursting the Wineskins* (Hodder and Stoughton, 1983), pp. 261–262.) Practical observation can supplement prepared exposition!

We can only conclude that Christian initiation is incomplete without that 'inundation' of the Spirit which combines both 'drenched' and 'drinking' – and that this experience is the vital ingredient of church unity. Indeed, without this it would be impossible to 'keep the unity of the Spirit through the bond of peace' (Eph 4:3). This could explain the many ecumenical disappointments and some of the unexpected by-products of the charismatic movement – when the water rises above the fences, the ducks begin to swim together!

24 THE BAPTISED DEAD
(1 Corinthians 15:29)

> Now if there is no resurrection, what will those do who are baptised for the dead? If the dead are not raised at all, why are people baptised for them? (1 Cor 15:29)

This is the only mention in the New Testament of 'proxy' baptism, in which one person undergoes the ceremony on behalf of someone else who will, nevertheless, be the beneficiary.

Some have seen it as a very early Christian practice developed to safeguard relatives who had died before full salvation – made possible by the first Easter and Pentecost – became available. As such, it would therefore have been one of those customs that would inevitably die out after the first few generations (since few people are concerned about the eternal destiny of their forebears further back than grandparents).

Others, notably the Mormons, claim it as a continued practice right through the 'latter days', since it has in this verse full biblical and apostolic sanction.

However, there are weighty objections to it being regarded as 'Christian' at all. The implications would be quite contrary to some major tenets of scripture.

First and foremost, it runs counter to the whole tenor of New Testament teaching, that moral choices cease at death. Beyond this life there is 'a great chasm' which none can cross (Luke 16:26). Decisions made during this life are decisive for our eternal destiny (Luke 12:20). The doctrine of a 'second chance' of salvation in the world beyond finds little basis in apostolic preaching. The only possible exception concerns just *one* generation – namely, those who were drowned in Noah's day (1 Pet 3:19–20 – see chapter 29).

Second, this would constitute the full-blown doctrine of 'baptismal regeneration' – the notion that the use of water and the use of right words effect salvation in and of themselves, even in the absence of repentance and faith in those benefiting from the baptism. The technical term for this mechanical, even magical, view of baptism is the Latin phrase *ex opere operato* (it 'works by itself').

Third, it relies on the possibility of vicarious faith – a faith which is exercised on someone else's behalf, with or without their consent and co-operation. It is true that there are some examples of this in the gospels, though there it is always concerned with the healing of disease or the exorcism of demons. But there is not a single case of someone acting as a 'substitute' in this way when it comes to the matter of personal and eternal salvation. Notice, for example, the strong emphasis on the need for a person's *own* response in apostolic preaching ('Repent and be baptised, every one of you . . .' – Acts 2:38; see chapter 15). Though there are expressions of collective responsibility for national sins in the Old Testament (Neh 1 and Dan 9 contain such), there is no case of vicarious repentance in the New. Indeed, it was to be a mark of the new covenant that each individual would be held responsible only for his own personal sins (Jer 31:29–30; Ezek 18:2).

As well as these general difficulties, there are indications in the text itself that Paul is not referring to a Christian custom. He speaks of its practitioners in the third person. Instead of asking 'Why do we . . .?' or 'Why do you . . . ?', he asks 'Why do they . . . ?' Added to this unusual (and presumably carefully chosen) wording are some significant omissions. There is no mention of repentance and faith, even of a vicarious nature, though Paul regarded both as essential preconditions for baptism. Nor does Paul state the purpose or the effectiveness of the practice.

The only point Paul makes is that those who engage in this physical rite on behalf of the dead do so because they believe in some kind of bodily existence beyond the grave (as distinct from the normal Greek view of the extinction of the body and the immortality of the soul, for which a 'material' sacrament would be totally irrelevant). The confidence of their 'superstition' is in marked contrast to the scepticism of the Corinthian Christians, who appear to have been infected by the doubts about bodily resurrection inherent to Greek philosophy (cf. Acts 17:32).

Clearly, Paul is using what is called an *ad hominem* argument: he is using an example of pagan confidence to shame his sceptical readers into a firmer faith. He is no more approving of the practice than was Jesus when he used a similar appeal to the shrewdness of a thoroughly dishonest crook; it is, alas, often true that 'the people of this world are more shrewd [or show clearer insight] in dealing with their own kind than are the people of the light' (Luke 16:8).

I possess a photograph, taken in Singapore, of a full-scale model of a car constructed entirely of bamboo canes and tissue paper; it would be bought and burned on a funeral pyre to provide the deceased with convenient transport in the next world. (I was amused to note that the paper wheels carried the Mercedes-Benz logo, presumably to guarantee eternal mileage!) If Paul were around today, he might well compare this naive belief in a 'material' after-life with radical theology's rejection of a 'bodily' resurrection, implying that the former demonstrate more faith than the latter! And many Christians whose ambition it is to have a Mercedes car in this world might be challenged by this Chinese practice to learn how to 'lay up treasure in heaven' by the proper use of money and material possessions (Matt 6:19–21; Luke 16:9).

Some of the points made above also raise questions about the appropriateness and effectiveness of infant baptism, whether it is understood 'sacramentally' (*ex opere operato*) or 'evangelically' (depending on vicarious repentance and faith in the sponsors – parents, 'godparents' and/or church members). What can be said from the verse under consideration is that if baptism on behalf of the deceased was neither a Pauline nor a Corinthian practice, it provides no precedent for proxy promises on behalf of the newly-born.

25 THE NEW CIRCUMCISION
(Colossians 2:9–12)

[9]For in Christ all the fulness of the Deity lives in bodily form, [10]and you have been given fulness in Christ, who is the Head over every power and authority. [11]In him you were also circumcised, in the putting off of the sinful nature, not with a circumcision done by the hands of men but with the circumcision done by Christ, [12]having been buried with him in baptism and raised with him through your faith in the power of God, who raised him from the dead. (Col 2:9–12)

Studying a New Testament epistle is like listening to one side of a telephone conversation. To understand what is being said, the other side of the dialogue must be reconstructed by deduction. (See Gordon D. Fee and Douglas Stuart, *How to Read the Bible for All its Worth* (Scripture Union, 1983), ch. 4. Fee and Stuart's book is quite the best Bible study aid I know.)

To appreciate how difficult this process of listening and reconstruction can be, the reader is invited to use his imagination and guess what the following exchange (of which he is given only one side) is about:

'Congratulations! How much does it weigh?'
(Silence.)
'What colour is it?'
(Silence.)
'How many gallons an hour does it use?'
(Silence.)
'Will your old implements fit it?'
(Silence.)

How soon did you guess that a farmer had bought a new tractor?

The cost and complication of mail in New Testament times meant that every letter was written for an important purpose, usually in response to a specific situation arising among those to whom it was addressed. So it is necessary to 'read between the lines' in order to identify the recipients' particular need for counsel or correction from the writer.

In the case of the Colossians, it is obvious that heresy had crept into their teaching ministry, with the inevitable bad effect on behaviour, particularly in personal relationships. The false doctrine seems to have been an amalgam of 'Gnostic' philosophy and Jewish ritualism. It is the latter that underlines the thrust of the verses we are considering. For Paul, such 'observances' as kosher diet, sabbath days and annual festivals belong to the world of 'shadows'; they may have the right 'shape' (more or less), but they lack any real substance.

Though he does not list circumcision in his compendium of erroneous practices, it must surely be in his mind. Verses 9–10 may be paraphrased thus: 'You have everything you could possibly need in Christ, including all the circumcision you will ever require.' To demand that Christians should be circumcised was a Judaising error that dogged Paul's mission to the Gentiles. He had to oppose it in Jerusalem itself (Acts 15) and almost everywhere else (see Rom 2:26; 1 Cor 7:19; Gal 5:2; Eph 2:11; Phil 3:2). The physical rite as such is obsolete and irrelevant to the new people of God in Christ (Col 3:11).

The rite of circumcision was given to Abraham as a 'seal' on his righteousness by faith (Rom 4:11 – note that it came *after* he believed; if there *were* any parallel between circumcision and baptism, the latter would have to follow this same order!). It was to be passed on to all male sons and servants in his 'household' as a 'sign' (which looked forward, whereas a seal looks backward) that God's promise was extended to Abraham's 'seed' – a single, male descendant who would inherit it (Gal 3:16). When that legatee arrived, in the person of Jesus, the sign reached its fulfilment and his circumcision was the last required by God. Note that while the 'sign' was being passed down its practical 'effect' was negligible. It did not actually make any change in the baby (other than the excision of the foreskin of the penis); it was merely the recognition that the boy was already a descendant of Abraham by his birth. However, failure to be circumcised would have had a profound effect, cutting the baby out of the line; not to be circumcised was regarded as breaking the Abrahamic covenant (Gen 17:14). Later, the rite of circumcision would also bind the recipient to the obligation of keeping every law of Moses, given to Abraham's descendants when they left Egypt. It was for this last reason that Paul so vehemently opposed its application to his Gentile converts, though he accepted it as a valid social custom with no spiritual significance (he even went as far as to circumcise Timothy so that he could evangelise Jews – Acts 16:3). As a religious rite, however, he clearly regarded it as having been abolished (1 Cor 7:19).

Yet many people today would say that circumcision has been fulfilled rather than abolished – it has been transmuted into another physical rite: Christian baptism. The one has simply replaced the other as the rite of initiation into the people of God. The 'continuity' between them is usually pressed by 'paedobaptists', who claim that baptism of babies, provided they can claim a Christian pedigree, is the valid perpetuation of the former practice of circumcising babies. The theological justification for this position is derived from a 'covenantal' interpretation of scripture which lumps all the different covenants together into one 'covenant of grace', thus making the conditions and application of this covenant the same throughout the Old and New Testaments (see chapter 34 and Appendix 1 for further details). The textual justification for this identification of baptism with circumcision is found in this Colossians passage (though it is the only place in the New Testament where the two subjects are mentioned together).

Let it be admitted that the words 'circumcision' and 'baptism' are here found in close association and, at first sight, in comparison with one another. However, a careful study reveals that they are actually set in contrast to one another. Had Paul simply said 'You don't need to be circumcised because you have been baptised,' there would be nothing more to say. If this is what he believed, he could have saved himself attending the Jerusalem Council or writing his letter to the Galatians! But neither he nor any other apostle ever made this simple equation: his train of thought is far more convoluted and needs careful unravelling.

At the heart of his argument is a clear distinction between the physical circumcision practised on the body by the Jews and the spiritual circumcision experienced in the heart by the Christians. The key phrase is 'not . . . done by the hands of men', which can hardly be a description of baptism! There is obviously a connection between this heart-circumcision and baptism, but not a total identification.

There was scriptural precedent for using the word circumcision in a spiritual, rather than a physical, sense. While its usual meaning in the Old Testament was that surgical operation which marked one of Abraham's descendants, the Israelite prophets were united in insisting that the physical operation needed to be matched by a moral purity, which they called the 'circumcision of the heart' (see Deut 10:16; Jer 4:4; 9:26). Foreigners were not to enter the temple, because they were uncircumcised in heart and flesh (Ezek 44:7). On most occasions this heart-circumcision was assumed to be the work of man, just as much as flesh-circumcision, but there is also a promise that one day the Lord himself will do it properly (Deut 30:6).

Paul would undoubtedly have been aware of this strand of prophetic teaching about circumcision, but his readers at Colossae would probably not recall it or even know about it. Nor was it necessary for them to do so. The argument does not depend on the double aspects of circumcision, but on the double meaning of the word 'flesh' (Greek: sarx). Though this could refer to the physical body, the apostle used it far more frequently to denote that sinful nature which had been inherited along with bodily life. Jewish circumcision only cuts off a small part of the physical 'flesh', but Christian circumcision cuts off the whole of the sinful 'flesh'.

This is accomplished through 'the circumcision of Christ' (v. 11). But what is the significance of the genitive ('of') – is it subjective or objective, is it done to Christ or done by Christ?

Is Paul referring to a once-for-all event in the life of Christ or to a repeated event in the life of every believer? To put it another way, when did, or does, this 'circumcision of Christ' take place?

Let us assume that it refers to a circumcision Christ himself had and see where that leads us. In its simplest sense, this could refer to the Jewish rite he underwent when he was eight days old (Luke 2:21). But Paul speaks of him 'putting off his flesh' – that is, not just part of it, but all of it. More likely, therefore, is the suggestion that this is a figurative reference to his death on the cross. Made in the likeness of sinful flesh (Rom 8:3), made to be sin who had no sin (2 Cor 5:21), he died to sin (Rom 6:10). He was not just 'shuffling off his mortal clay' but divesting himself of what had become a 'body of sin'. It was a total 'death to the flesh', in both senses of that word. As Lamb of God he 'took away the sins of the world' (John 1:29) in this 'putting off the flesh' at Calvary.

This understanding fits the context well, but it also provides a direct link between the 'objective' and 'subjective' meanings. What was done *to* Christ on the cross is also done *by* Christ in the believer. It was fundamental to Paul's theology that what had been historically achieved in the death, burial and resurrection of the Lord Jesus (1 Cor 15:3–4) must be existentially appropriated by the individual believer, who must be crucified, buried and raised with Christ in order that he, too, may 'put off the flesh' (this time the meaning will be totally spiritual, referring to his inherited sinful nature; no surgery on the body will be needed).

This identification with the 'circumcision of Christ' which separates the Christian from his sinful flesh commences with his repentance and faith but is consummated in the act of baptism. Baptism is 'into his death' (Rom 6:3). Submersion in the water applies his burial; emergence from the water applies his resurrection (note that the believer is 'buried' and 'raised' *with* Christ). Two things may be noted about Paul's language at this point. First, it is sacramental rather than symbolic; the rite is an instrumental agent rather than an instructional aid! Second, there is a surprising omission in Colossians of any direct link between baptism and the death of Jesus; only the burial and resurrection are mentioned (though this may not be too significant).

There is a profound paradox running through this whole section. While the flesh is alive, the person is in a state of uncircumcised death (Col 2:13), even if his body is circumcised! When the flesh has been crucified and buried through baptism, real life begins! The same 'power' that raised Jesus from the dead works through baptism to bring about new life in the believer. Since this 'power' is elsewhere defined as the Holy Spirit (Rom 8:11), Paul may here be referring to Spirit-baptism, which normally came immediately after water-baptism in apostolic evangelism. Other New Testament passages link baptism to resurrection in the same way (Rom 6:4; 1 Pet 3:21).

Such a 'high' view of baptism, in which God is more active than man, is saved from a mechanical, or even magical, efficacy by the strong emphasis on faith (note the phrase 'your faith' in v. 12). It is believers' baptism that achieves this effective identification with Christ's 'death to the flesh'.

There are, therefore, two reasons why this passage provides no encouragement for the practice of infant baptism. First, in the absence of the baptised person's faith, the rite degenerates into a ceremony which is practically superstitious or purely symbolic; either way, the biblical balance is lost. Second, Paul is not explicitly referring to *bodily* circumcision at all (though it was probably part of the background to his letter). Throughout the passage he is referring to *heart* 'circumcision', made 'without hands', by Christ and in Christians.

Had Paul been claiming, or even hinting at, a direct continuity between the two physical rites of circumcision and baptism – as successive rites of initiation within the same 'covenant of grace' – it is strange that he never used this line of argument at the Jerusalem Council (Acts 15) or in his letter to the Galatians, in which Jewish circumcision was the main topic, or in any situation where Judaisers were causing trouble among his converts. Nor would this explain why he opposed only the circumcision of Gentile believers; if baptism had 'replaced' circumcision, he ought to have discouraged the practice among Jewish believers also!

The interpretation of baptism given here emphasises the dissimilarity between the two acts. Circumcision was a recognition (made visible by the removal of part of the body) that a person had been born of the flesh into the Abrahamic covenant. Baptism, by 'burying' and 'raising' the whole body, recognises that a person has been born of the Spirit into the 'new' covenant, having died to the flesh. One requires a flesh connection with Abraham, the other a faith identification with Jesus. One was for males only; in the other there is 'neither male nor female' (Gal 3:27–28).

That baptism and circumcision were not regarded by Paul as equivalent acts of initiation has been conclusively demonstrated, on the basis of Colossians 2:9–12, by Bishop Lesslie Newbigin. In his *The Household of God* (London: SCM Press, 1953), pp. 36ff., he rightly observes that 'in all the terrible heat of the conflict about whether or not circumcision should be demanded of the Gentile converts, this equation [Circumcision in the Old Testament = Baptism in the New] is never hinted at either in Acts, or in Galatians or Romans'. On the contrary, he concludes that 'the tremendous struggle about circumcision was not a struggle about two alternative rites of initiation into the people of God. It was a struggle about the fundamental principles upon which that people is constituted.'

26   THE REGENERATING BATH
(Titus 3:5)

. . . he saved us, not because of righteous things we had done, but because of his mercy. He saved us through the washing of rebirth and renewal by the Holy Spirit – whom he poured out on us generously . . . (Tit 3:5–6)

The purpose of this epistle is very practical: to show that sound doctrine covers behaviour as well as belief. The salvation that God has worked in our hearts needs to be worked out in our lives (cf. Phil 2:12–13).

One stimulus to holiness is the constant remembrance of how much has already changed. It is good to recall both what we used to be like and the means God used to make us different. The immediate context of the verse under consideration is a vivid reminder of what kind of life the readers had previously lived, who had rescued them from this mess and how he had done it.

'Saved' is in the aorist tense and refers to a past event rather than a continuous process. This event set them free from their past sins (foolishness, disobedience, sensual bondage, malice, envy, hate, etc.). 'Doing good' could never have broken these habitual chains; they could no more have done it 'of themselves' than fly by pulling on their sandals! It took the kindness, love and mercy of 'God our Saviour' (v. 4 – almost certainly a reference to the Father, but the word 'appeared' includes the incarnation of the Son; it is unlikely that Paul is making a Christological statement).

But exactly how did this 'liberation' take place in human lives? What *means* were used to effect this deliverance? What actually happened to break these sordid patterns of behaviour? The answer is simple: water-baptism and Spirit-baptism (although the word 'baptism' is not used, we shall see that it is clearly implied). We have been 'saved' through a double event:

1. We have been saved 'through the bath of regeneration' (the NIV has 'washing of rebirth'). The word 'regeneration' (Greek: *palingenesia*) is made up of the word for birth or 'beginning' (Greek: *genesia*, from which the first book in the Bible is named) and the prefix 'again' (Greek: *palin*). So the first part of this 'saving' event consists of 'having a bath' that enables a person to 'begin again' or to be 'born again'.

Some would deny that this phrase has anything to do with water-baptism. The 'bath' would then refer to an exclusively 'spiritual' cleansing that takes place inside a person at the moment when they are 'born again' (see chapter 6 for a refutation of the view that the new birth is instantaneous). This approach is usually taken for a doctrinal reason; namely, a reluctance to attribute sacramental efficacy to the rite of baptism. The following reasons make this view unlikely.

The verbal form of the noun 'bath' (literally, the 'washing') is elsewhere used of the physical act of baptism (see Acts 22:16; Eph 5:26; Heb 10:22 – cf. also 1 Cor 6:11; 1 Pet 3:21). The noun itself can refer to a receptacle that holds water (as in 'The bathroom has a cast iron bath') or to the act of being in the water (as in 'I'm just going to have a bath'). The latter meaning makes most sense here. Most Bible commentators take this as a reference to water-baptism.

In what sense, then, can this be a 'bath of regeneration'? How can the physical act of man be a saving act of God? What is the link between the two? This matter has already been dealt with (in chapter 4), but a few comments may be added here.

The primary effect of baptism is retrospective. It both represents and accomplishes the final break with the old life of sin. It is a funeral – the burial of a life that is now dead. What crossing the Red Sea was to the Jew in relation to Pharaoh, baptism is to the Christian in relation to Satan. It marks the end of the old life of enslavement and the beginning of the new life of freedom. It is a burial that leads to resurrection, a death that leads to life.

However, new life needs more than a break with the past. It

is not just a new start in life that we need; it is a new life to start with! The negative break with the past needs to be supplemented with a positive boost into the future! That is the second aspect involved in being 'saved'.

2. We have been saved through 'renewal by the Holy Spirit, whom he poured out on us generously (or copiously)'. This does not refer to a continuous process, for the verb is again in the aorist tense, pointing to that experience of the Holy Spirit elsewhere described as 'receiving', being 'filled with' or 'baptised in'. Actually, this exact phrase 'poured out' is used of the day of Pentecost (Acts 2:17, 33) and of Cornelius' household (Acts 10:45). This is yet another confirmation that a 'pentecostal' reception of the Holy Spirit was the normal experience of *all* New Testament believers. The adverb 'generously' indicates a soaking rather than a sprinkling, and is not far off the word 'baptised' or 'drenched'.

Nor is the word 'renewal' (Greek: *anakainosis*, from *ana* = again and *kainos* = new) all that different from 'regeneration'. Both speak of being restored to an original condition (cf. Matt 19:28).

Both are the work of God. However, one stresses the beginning and the other the continuing of the process of restoration. Yet even the continued 'renewal' (cf. Rom 12:2; 2 Cor 4:16; Col 3:10) had a definite starting-point in the 'pouring-out' of the Spirit. Baptism in water ends the old life and begins the new; baptism in Spirit ensures that it continues until the original image of God has been perfectly restored.

Most commentators have noted the remarkable parallel between Titus 3:5 and John 3:5. Both deal with the subject of being 'born again' (though, surprisingly, it is comparatively rare in New Testament writings) and both mention 'water' and 'Spirit'. It is hard not to relate Paul's words to those of Jesus. The main difference between them would be in the preposition – where Jesus said a man was born again 'out of' (Greek: *ek*) the two baptisms, Paul said a man is saved 'through' (Greek: *dia*) them. Neither uses 'by', for they are both the means not the cause. A person can only be regenerated and saved by 'God our Saviour'.

27 THE ELEMENTARY TEACHING
(Hebrews 6:1–6)

¹Therefore let us leave the elementary teachings about Christ and go on to maturity, not laying again the foundation of repentance from acts that lead to death, and of faith in God, ²instruction about baptisms, the laying on of hands, the resurrection of the dead, and eternal judgment. ³And God permitting, we will do so.

⁴It is impossible for those who have once been enlightened, who have tasted the heavenly gift, who have shared in the Holy Spirit, ⁵who have tasted the goodness of the word of God and the powers of the coming age, ⁶if they fall away, to be brought back to repentance, because to their loss they are crucifying the Son of God all over again and subjecting him to public disgrace. (Heb 6:1–6)

It is probably impossible to find out who wrote this 'short letter' (13:22), but it is not too difficult to work out why it was written. Reading between the lines, these Jewish believers (probably in Rome – 13:24) were in grave spiritual danger as a result of the first wave of public hostility towards the 'Christians'. They had already suffered attacks on their property and persons, been thrown into prison and suffered public humiliation (10:33–34). They had not yet had to die for their faith (12:4); but the pressure was steadily increasing, and martyrdom was on the horizon.

The key to understanding the epistle is to realise that persecution was directed against Christians, but not Jews. Judaism was a 'registered' religion (a *religio licita*), but 'the Way', as Christianity was first called, was an outlawed 'underground' religion (a *religio illicita*). The same distinction exists under totalitarian regimes today.

So these 'Hebrews' had had no more than the usual social difficulties while they had been practising Jews. As soon as they came to faith in Jesus as their Messiah, however, real trouble began. At first, they had stood firm in the confidence of their fresh 'enlightenment' (10:32). As the novelty wore off and the troubles increased, they had obviously begun to wonder if it was all worth it (they were not the last to face this kind of doubt!).

The final clue to their predicament is that they had a ready-made escape route. By leaving the church and returning to the synagogue, they could avoid further persecution. However, to be accepted back by their Jewish compatriots, they would have to deny their faith in Jesus as the Son of God. No doubt they could rationalise the position by telling themselves they would still be worshipping the same God and could continue to be 'secret' believers in Jesus!

With this background in mind, every single sentence in the epistle to the Hebrews fits perfectly into one overall purpose. The author uses every conceivable argument to persuade these Jewish believers not to take this backward step, but to press on in 'the Way'. He does not pretend that it is likely to get any easier, but he encourages them to imitate the perseverance exhibited by their own Jewish heroes, as well as by their new Christian leaders and, above all, Jesus himself.

The main thrust of the letter is a careful exposition of the superiority ('better' is a key word) of Christianity to Judaism, even though the one derived from the other. To go back would be like exchanging the latest Rolls-Royce for a model 'T' Ford! However, the choice has more serious implications than that: in avoiding physical and temporal suffering, they are liable to bring upon themselves spiritual and eternal consequences.

So the general exposition is constantly interrupted by particular exhortations, directly addressed to the readers in personal and forceful language (2:1–4; 3:1, 6, 12–14, 19; 4:14; 5:11–6:12; 10:19–39; 12:1–13:25). They get longer and stronger towards the end of the epistle, going from sympathetic encouragement through stern rebuke to severe warning.

The verses we are studying (6:1–6) constitute the central portion of an extended exhortation (5:11–6:12). The section begins by expressing the author's frustration; he is aware that the complex comparisons of his exposition are probably a bit beyond his readers! It has been meat for the mature, rather than milk for babies. But by this time they should not only be able to receive such teaching; they should also be able to give it to others.

He appeals to these Jewish believers to 'leave' those 'elementary teachings' they heard when they became 'Christians' and 'go on' (a favourite expression of the writer) 'to maturity', which he defines as moral discernment rather than intellectual grasp. Yet he then proceeds to list those very 'elementary teachings' he wants them to leave behind. In recalling their 'beginnings', he will use their memory as a basis for his most terrible warning.

In doing this, he has given us an invaluable insight into his understanding of Christian *initiation*. This is the only place in the New Testament where the *four* elements are systematically set out. They are seen here as the four cornerstones, as it were, of a properly laid foundation to the Christian life. Yet there are some unusual modes of expression which require comment.

First, 'repentance from acts that lead to death'. The preposition 'from' (Greek: *apo*) is important. Many repent 'about' or 'over' their sinful acts, but not 'from' them! Acts of sin need to be followed by *acts* of repentance – renunciation, reformation, restitution and reconciliation (this was developed in chapter 2 and will be applied in chapter 32).

Second, 'faith in God'. The surprise here is that he directs this faith towards the Father rather than the Son. As Jews, they would already have had 'faith in God'. But this is probably not very significant, since this is very much a 'shorthand' list of reminders, not a handbook of instruction. No doubt at the time of their conversion it was expanded to mean 'faith in all God has accomplished through his Son, Jesus Christ'.

Third, 'instruction about baptisms'. Two features of this phrase have puzzled commentators. The use of a comparatively rare form of the word for 'baptism' (Greek: *baptismos*, used elsewhere only for regular 'washing' – Mark 7:4; Heb 9:10), rather than the usual word for the initiatory rite (Greek: *baptisma*) is one anomaly. Perhaps we need to remember that no word had yet become such a technical title for the sacrament as 'baptism' has become today, so that it has now lost all its Greek meaning of 'immersion'. The words used then were descriptive rather than definitive. Other words for 'washing' were also used of baptism (*apolouo* and *loutron*, for example). So we should not make too much of the vocabulary used here. But more disturbing is the *plural* of the word; what are the 'baptisms' referred to? There are at least five possible explanations (which I list in an ascending order of likelihood):

1. It simply means that there were usually a number of people baptised on each occasion.
2. Baptism in the trinitarian name involved a triple immersion (as in the Greek Orthodox churches today).
3. Baptism is a 'double' washing – of the body and the soul at the same time.
4. Enquirers need to know about both water-baptism and Spirit-baptism, since both are necessary.
5. There was a need for 'Hebrews' to be told the difference between Christian baptism and Levitical ablutions, proselyte baptism and, perhaps, John's baptism; though outwardly similar in mode, they are inwardly different in meaning.

The words 'instruction about' favour the last solution. They needed to be 'taught' about the many different baptisms, even if they were only given one in their Christian initiation (10:22).

Fourth, 'the laying on of hands'. Undoubtedly this was an expression of intensive prayer that the gift of the Holy Spirit might be received by the penitent and baptised believer. Verse 4 speaks about the results of this. The practice is paralleled in the book of Acts (8:17; 9:17; 19:6) and in other epistles (e.g. 2 Tim 1:6–7). What is unexpected is the implication that the laying on of hands was a normal and necessary element of initiation, used in every case to 'communicate' the Holy Spirit to the convert. Perhaps we need to recall that the only two recorded times when the Holy Spirit was given *without* the laying on of hands also contain clear indications why this was not done. On the day of Pentecost itself (Acts 2:2–4) there was no one else who had already 'received' to lay hands on them, so God himself laid his fiery fingers on them. With Cornelius' household (Acts 10:44), God again had to do it himself, since no one else would have done it for those Gentiles. Since these two 'exceptions' can be rationally explained, we are left with the 'rule' that the gift of the Spirit was invariably received through the laying on of hands right from the beginning, contrary to the opinion of some scholars that the letter to the Hebrews reflects a later stage in church history when the rite of 'confirmation' had crystallised. This physical act not only combined intercession with identification; it also included the notion of the transfer of power from one who already possessed it to one needing it (cf. Num 27:18–20 with Deut 34:9). The same thought of 'transfer' lies behind laying hands on the sick.

There follows an unexpected addition to these four basic Christian truths, which are all concerned with the present. The author adds two more foundational principles about the future: 'the resurrection of the dead' and 'eternal judgment'. These form a strange conclusion. Why is the resurrection of the dead, as distinct from that of Jesus, so important to Christian beginnings? And wasn't 'judgement to come' part of the original gospel preaching they had heard before embarking on their elementary teaching?

The problems arise only if we take these six subjects as an exhaustive curriculum for a 'beginners' class in Christianity (as some Christian teachers have been tempted to do from this very passage). But the writer has just told them he is *not* going to take them through such a course again! However, he is going to remind them of those things they had learned in the past and which will assist his argument and appeal now. In other words, this is a 'selective' list of particular items from their initial instruction which they most need to recall in their present situation. The six selected topics conveniently divide under two heads. On the one hand, they need to remember the four decisive steps taken in repenting, believing, being baptised and receiving the Spirit – all of them quite voluntary and, as we shall see, irrevocable. On the other hand, they need to remember two facts about the future – that they will one day rise from the dead and then be judged on how they have followed through from this beginning (as in 2 Cor 5:10). Their present situation must be set against their past initiation and their future examination in order to be seen in its proper light. Suffering feels rather different when viewed from an eschatological and not an existential perspective (cf. Rom 8:18).

This objective instruction had become their subjective experience; they knew the reality of it in their lives. They were enlightened, they tasted the heavenly gift, shared in the Holy Spirit and tasted the goodness of God's word and the powers of the coming age. To say that they could experience all this without having become Christians at all is to make the language here meaningless. This is usually done in the interests of a 'Calvinist' theology, which has a vested interest in their not having been 'born again', in view of the warning that follows. But we need to ask ourselves 'Why should the author want to move them on to "maturity" if they haven't even become infants yet?'

One might have expected a tender appeal to follow such a reminder – perhaps on the lines of 'Having had such a taste of the good life, are you ready to throw it all away?' Instead comes the toughest warning of the whole letter: 'If you throw all this away, you can never have it back again!' It is a tragedy that this passage is usually discussed in the context of the 'once saved, always saved' issue, which effectively diverts attention from the real issue. The writer is not discussing whether it is possible for a Christian to forfeit his salvation; he takes it for granted that this can happen! He is going much further than this by saying that if and when it does happen, it is then impossible for such an 'ex-Christian' to recover his salvation, since it is impossible to repent! Some sins cannot be repented of, including the public repudiation of Christ in times of persecution. To do this is to share the guilt of those who humiliated and crucified Jesus because they denied his claim to be the Son of God. That Peter offered forgiveness to those who were accomplices in the original deed does not alter this principle; they were acting in 'ignorance' (Acts 3:17), which a Christian cannot do. Other scriptures confirm the seriousness of such a denial (Matt 10:33 and 2 Tim 2:12, for example).

Having given such a severe warning of a very real danger – for to say that it is purely hypothetical robs the warning of its effectiveness – the writer assures his readers of his optimism rather than pessimism in their case (6:9–12). Though this terrible fate *could* be theirs, he is not expecting that it would be. He has real faith in the Holy Spirit's strengthening. God himself is on their side and wants them to succeed in the struggle. But a victorious outcome is not inevitable. It is vital for them to remain diligent, patient and faithful 'to the very end', if the hope of inheriting all that is promised for the future is to be made sure.

They had made a good start, but that will not win the race. A good finish is just as important. After listing many Old Testament heroes of faith, the writer says of them: 'All these people were still living by faith when they died' (11:13). He exhorts his readers to run with the same perseverance, looking to Jesus, the pioneer and perfecter of our faith, the one who himself enables us to start and to finish. Christianity is the way to die as well as the way to live!

28   THE WORKING FAITH
(James 2:14–26)

[14]What good is it, my brothers, if a man claims to have faith but has no deeds? Can such faith save him? [15]Suppose a brother or sister is without clothes and daily food. [16]If one of you says to him, 'Go, I wish you well; keep warm and well fed,' but does nothing about his physical needs, what good is it? [17]In the same way, faith by itself, if it is not accompanied by action, is dead.

[18]But someone will say, 'You have faith; I have deeds.'

Show me your faith without deeds, and I will show you my faith by what I do. [19]You believe that there is one God. Good! Even the demons believe that – and shudder.

[20]You foolish man, do you want evidence that faith without deeds is useless? [21]Was not our ancestor Abraham considered righteous for what he did when he offered his son Isaac on the altar? [22]You see that his faith and his actions were working together, and his faith was made complete by what he did. [23]And the scripture was fulfilled that says, 'Abraham believed God, and it was credited to him as righteousness,' and he was called God's friend. [24]You see that a person is justified by what he does and not by faith alone.

[25]In the same way, was not even Rahab the prostitute considered righteous for what she did when she gave lodging to the spies and sent them off in a different direction? [26]As the body without the spirit is dead, so faith without deeds is dead. (Jas 2:14–26)

Most evangelists ignore this passage when preaching the gospel. While acknowledging that it may contain a needed correction for complacent believers, they would not see its relevance for an enquiring unbeliever. In short, it has no bearing on Christian initiation. Yet James is clearly referring to the faith that can 'save' (v. 14), which is surely at the heart of the gospel.

Some go much further and question whether this short letter should be regarded as part of the canon of scripture at all! Luther's well-known dismissal of this 'right strawy epistle' is not an isolated attitude. A low opinion of its theological value can seemingly be held alongside a belief in its divine inspiration!

The 'problem' of James is largely felt by those who take Paul's understanding of salvation as a complete system of doctrine, by which other apostolic contributions to the New Testament are to be judged. This arbitrary bias does less than justice to other vital insights.

From this prejudiced standpoint, James can be, and often is, charged with being in direct conflict with Paul. Thus, his statement that 'a person is justified by what he does and not by faith alone' (v. 24) is seen as a direct contradiction of such Pauline statements as 'a man is not justified by observing the law [lit. 'the works of the law'], but by faith' (Gal 2:16). Little wonder that in the Reformation struggle for the principle of justification by faith alone, on the authority of scripture alone, the epistle of James was a somewhat embarrassing document!

Clearly this tension must be resolved if we are to benefit from James' vital contribution to our understanding of 'saving faith'. The Holy Spirit knew what he was doing when he guided the early church to recognise this letter of our Lord's brother as inspired scripture carrying apostolic authority for the whole church throughout the ages.

The apparent discrepancy over this fundamental article of faith can be resolved by a careful analysis of James' argument.

The key lies in his use of the word 'works'. James does not mean 'works of the law'. Paul, however, constantly uses it in this sense of keeping the commandments in order to 'earn', or at least 'deserve', the salvation of God. The thought that man can do anything to contribute to his salvation is utterly alien to the gospel of divine grace. Therefore Paul even repented of his good deeds as so much 'dung' (Phil 3:8–9; the word is a crude one referring to human excreta). There is no room in the same heart for self-righteousness and the righteousness of God.

James would wholeheartedly agree with all this; but he would emphatically denounce the deduction that man is no more than a passive recipient in salvation. James is emphasising that faith is an active appropriation of the divine righteousness. And Paul would wholeheartedly agree with James in that!

Neither Paul nor James would teach that 'faith' consists of attaining moral standards in one's own strength. The basic need of human nature is precisely its inability to keep the commandments of God (even the zealous Saul of Tarsus only managed nine out of ten – Phil 3:6 needs to be balanced with Rom 7:8). To clinch this total distinction between 'faith' and 'works of the law', it only needs to be pointed out that the two examples or 'models' of faith cited by James were both breaking the law of God! A prostitute is commended for bearing false witness and a father for attempting to kill his own son!

Nor is James referring to 'works of love'. This point is more subtle. At first sight, it looks as if this is what he does mean (vv. 15–17), and this interpretation has been welcomed as a possible basis for reconciling his teaching with Paul's, who also spoke about a faith that 'expresses itself through love' (Gal 5:6). But the implication that faith needs to be supplemented by acts of welfare towards the needy is really no different from saying that it needs to be supplemented by acts of morality. Both dilute the doctrine of grace.

We need to realise that the little vignette of neighbourliness in verses 15–17 is not meant to be a particular example of the 'works of faith', but a general illustration of the principle that profession without action is useless in any sphere of life – in this case, confrontation with a brother in need. Sympathy for suffering, like faith in God, doesn't show in what we say, but in what we do. Notice that James shared the same ability as his brother Jesus to drive home a profound truth through an everyday situation.

So James is not saying 'Faith without works of love is useless,' though liberal theology would welcome that, but 'Faith without works is as useless as love without works.' In other words, for James the word 'works' means simply '*actions*' – rather than all that is conjured up in the evangelical mind soaked in Pauline theology! Many modern translations have recognised this need to use another equivalent without such offensive connotations – some use 'deeds', but the general and more helpful trend is towards 'actions'.

What, then, does James mean by the 'actions of faith'? Since giving a hungry brother food is not what he means, he turns to two actual situations in the Old Testament (in contrast to the hypothetical case supposed in v. 15). He wants to show 'faith at work' or 'faith in action'. As if to underline that he is not talking about morality, he chooses a bad woman and a good man. As if to underline that he is not talking about welfare, he chooses one deed which saved lives and another which nearly destroyed a life. What, then, did the actions of Rahab and Abraham have in common? They both acted in a way that jeopardised their present security – because both were trusting God to safeguard their future. Taking such risks is of the essence of faith. It is having enough confidence to act on one's convictions, particularly where these are rooted in God's revelation of himself.

This kind of faith is in stark contrast to much that often passes for it. Today people are often told they have become Christians and are eligible for baptism and church membership on no other ground than a 'profession of faith'; what they *say* in words. James would have none of it: only possession of faith would satisfy him. The evidence for this would be visible rather than audible, discerned by observing what a person did rather than listening to what they said (v. 18).

With powerful satire, James points out that a credal recitation of impeccable theology is no better than demons can manage, good monotheists all of them! And their 'confession' at least contains some emotional content – they tremble in fear, but they have no faith. James may be hinting that it is some time since his readers showed even that much response to the awesome fact of God's monopoly of power.

Reading the earlier part of James 2, one is left with the impression that apostolic Christianity was already degenerating into respectable 'churchianity' by the time this letter was written. In such a setting faith tends to fossilise into verbal repetition; worshippers can go for weeks, months and even years without ever exercising the faith they profess so regularly in church. It may be doctrinally accurate but it is no longer dynamically adventurous. The pattern is all too common.

James wants to make sure that we realise 'faith' is not the articulation of sound theology. It is not so much *accepting* the truth of God's word as *acting* on it. Profession without practice is as useless to ourselves as sympathy without succour is useless for others. Such a faith cannot 'save'. It is as 'dead' as a cadaver in a mortuary!

[18]For Christ died for sins once for all, the righteous for the unrighteous, to bring you to God. He was put to death in the body but made alive by the Spirit, [19]through whom also he went and preached to the spirits in prison [20]who disobeyed long ago when God waited patiently in the days of Noah while the ark was being built. In it only a few people, eight in all, were saved through water, [21]and this water symbolises baptism that now saves you also – not the removal of dirt from the body but the pledge of a good conscience towards God. It saves you by the resurrection of Christ, [22]who has gone into heaven and is at God's right hand – with angels, authorities and powers in submission to him. (1 Pet 3:18–22)

Some scholars have suggested that this whole epistle is a 'baptismal tract', a kind of 'catechism for candidates'. It is certainly an excellent Bible study for beginners, covering many things that a new Christian needs to know and do.

But there is much here for mature believers also. In fact, Peter seems to have been one of those rare Christians who are equally good at evangelising and pastoring. After all, Jesus called him to be a fisherman and a shepherd (Mark 1:17; John 21:15–17)!

Both the enquirer and the believer need to be told that the Christian life will involve suffering. Paul was as honest as Peter in making this clear (cf. Acts 14:22); both were following the example of Jesus (John 16:33).

The scarlet thread of suffering runs right through this letter. Probably written against the background of the first wave of persecution under Nero, one of the main concerns of the author is to help his flock scattered over Asia Minor (now

Turkey) to maintain their moral integrity in the face of opposition – not just from the general public but now also from the state authorities (he anticipates this will spread from Rome throughout the Empire – see 1:1; 4:12; 5:13).

The tensions of living under a hostile regime repeatedly surface in the letter. The follower of Jesus must live a blameless life, yet will find himself accused of crime. He must be a loyal citizen, yet will be treated as a traitor. He must be open and honest, yet will be the subject of slander.

To suffer for doing wrong is acceptable to human nature (cf. Luke 23:41) but to be the innocent victim of injustice is a severe test. Such was to be the general experience of Christians for the next two centuries. Peter himself would be one of many martyrs.

Under such pressure it is easy to imagine that 'righteousness only brings more trouble' (Ps 73:1–22 is a classic example), which tempts one to revert to the 'ways of the world'. The antidote is to keep an eternal perspective (Ps 73:23–28 achieves this). What happens to the body is seen as relatively unimportant; maintaining the life of the spirit is the vital objective.

This, then, is the background to our passage, which contains an unusual association of ideas, together with one unique revelation. The style is 'rambling' rather than logical; the thread holding it together is an overall concern rather than a linear argument. It is a painting rather than a photograph.

After making the valid observation that it is morally preferable to suffer for doing what is right than what is wrong, it is natural for Peter to illustrate this by speaking of Christ's own demeanour on the cross, in the face of that greatest injustice of all. He has already made this point effectively (in 2:21–23), but this time his train of thought takes him in an unexpected direction. The point he makes is that the destruction of Jesus' body was the liberation of his spirit (small 's'; Peter refers to his human spirit, not the divine Spirit). Far from curtailing Jesus' ministry, his death extended it!

From one point of view (Greek: *men*), Jesus was killed in flesh; but from another point of view (Greek: *de*), Jesus was enlivened in spirit. This is not a reference to his resurrection three days later, which was the enlivening of his body again. It is a comment on his state during the three days between his physical dissolution and his resuscitation. That he was fully conscious and active during this period is nowhere else stated in the New Testament, though Jesus' words to the dying thief clearly imply it (Luke 23:43).

This striking insight is immediately followed by an extraordinary piece of information. During this time, Jesus visited the abode of the departed (in Hebrew: *sheol*; in Greek: *hades*). (This is the true meaning of the statement 'he descended into hell' in the Apostles' Creed – it was *not* the place of eternal punishment, which is entered only after the final judgement.) Here Jesus preached to 'the spirits in prison', a phrase indicating those being kept in 'custody' until their trial on the judgement day (cf. 2 Pet 2:4 and Jude 6). The particular group Jesus addressed is identified as the generation drowned in the flood at the time of Noah. All this happened between Christ's death and resurrection.

Peter is the only New Testament writer to tell us about this, (though one gospel mentions another effect of Jesus' death on the world of the departed, namely that many former 'saints' were released from Sheol and returned to the streets of Jerusalem and were recognised as they walked about – Matt 27:52–53). But where did Peter get this information? Surely from his unrecorded meeting with the risen Jesus on the first Easter Sunday (1 Cor 15:5).

To ask why Jesus did such a thing is to enter the realm of speculation, since scripture offers no rationale. Was it to announce that the most severe act of God's judgement had now been matched by a decisive intervention of his mercy? But to proclaim this without offering an opportunity of salvation to the hearers would be a tantalising torment utterly alien to the Lord. We can only assume that it was with a view to their repentance. But why should this particular group have the unique privilege of a 'second chance' after death? Presumably because they were the only generation to experience divine judgement of such a full and final kind before the day on which the rest of the human race stands trial – and could therefore plead unjust treatment, God having promised never to do the same to any other generation. God will give no one a chance to accuse him of being unfair (cf. Gen 18:25).

Unwillingness to take Peter's narrative at its face value is usually due to theological reservations. The incident is seen as contradicting the general biblical teaching that the moment of death fixes our eternal destiny (Luke 16:26). The door would be opened for those who want to believe they will have a 'second chance' to accept salvation beyond the grave, on the naive assumption that those who have tasted hell will really want to go to heaven. Fears that this will remove the moral and spiritual motivation to repent in this world are valid, but they can be dispelled by pointing out that Peter's words can only be applied to Noah's generation and to no others. This sole exception therefore does not compromise the general rule.

Mention of the flood reminds Peter what an appropriate example may be found in Noah's family of those who maintained their moral integrity in a grossly immoral society – and survived the judgement that came upon it. The ark carried them 'safely' through the flood; they were 'saved through water' (Greek preposition: *dia* = by means of). The exact significance of the phrase is debatable. It means more than being kept from drowning in the water. Some think it means that the same water which drowned others actually 'upheld' the ark and was quite literally the means of their survival. The most likely suggestion is that the flood actually 'transferred' them from a dirty world of sin into a clean world of righteousness.

This cleansing and liberating effect of the flood leads Peter naturally to thoughts about Christian baptism. The two events, one universal and the other individual, can be thought of as 'type' and 'anti-type', the one symbolising and 'prefiguring' the other. As the water of the flood 'saved' Noah and his family (all adults, no babies!), so the water of baptism 'saves' the believer. This claim for baptism is made twice (in v. 21) and is perhaps the strongest *instrumental* language used of baptism in the New Testament (though Mark 16:16 and Tit 3:5 also use the word 'saved' of baptism – see chapters 8 and

26). Those who have a phobia about 'baptismal regeneration' have real difficulty with this statement and tend to ignore it (as they do the word 'water' in John 3:5). Peter, maybe anticipating this later misunderstanding, hastens to explain the meaning of 'saves'. Baptism has a cleansing effect in the moral rather than the material realm, removing defilement from the conscience rather than dirt from the body.

At this crucial point, Peter's Greek is unfortunately ambiguous! The phrase translates literally: 'an acceptance (or answer) into God of a good conscience'. But who is doing the accepting/answering: man or God? Both possibilities have been incorporated into modern translations:

1. 'the pledge of a good conscience to God';
2. 'the plea for a good conscience from God'.

These renderings lead to rather different views about baptism, though the overall thrust of the passage is not deeply affected.

The 'pledge' version is simply a promise to live a good life in the future, an acceptance that life must now be lived in obedience to the Lord (a *sacramentum* was originally the oath of allegiance taken by a newly recruited soldier, promising obedience to Caesar). But why should such a resolution have to be made in water, and what possible parallel could there be between this and Noah's flood? Above all, this interpretation empties the word 'saves' of any redemptive content.

The 'plea' version fits the immediate context better. Baptism is not for an outward cleansing of the body, but for an inward cleansing of the conscience. As surely as all the evil of the ancient world was washed away in the flood, so the penitent believer will be 'flushed' of all his guilt and shame. As Noah emerged from the ark into a sin-free world, so the believer can enjoy the liberty of a 'laundered' life! Such an efficacious view of baptism is entirely consistent with other apostolic writings (Acts 22:16; Eph 5:26; Heb 10:22; note that the latter also links 'conscience' and 'water').

Before settling on either of these alternatives, a third possibility needs to be mentioned – somewhere between the two and rather more subtle. Noah had lived righteously before the flood (Gen 6:19), and when he entered the ark he was trusting the Lord to vindicate his good conscience by bringing him safely through the waters. In a similar manner, it may be supposed, the penitent believer is asking God to confirm that he is 'righteous' (in this case, justified) in his sight by not harming him in the waters of baptism! This is not such a wild suggestion as it appears, when we consider that the Lord's Supper taken unworthily can cause sickness and even death (1 Cor 11:30). However, this would limit the divine activity in the sacrament to the negative function of judgement, whereas the language implies the positive purpose of salvation. And there is also the practical objection that though such a fate must have been deserved on many occasions, God has not used the rite for this purpose to my knowledge!

Whichever translation/interpretation is preferred – and I favour the second – one thing is clear in all of them: baptism is for those with a conscience, whether a good one seeking vindication or a bad one seeking purification. It is therefore a conscious and responsible act, undertaken voluntarily. To apply it to babies without any awareness of a good or a bad conscience would therefore seem totally inappropriate. Michael Green, when discussing this passage in his *I Believe in the Holy Spirit* (London: Hodder & Stoughton, 1975), p. 128, makes the following comment:

> The word translated 'pledge' is variously interpreted . . . But in any case it speaks of the genuine commitment on man's side. And the allusion to the ascension of Christ to God's right hand hints at the power released in the life of the baptised when the candidate does not merely go through a ceremonial washing, but turns in obedient repentance and faith to Jesus Christ. That sort of baptism saves us.

Baptism is therefore a combination of human and divine activity. The person being baptised makes a plea to God as he is immersed (Acts 22:16 describes this as 'calling on his name'). God uses the occasion to effect an inner cleansing, which sets the person free from past guilt (Acts 22:16 describes this as getting your sins washed away). It is the meeting-point between active grace and active faith. Both are essential to 'efficacious' baptism.

Finally, the 'deliverance' which baptism effects is only possible because Christ himself has risen from the dead and ascended into heaven, giving him total control of all supernatural powers, both good and evil. As Noah's flood cleansed the world of the perverted sex and violence introduced by demonic corruption (Gen 6:1–11), so the water of baptism sets us free from the 'dominion' of those same forces (Rom 6:3–14). Baptism is sacramental precisely because it is supernatural.

30   THE SHUT DOOR (Revelation 3:20)

> Here I am! I stand at the door and knock. If anyone hears my
> voice and opens the door, I will come in and eat with him,
> and he with me. (Rev 3:20)

'A text out of context becomes a pretext.' If ever that cliché
was true, it is with the use of this verse in evangelistic
preaching and counselling!

Holman Hunt's picture 'The Light of the World' is both an
effect and a cause of the widespread misinterpretation and
consequent misapplication of this scripture. Apart altogether
from the effeminate representation of Christ (girls were used
for the figure and head), with its ecclesiastical robes, the main
error is the door on which Jesus is knocking, which should
have been a church door (it was actually a barn door in an
orchard in Ewell, Surrey).

The statement in Revelation 3:20 is not addressed to unbelievers, but to believers; and it is not addressed to individual
believers, but to a community of believers in the city of
Laodicea.

Jesus is knocking on the door of one of his own churches! He
is outside the fellowship, though the people imagine he is still
inside. It is a sobering thought that a church can continue its
life without Christ, even considering itself prosperous and
successful, while remaining blind to its spiritual poverty.

To be half-hearted is more offensive to the head of the
church than to be indifferent! Says the Spirit of Jesus to them:
'Lukewarm churches make me sick,' a reference they would
understand only too well as the hot springs outside Laodicea
had become a lukewarm stream by the time the water reached
the city, and drinking it at that temperature, full of salts as it
was, acted as a powerful emetic.

The church's real problem was self-delusion. Someone who was as utterly 'real' as Jesus, the 'Amen' (= truly, verily, honestly), the 'faithful and true witness' ('true' and 'real' are the same word in Greek), cannot be 'at home' in the midst of such unreality and self-deception. To be cold towards the truth is a genuine rejection and to be hot about it is genuine acceptance; but to be tepid about truth is deeply offensive. Artificiality in religion is hypocrisy, and nothing angered Jesus more.

The good news is that it only takes one member to get up and open the church door to get Christ back inside the church! To 'hear his voice' means to accept Jesus' diagnosis of the church's real condition. To 'open the door' means to admit being part of the sickness and to seek his healing. The church as a whole cannot be put right unless and until individual members are willing to be restored to a real relationship with Jesus. Any person in the church who is willing to do this will rediscover the joy of renewed fellowship with the Lord, such as is enjoyed by friends around a supper table. Commentators may not be entirely wrong in sensing here a reference to the Communion table, or at least to the early practice of the Love-feast or Agape-meal. It means that at least one member would again experience the real presence of Jesus at such gatherings, even though, for the rest, it would still be a formal ceremony, however richly adorned!

This whole message is so relevant and is often desperately needed in many churches – in the successful ones even more than in the struggling; and in the warm ones even more than in the cold ones! But it has nothing to do with conversion or becoming a Christian.

Its use in evangelism inevitably over-simplifies initiation. It becomes simply a matter of asking Jesus to come into your life or receiving Jesus into your heart or opening the door to let him in. Such euphemisms are alien to the New Testament. The picture of Jesus seeking entrance is to be found nowhere else. The reality is quite the opposite! It is the sinner who is on the outside knocking, seeking to enter the kingdom (Luke 11:9). The question is not 'Shall I let *him* in?' but 'Will he let *me* in?' (Matt 25:10–12). In fact, Jesus himself is the door of salvation; we can only enter through him (John 10:7–9).

Only occasionally, the New Testament speaks of 'Christ in' us (Col 1:27 is one of the few verses containing this expression). Far more frequently, the New Testament speaks of us being 'in Christ'. 'Conversion' is not so much Christ coming to be in us, as us coming to be 'in Christ'. We are baptised in water into Christ (Acts 19:5; Gal 3:27); we are baptised in Spirit into his body (1 Cor 12:13 – see chapter 23).

As unbelievers, we are already 'in God' (Acts 17:28). As penitent, baptised believers we are 'in Christ'. But there is a real change when we come to consider our relationship with the Holy Spirit. After Pentecost, it is he who is received, not Jesus (see chapter 5), and he who dwells in us. We are 'in Spirit' and the Spirit is 'in us'; but it is the latter aspect that gets most frequent mention (for example, Rom 8:9–11 contains three references to the 'indwelling' Spirit). This may be one reason why prayer is usually addressed to the Father and Son in the heavens, outside us, rather than to the Spirit, in the heart, 'inside' us. Psychologically, it is easier to pray aloud (as Jesus expected us to do, even when alone – Luke 11:2; cf. Matt 6:6–13) to someone we can imagine 'outside' us; to talk to someone inside us would seem strange, and more akin to oriental meditation techniques. The biblical posture of prayer seems to have involved the 'lifting up' of voice, hands and eyes (cf. John 17:1; Acts 7:55–59; 1 Tim 2:8, etc.).

It would be better, in view of the confusion it causes, to stop using this text altogether in the context of initiation. It may be objected that God has 'blessed' its mistaken use for the salvation of many. But God's mercy is entirely at the disposal of his own choice (Matt 20:15; Rom 9:15); and if he waited till our exposition was perfect before he saved anyone, who would ever be saved? His freedom, however, is not ours. We are under a solemn obligation to study his word so carefully that we are workmen who are not embarrassed by shoddy or slothful craftsmanship but who 'correctly handle the word of truth' (2 Tim 2:15). Impressive eisegesis is no substitute for accurate exegesis! To put that in less technical terms: once we know what is really in a text, we can no longer preach what we thought it meant, however much God blessed our earlier naivety and ignorance. The preacher of the gospel must share our Lord's own passion for truth: 'if it were not so, I would have told you' (John 14:2).

The danger of using this verse to 'lead someone to Christ' is that vital elements of initiation will be ignored. It does not mention repentance from sin, baptism in water or reception of the Spirit. It would be much more appropriate to quote a text that specifically deals with what an enquirer needs to do (like Acts 2:38, for example). It could unfortunately be the case that the 'simplicity' of Revelation 3:20 is actually preferred by some people, because it saves the counsellor a lot of time and trouble working through the other steps involved. In fact, in united crusades which depend on the support of a wide variety of churches, it may be used to avoid such 'controversial' topics as baptism in water or Spirit! However, this evasion of the full New Testament challenge does more harm than good – in the short term to the experience of the 'convert', and in the long term to the quality of the church. This whole matter is taken up in the next chapter.

I fully realise this chapter may rob some preachers of their favourite evangelistic sermon! Let them draw comfort from the fact that apostolic evangelism was quite effective without the appeal of this verse. It wasn't even written until most of the Twelve were dead! The response to our preaching will be of greater quantity and better quality if we are determined to continue steadfastly in the apostles' doctrine of initiation and appeal for a whole response to the gospel. And if we expound this verse in its true context, we might find ourselves with an even more powerful sermon than we had before – this time a prophetic message for the church rather than an evangelistic message for the world.

Part Three

TODAY'S TYPICAL DECISION – The pastoral dimension

From a treatment of the passages containing 'yesterday's normal' pattern of initiation, we turn to 'today's average'. By 'normal' I mean what should happen; by 'average' I mean what does happen. In the New Testament period these two were one and the same thing – what should happen did happen! Taking apostolic evangelism as our standard, we can now state the converse truth – what did happen then should happen now. But sadly so often it doesn't.

We saw in the first chapter that different streams of Christian thought have emphasised different aspects of initiation: liberals stress repentance, evangelicals stress faith, sacramentals stress baptism and pentecostals stress the Spirit. An over-emphasis on one element can down-grade and even distort the others. With the differences of emphasis have come disagreements over the significance of each part, especially when it is seen as isolation from the rest, and this is particularly true of water-baptism and Spirit-baptism.

The tragic effects of the resulting confusion surface when the different streams attempt united evangelism. The 'lowest common denominator' factor takes over. The full gospel in the New Testament and, in particular, the full response to that gospel, suffers reduction by being limited to those elements widely agreed by participating churches. Both are defined in minimal and general terms. Most evangelists are willing to accept this compromise for the sake of a broader sponsorship and a bigger opportunity. The old Christians will then give their support to the objective of making new ones!

However, it is these new Christians who are made to suffer. They are often 'badly delivered' and are either stunted in growth or (in some cases) do not survive at all. In recent years the crucial importance of adequate follow-up has been increasingly recognised and losses are reducing. It is not yet fully realised that the delivery itself is as demanding as the post-natal care. A good start is as vital to life as to a race (1 Cor 9:24; Heb 12:1).

One of the reasons for slipshod spiritual midwifery is the pressure of time. As with natural birth, some deliveries are remarkably quick: the Philippian jailer was a case in point, though it took an earthquake to bring on his labour pains. Others take more time: for Paul himself, it was three days. It is quite unreasonable to hope to complete the process in a few moments at the end of a meeting, especially if relatives and friends are being kept waiting.

To meet this contingency, the whole procedure has been severely condensed into a précis that may represent the 'bare minimum' required from someone about to die (see chapter 9 on the dying thief), but which is quite inappropriate and even grossly inadequate for someone who is expected to live! The result is a fairly standardised 'formula', popularly known as 'the sinner's prayer', widely used in preaching and in print. But it is not mere pressure of time that has formulated this 'prayer'. Behind it lies a theological understanding that it covers all that is necessary to be 'born again'. Sincere repetition is considered sufficient for eternal salvation.

THE 'SINNER'S PRAYER'

It is time to look at such a 'sinner's prayer' in more detail (this example, which is a version used by the Billy Graham Evangelistic Association, is one of the most widely employed and differs little from most others):

Lord Jesus, I know I am a sinner. I believe you died for my sins. Right now, I turn from my sins and open the door of my heart and life. I receive you as my personal Lord and Saviour. Thank you now for saving me. Amen.

We shall evaluate this in the light of the 'four spiritual doors' already outlined in this book. In doing so, we are not so much saying that this prayer is bad, as that it could be much better. It is fully recognised that in its present form it has served as a real step in the right direction for many, though we have no way of knowing how many have used it to no immediate or lasting effect. What is questioned is the suggestion that it is the full journey into life in the kingdom.

Repentance

In the New Testament this is always commanded by and directed to God himself rather than Jesus. Jesus died to bring us to God, to reconcile us to God. It is God we have sinned against (see chapter 2). It is to God that we need to apologise, rather than Jesus.

There is no specific mention of particular sins (plural). This is the main weakness of a 'general confession'. Nothing definite is being faced. It is unlikely that such a vague though comprehensive acknowledgement will be followed by any 'deeds' of repentance – renunciation, restitution, reconciliation, reformation – since all these spring from a realised identification of actual wrongs.

Faith

We have already questioned the whole concept of 'receiving' Jesus (see chapter 5) and of 'opening the door' to him (see chapter 30 on Rev 3:20). Neither of these is a New Testament definition of what it is to 'believe in' Jesus. The sinner should be asking the Saviour to open the door and 'receive' him!

It is also very doubtful whether repeating someone else's words is what the New Testament means by 'calling on the name of the Lord'. As we shall see (in chapter 33), it is much more helpful to encourage enquirers to address the Lord directly in their own words, which are then much more likely to come from the 'heart' than the head.

But the main weakness of this petition is its emphasis on the words of faith rather than the works of faith (see chapters 3 and 28). No 'actions' are involved in this prayer, yet faith without actions 'is dead' and cannot save (Jas 2:14, 26). Nor is there any mention of the need to 'go on' believing.

It is also doubtful if 'Thank you' is appropriate at this stage. If water-baptism is 'for the forgiveness of sins' (Acts 2:38) and Spirit-baptism is that first 'proof' that God has accepted the penitent believer, it would seem that 'Please' would be more fitting at the stage of first asking for salvation.

Baptism

This is the first 'action' of faith, as well as expressing repentance. It is fundamental to becoming a disciple (Matt 28:19), to being saved (Mark 16:16), to being born again (John 3:5), to having sins forgiven (Acts 2:38) and to gaining a clear conscience (1 Pet 3:21).

Yet there is never any mention of baptism in 'the sinner's prayer' or, usually, in the verbal or printed counselling that accompanies it! That is because it is no longer understood as an evangelistic response but as an ecclesiastical rite which can be left in the hands of the denomination a 'convert' chooses to join.

Reception of the Holy Spirit

The Holy Spirit is rarely introduced at this stage. Just as the first person of the Trinity is often omitted from the 'prayer', so the third person is invariably ignored. The petition is virtually 'unitarian', leading to a truncated relationship and experience which falls well short of the full trinitarian evangelism of the apostles ('repent towards God, believe in the Lord Jesus and receive the Holy Spirit').

Even when the Spirit is mentioned, it is assumed that he will be given automatically. There will be no need to say anything else, much less to 'go on asking' (as in Luke 11:13), or to do anything more, like laying on hands (as in Acts 9:17; 19:6; 2 Tim 1:6; Heb 6:2).

And because nothing usually 'happens' when the sinner's prayer is repeated, it is implied that the reception of the Spirit is normally unconscious. Indeed, many 'How to become a Christian' booklets cover themselves by emphasising that converts may not 'feel different'; some even tell them not to 'expect' to! It is hard to imagine a greater contrast to the New Testament approach to counselling. If 'nothing happened' in those days, it was universally assumed that the Spirit had not been received at all (see chapter 16) and when 'something happened', it was impossible to deny that the Spirit had been received (see chapter 18).

So the sinner's prayer is good as far as it goes, but it does not go nearly far enough. It contains omissions and distortions. Said slowly and sincerely, it takes less than half a minute! More carefully phrased, it might serve as the beginning of a response to the gospel; but it is dangerously misleading to regard it as a complete response, covering all that is necessary to 'become a Christian'. It should only be used after a person has truly repented in thought, word and deed (see chapter 2) and before leading them on into water-baptism and Spirit-baptism. Nothing in the prayer should suggest that it is all done at that moment. In the example quoted above, it is assumed that the one praying is 'saved' by the end of the prayer, which is not true to scripture (see Mark 16:16; Acts 2:38; 22:16; Tit 3:5 and chapter 36 of this book).

The result of putting the emphasis on profession rather than on possession of faith, and of the over-simplification of initiation, is to open the door to unscriptural language. Instead of saying that a person has 'repented', 'believed', 'been baptised' or 'received the Spirit', a flood of euphemisms has been adopted to act as substitutes for these New Testament terms. Enquirers are exhorted to 'make a commitment', 'hand your life over', 'dedicate yourself', 'make a decision', 'open your heart', 'give yourself', 'let him come in', etc. All are 'blanket' phrases which reduce initiation to one single step, which perhaps explains the motivation behind their invention. But they are quite alien to apostolic evangelism, which is significantly void of all such terminology.

The result of this approach is to leave many 'Christians' inadequately initiated or, more simply, 'badly birthed'. The foundation is badly laid; one or more of the four cornerstones is missing. To change the metaphor, their 'engine' will not be firing on all four cylinders, which may not become apparent until they tackle their first steep hill, which John Bunyan called 'Difficulty'. Of course, these remarks apply just as much to the millions who have had baptism without faith (as babies) as to those who have had faith without baptism. Some might object that the latter case is far 'safer' eternally than the former. But that kind of 'evaluation' or antithesis is utterly foreign to New Testament thought, which never considers such an alternative. For the apostles, faith and baptism were the inside and the outside of the same thing. It was as unthinkable for someone to profess faith without obeying the Lord's very first command to be baptised as it would have been to baptise someone before they had believed. For them 'Whoever believes and is baptised will be saved' (Mark 16:16; we have already noted that a person will be 'condemned' for lack of faith, not lack of baptism). But it could be argued that the lack of a conscious relationship with the Holy Spirit is an even greater handicap to the new Christian than not having experienced water-baptism. Perhaps the majority of today's Christians have tried to begin living the Christian life without having 'received' the Holy Spirit, in the New Testament sense of consciously experiencing his outpouring.

DEALING WITH INADEQUATELY INITIATED CHRISTIANS

This book is primarily addressed to those whose ministry is to such new Christians, and is an urgent plea to give them the *whole* package which is theirs in Christ – and at the time when they most need it. But it is obvious that this enlarged view of initiation has pastoral, as well as evangelistic implications. Indeed, one vicar's reaction on hearing this teaching was to agree that it was true to scripture but to declare his intention never to preach it from his pulpit because he already had quite enough problems with his members! All of this raises the delicate question of applying these concepts to Christians of long standing – and often of 'high standard' – who have managed to live faithfully and fruitfully for many years without one or more elements of New Testament initiation. If the four spiritual doors are taught properly to new converts coming into the church, it will not be long before many of those who are already in will begin to feel uncomfortable by comparison, and even vulnerable and threatened.

There are two possible approaches to such discomforted and defensive believers: to comfort them or to 'complete' them.

To comfort them

This is certainly the easier solution – to assure them that God's blessing on them proves that he is satisfied with them, that they are all right as they are and have all they need. Indeed, it is often considered hurtful and unloving to suggest that such 'saints' lack anything, which could do more harm than good to their spiritual peace and progress.

The dying thief is often cited as a precedent in this context; he was saved without water-baptism or Spirit-baptism (see chapter 9 for a critique of this argument). This executed criminal has given more comfort than he could ever imagine! He has inspired many to hope to scrape into heaven with minimal qualifications. More often, 'great' Christians are used for 'comfort' in a similar way – Salvation Army generals who were never baptised in water, great preachers who never spoke in tongues, etc. Immature 'baptists' and 'pentecostals' are unfavourably compared with such outstanding 'saints' and erroneous conclusions are drawn as to what is 'necessary' for full salvation.

There is a fatal flaw in such odious comparisons. The proper response should be to point out how much better these 'great' Christians would have been had they received all God wanted them to have. How much more effective those with the fruit of the Spirit would have been had they had the gifts as well; and how much more attractive those with the gifts of the Spirit would have been had they had the fruit as well.

In the long term, it is more of a hindrance than a help to spiritual maturity to be told that no more is needed. To suggest that something commanded of every believer in the New Testament is in fact optional is entirely unwarranted. This may be the simplest solution, but it is not the best or even the right one. There is an apostolic alternative.

To complete them

This is the proper way – to find out which dimensions are lacking and take positive steps to make up the deficiency. The apostles Peter, John and Paul may all be found doing this in the book of Acts (see chapters 16, 18 and 20). They did not waste time *discussing* the spiritual or eternal standing of those who lacked one or other element of initiation; it was a situation to be *doing* something about! Whatever was needed must be supplied as soon as possible.

This is the kindest and most loving approach, since it seeks the very best for a fellow believer; it cannot be content with less. It is of the essence of a truly pastoral (and evangelistic) concern to 'supply what is lacking' (1 Thess 3:10).

So many later problems can be traced back to an inadequate initiation: the past may never have been brought to a proper conclusion; the need to exercise trust by taking risks may never have been explained; the 'old man' may never have been given a proper funeral; supernatural power may never have been personally experienced. When these omissions are rectified, later problems are often reduced in size or even disappear altogether (it is a sound approach to many pastoral problems to enquire first about a person's conversion, to see if it was 'complete'). At the very least, a Christian will be much better equipped to tackle the problems of living the Christian life when he has a sure foundation under him.

This digression has been necessary because some readers may have become more concerned about the condition of 'old' Christians than the conversion of 'new' ones! The above remarks are not intended to discourage or disenfranchise such but to encourage and enrich them. However, the fear of upsetting 'saints' must not be allowed to rob sinners of a proper start in life. Too often our evangelistic counselling has been tailored to avoid offending the ninety-nine already in the fold (or, more probably, their shepherds!). It is the lost sheep who lose out, every time. Even if a fuller understanding of New Testament initiation creates problems for ourselves, that does not give us the right to withhold any part of it from others. Why should they have a poor beginning just because so many of us did?

It is time to look at the practical help that can be given to enable 'disciples' to pass through the 'four spiritual doors' into the kingdom of heaven on earth – whether they are just beginning the Christian life or have been on 'the Way' for some time. One easy way for the counsellor and the enquirer to remember them is the alliterative method – using the consonants of the word 'RuBBeR': *R*epent, *B*elieve, be *B*aptised and *R*eceive the Spirit. We shall now look at each of them in turn, considering them this time from a practical rather than a theological perspective.

32 HELPING DISCIPLES TO REPENT

Time taken to make sure repentance is real is time well spent. A blanket 'sorry' does little good and often leaves the umbilical cord to the past intact. Repentance is the first step into the kingdom, and it must not be rushed. The enquirer needs help in three basic areas – to be serious, to be specific and to be sensible. The counsellor has need of the gifts of the Spirit, particularly words of knowledge or wisdom and, above all, discernment.

TO BE SERIOUS

A person can be very clever, very rich, very attractive, very gifted, very powerful – and still very foolish! Real wisdom is not first of all a store of accumulated experience; it begins simply by *doing* the right thing. To turn from sin to God is the most sensible thing that anyone can ever do. But few do it until they are highly motivated.

'The fear of the Lord is the beginning of wisdom' (Prov 1:7). It is doubtful if anyone makes a genuine moral change unless this fear is present. It is the result of realising the ultimate consequences of continuing in wrong habits of thought, speech and behaviour.

The obverse side of the good news that the kingdom of heaven is being re-established on earth is that the inevitable climax to the process will be a crisis of judgement. Half of Jesus' parables are about the present process of infiltration and half are about the future crisis of separation (sheep from goats, wheat from tares, good fish from bad).

Judgement will be individual, each person being accountable to the Lord for his or her entire life. Every thought, word and deed has been faithfully recorded. Books will be opened and unlike the television programme *This is Your Life*, the unsavoury disclosures will not have been edited out. The trial will not be prolonged, since all the facts will be fully known to the judge, who will be strictly impartial and absolutely fair. There will be no appeal against sentence, since there is no higher court. Nor will a single human being be able to plead 'Not guilty', when confronted with their real record.

Lest any should think that God does not understand the pressures of living in this world, he has delegated the responsibility of judgement to a man, Jesus (Acts 17:31). The same one who did everything he could to warn and win us will at the last reject those who have heard of him but ignored him, which means that Pilate, Herod and Judas will all stand before Jesus' judgement seat.

The punishment is to 'perish'. The word means much the same in Greek as in English – not ceasing to exist, but rotting to the point where the original purpose of being made is no longer possible (a 'perished' man is as useless to God as a 'perished' tyre is to man). Hell is God's incinerator for perished 'goods' (cf. 'very good' in Gen 1:31 with 'being evil' in Luke 11:13). Every disaster is a reminder of this terrible fate (Luke 13:5). Our greatest fear should not be of cancer, redundancy or nuclear holocaust – but of the one who can destroy body and soul in hell (Luke 12:5).

All our knowledge about hell comes from the lips of Jesus himself, as if God would trust no one else to convey such dreadful revelation. Many attempts have been made to find an alternative to such an appalling possibility – second chance, temporary suffering (purgatory), conditional immortality (total extinction). All of these would be preferable to unending torment, but none of them can be squared with Jesus' description of the ultimate horror. Perhaps the feature he highlighted most frequently was the mental agony of hopeless frustration (Matt 25:30; Luke 16:24). To live without God for ever and ever, and to be among totally corrupted people and among utterly perverted 'animals' who were once human (Dan 4:16) – all the while realising there is no hope whatever of escaping from the company or the conditions (Luke 16:26) – that is hell, and any sacrifice in this life is worth making to avoid entering it.

Such are some of the truths that need to be clearly communicated to someone desiring to become a Christian. The above paragraphs are virtually a paraphrase of John the Baptist's call to 'flee from the coming wrath' (Luke 3:7). He knew that the same King who would 'baptise in Holy Spirit' would also one day baptise 'in fire', burning up the chaff (Matt 3:11–12) – though the two would not be simultaneous, as he perhaps expected (Luke 7:19). When Paul preached the gospel, he always began with news about God's anger, simmering in the present (Rom 1:18–32) but one day to boil over (Rom 2:5–11). On that day all classes and types of people, from the highest to the lowest, would rather be crushed under a landslide than look into the furious faces of the divine Father and Son (Rev 15:6–7).

It is of the essence of judgement that a person is both accountable and responsible for his own actions and character. Behaviourist psychology has undermined this concept, treating human beings as overgrown Pavlovian dogs (which could not help 'drooling' when the meal bell rang, whether there was food or not). We have been taught to consider ourselves as helpless victims, determined by heredity and environment and unable to help ourselves. Even Christian thinking has been influenced by this outlook; there can be a greater desire for 'inner healing of the emotions' than for 'forgiveness of sins'. But it is not what has been done to us that has made us what we are; it is what we have done with what has been done to us that has made us what we are. No one can avoid being wrongfully hurt in this world; but we choose to be bitter and resentful about it. God alone knows what we could not help; but by the same token he knows what we could, and judges us for these choices made by our wills.

To regard a person as responsible for themselves is to accord them full human dignity. To assume they have made wrong choices is to accept the biblical truth of human depravity. To speak of judgement to come is to remind them of human destiny. Sin is that serious. Any one sin could permanently disqualify us from an inheritance in the coming kingdom (1 Cor 6:9–10; Gal 5:19–21; it is sobering to realise that these warnings were given to believers, not unbelievers).

Such teaching about 'eternal judgement' is integral to Christian initiation (it is in the list of 'elementary teachings' in Heb 6:1–2 – see chapter 27). This, then, is the basis of that 'repentance from acts that lead to death'.

TO BE SPECIFIC

We have already seen the danger of a 'general confession'. True repentance is not from general sin, but from particular sins. At the very least, the sins that are being repudiated need to be named.

How can a counsellor help someone to be definite? There are at least three possible methods.

First, by *a guided conversation*. In this, the counsellor firmly presses beyond vague statements to personal details. Specific questions need to be asked: 'Why do you want to become a Christian?', 'What sins do you need to be saved from?', 'What secrets are you hiding from others?', 'Have you ever been involved in occult practices?' This must not be done in any spirit of morbid curiosity, and the counsellee must feel that confidences will be kept. But it is a loving thing to do, since bringing such things to light is often the first step of liberation from the kingdom of darkness. Exposing hidden sins can begin to release their hold as well as reduce the torment of secret guilt.

Second, by use of *a detailed list*. Some counsellors today use a prepared 'compendium' of forbidden things, to be checked off by the would-be disciple. (Basilea Schlink's superb book *The Christian's Victory* (Marshall, 1985) deals with forty-five of the most common sins, especially those that afflict the spirit rather than the flesh.) The use of such lists can be efficient and effective, particularly in prodding the memory. It is, alas, increasingly necessary to work through particular examples of occult involvement and sexual perversion, since both lead to bondage, needing deliverance as well as forgiveness.

The temptation with such 'catalogues' is to concentrate on the cruder and simpler sins (stealing, fornication) rather than the more complex and subtle (pride, greed); but the latter can easily be included by giving specific examples (collecting antiques, gambling on the stock exchange, etc.). John the Baptist made such practical suggestions (Luke 3:10–14 – note particularly: 'Be content with your pay'!).

The New Testament contains such lists (Matt 15:18–20; Mark 7:21–23; Rom 1:29–32; 13:13–14; 1 Cor 5:9–11; 6:9–10; 2 Cor 12:20–21; Gal 5:19–21; Eph 4:17–19; 4:25–31; 5:3–4; Col 3:5–6, 8–9; 1 Tim 1:9–10; 2 Tim 3:1–5; Tit 3:3–5; 1 Pet 2:1; 4:2–4; Rev 21:8; 22:14). The twenty-one New Testament lists contain just over a hundred different sins. A wise counsellor will have studied them and be able to carry an 'outline' in his head for reference. The classification may be done in a variety of ways: sins of thought, word and deed; sins against God, others, self; sins of omission and commission.

In the New Testament sins are not 'graded' into categories – for example, 'venial' and 'mortal' (though there are the 'unforgivable sin' and the 'sin that leads to death', both of which are apparently hopeless cases – see Matt 12:32; 1 John 5:16); nor should any sin be regarded as more serious than another, since all sin breaks the relationship with God.

Study of the New Testament lists will soon convince the reader that most of the 'Ten Commandments' in the law of Moses are taken up, with deeper meaning and wider application, into the 'law of Christ'. The exception is the fourth, concerning the sabbath, which is never applied to Gentile believers, being 'fulfilled' in quite a different manner (see Rom 14:5–6; Col 2:16–17; Heb 4:9–11; see also D. A. Carson (ed.), *From Sabbath to Lord's Day* (Zondervan, 1982).) The Mosaic law can still be used as a 'tutor' to bring us to Christ (Gal 3:24), 'indeed it is the straight-edge of the Law that shows us how crooked we are' (Rom 3:20 – J. B. Phillips' paraphrase).

A contrast with the virtues can be as effective as a comparison with the vices. In particular, a confrontation with the balanced perfection of character, conversation and conduct of the Lord Jesus himself can bring profound conviction of sin (Luke 5:8). Deep down, everyone who has heard of him knows that that is how life ought to be lived and how it has not been lived by the rest of us. To gaze at him is to be convinced that 'all have sinned and fall short of the glory of God' (Rom 3:23).

Third, by *an immediate revelation*. It is at this level that the aid of the Holy Spirit in counselling is so invaluable, though the two previous 'techniques' need to be used under his control as well.

On the one hand, he can bring the 'root' sins back from the subconscious memory into the conscious thought of the one being counselled. We never actually forget anything we have ever thought, felt, said or done (note how often a sight, sound or even a smell can trigger recall); but we do have difficulty remembering when we need to. The Holy Spirit can help us precisely at this point (John 14:26). Counselling can begin with a prayer for his assistance in recall.

On the other hand, the Spirit can give a 'word of knowledge' which guides the counsellor to a major 'tap-root' of sin, which the counsellee may be consciously or unconsciously hiding. Just as Jesus 'knew what was in man' (John 1:48; 2:25; 4:18) and could 'pinpoint' the real problem (for example, the acquisitiveness of the rich young ruler – Mark 10:17–22), so his Spirit can give similar insights today. I recall trying to help a girl who had responded to every evangelistic appeal for eighteen months, hoping life would change but finding no difference; the Holy Spirit prompted me to ask 'Who are you living with?' – which laid bare the whole problem, but led to the same result as the rich ruler: she went away sad, unwilling to let go of a man who would not marry her. Full of regret, she would not repent.

TO BE SENSIBLE

There are two aspects to this need – the emotions that accompany repentance and the actions that should follow it.

There is an ever-increasing need to distinguish between psychological guilt (what we feel about ourselves) and moral guilt (what God feels about us). The former is often conditioned (by upbringing, temperament, etc.) and artificial (self-hatred and self-pity are quite destructive, often hindering repentance). Moral guilt is objective rather than subjective, an ability to step outside one's own state and see the sin for what it really is. The parable of the 'Prodigal Son' is a perfect example. The son's feelings changed from regret and remorse to real repentance when he encountered his father's love and realised the enormity of his neglect. How easily our emotions distort our judgement:

> Once in a saintly passion,
> I cried, in desperate grief:
> 'O Lord, my heart is black with guile;
> Of sinners I am chief!'
> Then stooped my guardian angel
> And whispered from behind:
> 'Vanity, my little man,
> You're nothing of the kind!'
>
> (source unknown)

This short poem highlights the danger of distorted emotion, which can be quite self-deceiving, shutting a person off from reality: for example, a man can be more easily convicted about masturbation than murder. Sometimes the sins the sinner is most worried about are not the real barrier between that person and God. Grief over one can disguise guilt over another. The heart is adept at deceiving itself. To be sensible is to have a sense of proportion, a right scale of values. This comes from the application of scripture to the sinner by the Spirit.

It is also important to be realistic about the actions as well as the emotions of repentance. With some sins, it is impossible to go back and put them right. With others, it would be unwise even to try; digging up the past can do positive harm. This is where the gift of the Spirit called 'the word of wisdom' can be so useful. A man confessed adultery to me, but wondered whether he should confess it to his wife, who was a permanent patient in a mental home; the Lord gave me this word for him: 'She is now a child to me, says the Lord, and you do not tell a child such things' (the husband was at that point totally relieved of his guilt and is now living right and loving his wife as he should).

The most difficult situations to straighten out are those involving divorce and re-marriage. What did Jesus tell the woman at the well in Samaria to do about her predicament? Marry her latest 'man'? Go back to the fifth husband? Or the fourth, third, second or first? Remain single for the rest of her life? If we only knew! This is not the place to deal with this complex issue (it requires a separate book). However, I have always found it wise to make sure that before looking at their individual circumstances the following two points are clearly understood and accepted by the parties concerned. First, that forgiveness does not cancel all previous contracts – from a mortgage to a marriage (imagine telling a creditcard company that all your debts have been paid at Calvary!); regeneration doesn't 'convert' either a married or a divorced person into a bachelor or spinster again! Second, whatever exceptions there may be in scripture (I accept Jesus' exception of adultery but not the so-called 'Pauline' exception of desertion – Matt 19:9; 1 Cor 7:15; 'bound' in the latter text is not Paul's usual word for the marriage bond, as in v. 39 or Rom 7:2), the *rule* of the Lord is quite clear: re-marriage is adultery in God's sight. The person who is forgiven the sin of adultery is not free to continue in it (John 8:11). For many, the 'fruit worthy of repentance' will be to remain single or be reconciled to their former partner (1 Cor 7:11). Once these two principles are wholeheartedly accepted, it is then possible to seek wisdom from the Lord for the best way forward, particularly where children are involved, for whom the Lord has a special concern (Matt 18:10; Luke 17:2).

However, most 'deeds of repentance' are much easier to define, if just as hard to do. It is essential to be positive and to put right what can be put right. Debts can be paid off, apologies made, crimes confessed to the police. One convert known to me did this, got the lightest possible sentence, was nick-named 'the Bishop' by his fellow prisoners because of his enthusiasm to tell them about Jesus, and boasted that he was the only evangelist in Britain entirely financed by Her Majesty the Queen! To do good to those who have done harm is extremely effective in expelling bitterness and resentment.

In encouraging such reformation, restitution and reconciliation, it must be made crystal clear that this is not in any sense doing penance or making atonement for past sins, even though such actions do ease the conscience and relieve feelings of guilt. Deeds of repentance in no way 'earn' divine grace. They are more to be seen as expressions of a genuine desire to be saved from sins and of deep gratitude for the wonder of forgiveness. It is not through repentance that we are saved, but through faith, though both are the gift of God as well as the act of man (Acts 5:31; Eph 2:8).

Repentance begins at initiation, but it does not end there. It may be described as a 'way of life'. Indeed, there will normally be much more repentance after 'conversion', though it must begin before. It is one of the marks of a 'saint' that they become more and more aware of being a 'sinner'. Continuing repentance is essential to the process of sanctification. As spiritual maturity brings increasing discernment between right and wrong (Heb 5:14), there will be more, not less, need for repentance. The most penitent are usually the most holy. Thus, repentance will be extended into the rest of life.

It will also be extended into the whole of life. As a Christian matures he becomes aware that evil is corporate and collective as well as personal and individual. He learns to identify the sins of the church, the nation and the world – to feel their guilt and express penitence for them. He develops a 'social conscience' which will lead to deeds of repentance in 'social action'. Above all, this will be reflected in his intercessory prayer, which will echo Jesus' own plea: 'Father, forgive them, for they do not know what they are doing' (Luke 23:34).

However, this double 'extension' of repentance, into the rest and the whole of life, belongs to life in the kingdom. It is both unrealistic and inappropriate to introduce these aspects into initiation. While it is perfectly legitimate, and necessary, to demand proof of real repentance, it is impossible to expect total repentance (i.e. from every sin ever committed); that would be to look for sanctification before justification (which is the basic error of all other religions, including Judaism). Similarly, at the moment of entering the kingdom, a sinner needs only to face up to his own sins; his only concern with collective vices and crimes is his personal part in them, if any. In a sense, he is choosing to take his trial before the day of judgement, pleading 'Guilty', and obtaining acquittal in the name of Jesus.

To get this verdict, repentance must be followed by faith. When repentance is made the sole or primary element in initiation, as 'liberal' thinking tends to do, the result is dangerously near salvation by works, which appeals to a 'Do-it-yourself' age. The emphasis is then on what man does for God rather than what God does for man. We are not justified by works of the law – or by works of repentance! We must help people to repent; we must also help them to believe.

The world says 'Seeing is believing.' The Bible says 'Faith comes from hearing' (Rom 10:17). It is therefore widely assumed that only 'blind' faith is true faith; that the gospel must reach the human soul through the ear-gate, but not the eye-gate.

Certainly faith penetrates beyond the visible (Heb 11:1, 27); and there is a special blessing for those who, without seeing him, believe that Jesus is alive (John 20:29; note that Thomas was no more a 'doubter' than the other ten apostles or even the women at the tomb – see Mark 16:9–14). But is this the whole truth? Is a world that wants to see some evidence for the truth of the gospel asking for that which it must not be given and, some might add, which it cannot be given? Was Nietzsche so terribly wrong to say that he would want to be saved if Christians looked more saved?

WORDS, DEEDS AND SIGNS

We may begin to unpack these questions by noting how in the four gospels sight often led to faith. Those Jews who 'received' Jesus, 'believed in his name' and were 'born of God', so often did so because they had seen his miracles. The supreme climax of this effect was the raising of Lazarus (John 11:45). This is why John's gospel speaks of the miracles as signs, physical events so unnatural as to point beyond themselves to supernatural realities. Jesus never discouraged those who came to faith in himself by this route. But he was highly critical of those who were only wanting the physical benefits of his ministry rather than the spiritual blessings behind his miracles

(John 6:26) – an attitude all too common in our own materialistic age. And he refused to perform miracles to satisfy the curiosity of hostile sceptics (Matt 16:1–4); though he did promise them the 'sign of Jonah'. We need to remember that had no one *seen* the risen Jesus, there would be no such religion as Christianity (cf. Luke 24:24): Jesus would be regarded simply as a prophet (as both Judaism and Islam consider him).

Peter had no hesitation in using as evidence for Jesus' resurrection and ascension (and that these events proved that he was now the '*Lord* Jesus *Christ*') the fact that he had 'poured out what you now *see* and *hear*' (Acts 2:33). Later Peter and John seized the opportunity of the spectacle of the man who 'asked for alms' to lead the crowd to faith; they saw the miracle and heard the message (Acts 3:9–10; 4:4). 'Signs and wonders' were obviously one of the main factors in the spectacular growth of the early church (Acts 5:12–16).

Paul also understood the communication of the gospel in these terms. In fact, he refers to three dimensions – word, deed and sign (some prefer the alliterative list 'words, works and wonders'). Informing the Roman church about his evangelistic methods among the Gentiles, prior to his visit to the metropolis, he wrote: 'I have won them by my message and by the good way I have lived before them, and by miracles done through me as signs from God – all by the Holy Spirit's power. In this way I have fully accomplished my Gospel ministry all the way from Jerusalem to Illyricum' (Rom 15:19 – Living Bible paraphrase; cf. 1 Thess 1:5).

What is striking in this description of Paul's method is that two dimensions are for the eye and only one for the ear. The truth of what is said is confirmed by what is seen, in human deeds and divine signs. The human 'deeds' are not primarily acts of social provision or political pressure, necessary outworkings of the gospel though they may be. Jesus' definition was in terms of a much higher 'standard of living', moral rather than material; he spelled it out in the Sermon on the Mount – no anger, no lust, no divorce, no swearing, no revenge, no public piety, no worry, etc. (see Matt 5:16 and the whole of Matt 5–7). The divine 'signs' are primarily the healing of disease and deliverance from demons (Matt 9:1), though they are not confined to these (cf. Paul's 'blinding' the Cypriot sorcerer, repeating his own experience on the Damascus road and leading to the Governor's conversion – Acts 9:9; 13:11).

All this ties in with the gospel of the *kingdom*. The good news is that the kingdom of God (his 'rule' rather than his 'realm') has been re-established on earth by the coming of the King. He has now ascended to the throne of the universe, while his subjects on earth, already enjoying the benefits of his rule, are preparing all who believe for its full and final establishment, following the King's return to this planet. Truly an 'incredible' programme, quite beyond human experience or imagination (Isa 64:4, quoted in 1 Cor 2:9). The kingdom 'there and then' is also 'here and now' (half of Jesus' parables point to a future crisis for the establishment of the kingdom on earth; the other half point to a present process). Is it unreasonable for people to expect some visible indication that the kingdom is already here? The early disciples were able to claim that Jesus was already sovereign by pointing to the divine signs; and that they were already his subjects by pointing to the human deeds. The kingdom could and should be demonstrated as well as declared (Luke 10:9). This is precisely what Paul meant when he said his preaching at Corinth was 'with a demonstration of the Spirit's power' (1 Cor 2:4; cf. Acts 14:3).

ARE SUPERNATURAL 'SIGNS' OBSOLETE?

It is usually acknowledged that the apostolic preaching was attested in this way (2 Cor 12:12), but it is frequently argued that this was not to be the evangelistic pattern throughout church history. The contention is that once apostolic doctrine was completed and committed to writing, such miraculous authentication was rendered obsolete. Faith would then have to believe in past (i.e. unseen) miracles as evidence for the truth of the message! The visible print is then considered an adequate substitute for manifest power! Neither scripture nor church history give support to the notion that God withdrew miraculous confirmation of his word when it was transferred from oral to written form. (For example, John Wesley's letter of 4 January 1749 to the sceptical Dr Conyers Middleton about prophecy, tongues and healing is a classic defence of continuing supernatural gifts. See his *Letters* (Epworth, 1931), vol. 2, pp. 312ff.)

There is one clear scripture which contradicts the view that God caused supernatural 'signs' to cease, though it is not part of the original text (namely, Mark 16:15–20). Even if it is a later addition by an early church editor, it is all the better evidence for the post-apostolic outlook! Here is the missionary mandate for the church in 'all the world' and to the 'end of the age'. The promise is that miraculous events will accompany all believers, not just the apostles, whenever and wherever the gospel is preached. To reinterpret these 'signs following' as 'many conversions' or 'changed lives' is an abuse of biblical terminology and a cover-up for the absence of the signs predicted.

The onus of proof rests with those who assert the withdrawal of 'signs and wonders'. One thing they cannot deny – the Holy Spirit himself has not been withdrawn. Until clear biblical or historical grounds can be given for a radical change in his mode of operation, the demonstration of his power and the distribution of his gifts remain as integral and convincing features of full gospel communication (Heb 2:4). Let it be added that the printed, and even the preached, word could be disseminated without the Holy Spirit (for example, an unbeliever could be paid to distribute tracts and some might be saved as a result!) – but the human deeds and divine signs are impossible to reproduce without his presence (which must be why Jesus commanded the disciples to wait in Jerusalem until they 'received power'). Even a 'scriptural' knowledge about his death, resurrection and ascension is apparently not enough to be his 'witness' (cf. Luke 24:27 with Acts 1:8).

THE VALUE OF A REASONED DEFENCE

In helping others to believe, one other kind of 'evidence' for the truth of the gospel needs to be considered. We refer to the role of 'apologetics', the need and ability to give a 'reasoned defence' of the faith. It is a half-truth to say that no one was ever argued into the kingdom (Agrippa's reaction to Paul's persuasiveness is often quoted to support this view; Acts 26:28). Barriers to truth can be removed by demonstrating that the case for Christianity is reasonable. (For example, the writings of C. S. Lewis, Francis Schaeffer, Bernard Ramm and Josh McDowell have helped many in this way; they provide an excellent store of 'ammunition'!). To believe is not to commit intellectual suicide. Faith and reason travel the same road towards truth, though faith goes much further up the road. Was it not Abraham Lincoln who said 'Accept as much of the Bible as you can on the basis of reason, take the rest on faith; and you will live and die a happier man'?

On the one hand, there is a growing body of evidence for the historical accuracy of the Bible, particularly in the archaeological field. Then there is the inherent authenticity of the scriptures themselves; the circumstantial details of the resurrection narratives would be enough to convince any legal jury that the event had taken place. Many of the so-called 'contradictions' can be shown to be superficial or merely apparent. The history of the text itself encourages increasing confidence. The fact that nearly six hundred separate predictions have come true (the remaining fifth are almost all about the end of the world) is more impressive than superstitious astrology or scientific futurology. The average unbeliever is largely unaware of how much cumulative evidence can be amassed in favour of the truth of God's word.

On the other hand, an effective apologetic must tackle the general philosophical outlook of the Bible as well as the particular historical details. The scriptures certainly do not teach *atheism* (the belief that 'there is no God', which requires a lot of faith to accept!), *agnosticism* ('I don't know whether there is a God or not'), *pantheism* ('everything is God'), *humanism* ('man is God, having come of age') or *deism* ('God created the world but cannot control it'). The true biblical philosophy is *theism* ('God created and controls the universe') – the view which makes most sense of nature and history.

In presenting particular evidence or making general sense, we are obeying the scriptural injunction 'Always be prepared to give an answer to everyone who asks you to give the reason for the hope that you have' (1 Pet 3:15). However, the 'reason' is subjective as well as objective and should include experience as well as evidence. Two words of warning may conclude this section. First, it is necessary to discern whether a questioner has genuine difficulties which he wants to resolve or is simply putting up defensive flak around his determined scepticism (in the latter case, however many problems are satisfactorily solved, more will be found!). Second, while genuine mental barriers need to be faced, it must be pointed out that the primary problems keeping us from faith in God are moral (our deepest need is forgiveness, not enlightenment).

HELPING PEOPLE TO ACT IN FAITH

Having presented the gospel in word, deed and sign through the ear and eye to the heart and mind, and being satisfied that the truth of it has been fully accepted, the next step is to help a person to act in faith, for believing is primarily of the will – it is to be done (see chapter 3). There are two practical steps to be taken.

First, faith needs to be expressed in words. Negatively, it is not helpful to provide the words, either in a sample creed or as a 'sinner's prayer'. The enquirer may be more conscious of the person whose words they are repeating than the One to whom they are addressed. Above all, the degree of sincerity will vary in proportion to the appropriateness of the 'liturgy' to the emotions and thoughts of the speaker. Positively, it is far better to let a person address the Lord directly, finding his or her own words, however simple or stumbling they may be. A discerning counsellor, listening carefully to what is not said as well as what is said, will realise what further help the person may need and whether they have genuinely 'called on the name of the Lord'. They should be encouraged at this stage to use the human name 'Jesus' and, when they understand its meaning, to call him 'Lord'. In particular, the personal pronouns, or their absence, should be noted; not just 'I believe you died and rose again' but 'I believe you died to stop *me* sinning and rose again to help *me* find real life.' It may be necessary to encourage a number of short prayers, interspersed with counselling, expressing each aspect of faith as it is realised.

Second, faith needs to be expressed in deeds. It is important to help someone to begin to live by faith, and to go on doing so for the rest of their lives. The best way to achieve this is to identify some particular need or situation requiring the immediate help of the Lord. This may then be talked through; it should be clearly explained that faith is not believing that God *can* help, but that he *will*. It is vital to discover the person's level of faith before praying with them. The best way is to suggest a variety of ways in which the Lord might act in the situation (from a small to a total change in the situation) and ask which of these the disciple believes will happen. It is sometimes helpful to suggest a specific time by which the particular answer is expected. My own 'technique' to discern the level of faith is to issue a direct challenge ('So you really believe the Lord will send you twenty pounds by the end of the month, do you?') – but instead of listening to the answer, I look straight into the other person's eyes! The eye is the 'light of the body' and doubt always shows in a 'shifty' look; only if the pupils remain rock steady and the person openly returns the gaze do I feel free to pray confidently that the promise of Jesus to 'two agreed on earth' will be fulfilled (Matt 18:19). It is often necessary to 'cut down' the size of the petition to the level of a new believer's faith; but it will be far more helpful to pray for something small that does happen than for something large that doesn't! This will not only impart a gift of faith to them; it will also encourage their faith to continue and grow.

Of course, it is assumed that a good counsellor will have told the disciple that the very first practical expression and exercise of faith is to bury his old 'dead' life and wash its 'dirt' away in the waters of baptism. If he is really trusting Jesus for forgiveness, he will readily obey him in submitting to this rite of cleansing (Acts 2:38).

34   HELPING DISCIPLES TO BE BAPTISED

This might have been the shortest and simplest chapter in the book! There are only two things that need to be done.

First, it is absolutely essential to make sure that the candidate has genuinely repented and truly believed (see chapters 2, 3, 32, 33), remembering that profession in word is no guarantee of possession in deed. Once these two qualifications are established, there is no need to delay a moment longer.

Second, it is necessary to find a place where there is enough water (John 3:23). Immersion seems to have been the New Testament mode of baptism (the word itself indicates this as well as its use) and certainly conveys the New Testament meaning (a combined 'bath' and 'burial'). In England this is comparatively easy: an increasing number of church buildings (including Anglican) have installed pools, many communities have facilities for swimming in leisure centres and the country is blessed with many rivers and lakes, to say nothing of being surrounded by sea. In Russia, the ice of a frozen lake is broken into, the candidate being thawed out later! Sometimes in those places where droughts are frequent, a grave is dug, lined with a cotton shroud in which the candidate is 'buried' and precious water is sprinkled on the sheet until it is saturated. Where there's a will, there's a way!

BAPTISMAL PRACTICE

The efficacy of the act does not depend on the exact amount of water used, since it is not the washing of the body that is the essential event (1 Pet 3:21). But the nearer we can get to representing both the bath and the burial, the more meaning-ful it will be to the candidate. Those who have been 'sprinkled' as believers often feel 'short-changed'; there seems to be no real reason why their baptism could not be 'completed' with an immersion, thus adding the 'burial' aspect to the 'bath' (the wording used at the time being suitably adjusted).

Nor does its efficacy depend on the spiritual state or status of the person doing the baptising. John the Baptist was not even baptised himself, though Jesus accepted baptism at his hands (Matt 3:14). Today one might not be totally at ease being baptised by someone who was not prepared to be baptised himself. Neither is there anything in the New Testament to suggest baptism can only be administered by any particular 'ministry' (and the scripture contains no hint of an 'ordained' ministry with a monopoly of the sacraments). Indeed, the apostles, following the example of Jesus, left the baptising to their helpers (cf. John 4:2 with Acts 10:48 and 1 Cor 1:13–17). Paul himself was baptised by an 'ordinary' brother called Ananias (Acts 9:17–18). The vital element is the submission to another, of which the Lord himself is a perfect example. The bathing and burying is done *for* us, not *by* us; a 'corpse' does not assist at the funeral!

However, 'everything should be done in a fitting and orderly way' (1 Cor 14:40). If mature Christian leaders are available, it is good to ask them to do it. And for the sake of others, as well as the candidate, it is preferable to have a public rather than a private ceremony. This public 'testimony' may be what Paul is referring to when he reminded Timothy of his 'good confession in the presence of many witnesses' (1 Tim 6:12). But it must be emphasised that this 'wet witness' is not the real purpose of baptism, however profound its influence on the spectators.

There is certainly good biblical warrant for expecting the candidate to take a full vocal part in the proceedings, but this will primarily be directed to the Lord himself – confessing actual sins (Matt 3:6) and calling on the 'name' of Jesus (Acts 22:16) for the forgiveness of those sins (Acts 2:38). To address him in this way is more important as an expression of repentance and faith than giving a potted history of one's conversion to the bystanders; the latter may be a helpful addition, but is an unhelpful substitute for the former.

Immediately after the candidate has been 'submerged' and has 'emerged', hands should be laid on, with earnest prayer for the reception of the Holy Spirit, if he has not already been received (cf. Acts 10:47 with 19:5–6; see also the next chapter). At this point, it is helpful if others present turn their attention from the baptism to the Lord, engaging in whole-hearted praise and adoration; in such an atmosphere it will be much easier for the candidate to 'overflow' as the Spirit is 'outpoured'.

The memory of this event/experience will remain a source of inspiration and encouragement for the rest of the person's life. Whether he came to repentance and faith slowly or quickly (the New Testament is quite indifferent to velocity!), he can now date the end of his old life and the beginning of his new life (as one pastor says to his candidates: 'It's your funeral; enjoy it!'). Baptism is to discipleship what a wedding is to a marriage.

In both baptisms and weddings, the full meaning of what has been said and done may not be realised at the time (did any loving couple really understand the implications of 'for better, for worse; for richer, for poorer; in sickness and in health; till death us do part . . .'?). This does not matter. The passing years will draw out the full significance and deeper appreciation. Most of the New Testament teaching on baptism is given afterwards (cf. Rom 6:3–4). The ceremony needs to be frequently recalled, but never repeated. A couple should only be married once and a Christian should only be baptised once.

This brings us to the thorny problem of 're-baptism'!

RE-BAPTISM – IS IT APPROPRIATE?

In Europe, and particularly in the British Isles, many, if not most, people have already been through a 'christening' ceremony as a baby, which the churches practising this believe to have been full Christian baptism. Though a person has no conscious recollection of it, draws no regular inspiration from it and cannot see any connection between that and his later 'conversion', he is nevertheless forbidden to consider 'being baptised again'. Having died to his sinful life, a proper funeral is denied him! Whenever he reads about the New Testament mode, meaning and moment of baptism, he often feels that his parents and church have between them robbed him of a 'normal' Christian birth.

Christian ministers who are convinced of the validity of baby baptism will seek to help a new Christian 'read back' into their christening the full meaning of Christian baptism, though there are real difficulties in doing this without making the original event purely symbolic or practically magical. Many admit that its meaning for a baby has to be different from its meaning for a believer.

Others seek to put the emphasis elsewhere, focusing attention on 'confirmation', for example, as the 'completion' of baby baptism, insisting that repentance and faith can just as easily follow baptism as precede it (though this separates the effect of baptism from the event, usually by at least a decade!). More recently, the unusual suggestion has been made of 'confirmation by immersion'; those who administer such a hybrid rite persuade themselves it is not a baptism, but those who receive it increasingly think of it as that!

Those who take the church as the authoritative voice of the Lord are likely to adopt these expedients, though often with regret. Those who take the Bible as the authoritative voice of the Lord will find it much less easy. Since this book is more likely to be read by the latter, we must grasp the nettle.

Someone in this dilemma must be prepared to spend time and thought in seeking a convincing answer to the question *Am I baptised in the sight of the Lord?* The answer will come from the scripture and through the Spirit, though part of the quest will consist of listening to what others have to say.

I have advised the following approach. First, study all the New Testament passages on the subject (there are over thirty of them, but they have been conveniently arranged as a month's daily Bible readings in Stephen Winward's *The New Testament Teaching on Baptism*, published by the Baptist Union). Throughout the study ask yourself 'Does this apply to me; can I claim this for myself?' Second, talk to Christians of differing views, on the principle that if a man has talked us into something, another man can talk us out of it; but if God is talking us into something, whatever a man says only makes us more sure! Third, find out why and how the church introduced and continued the practice of baptising babies (Appendix I is included for that very purpose, though 'paedobaptists' will no doubt consider my account biased; they can recommend their own summary to be studied alongside mine). Fourth, get alone with the Lord, lay the options before him and ask him to give you peace over the one he wants you to follow and unease over any others. Fifth, apply the test of time: human impulses fade, but the Lord's guidance gets stronger, until there is really no choice but to obey or disobey.

Should this process lead to a decision to seek baptism as a believer, a person should speak first to the leaders of his or her fellowship – to seek their blessing at least, even if they feel it impossible to give their co-operation or approval. It is important to clarify at this stage whether they are willing to continue their pastoral responsibility in other matters, should the person go elsewhere for baptism; if the answer is negative, then consideration has to be given as to what part of the body of Christ can be a continuing spiritual home, so that the 'new' shepherds can then be approached with a view to performing the baptism.

Finally, I would make a sincere plea to 'paedobaptist' clergy to respect the conscience of individuals in their care. A good shepherd is not primarily concerned with submission to himself or even to his section of the body, but with submission to the Head of the church and to his Father, who is all in all. When a sheep is convinced about obedience to the Chief Shepherd in a particular matter, this should be encouraged unless the course of action is clearly forbidden in scripture. The believer should be allowed to follow conscience and conviction.

Re-baptism must not be treated as if it were the unforgivable sin. It should certainly not be made a matter of discipline, much less excommunication. After all, the 'sin' is motivated by a determination to be obedient to the Lord in all things, to fulfil all righteousness (Matt 3:15). It is hardly right to be penalised for that! And there is some precedent for 're-baptism' in the New Testament. Paul had no hesitation in doing it when the previous baptism, though it expressed repentance, lacked saving faith in the Lord Jesus (Acts 19:1–6; see chapter 20). Peter probably did the same on the day of Pentecost, since it is highly unlikely that none of the three thousand had been baptised in the Jordan by John. The real question is: What makes a baptism 'Christian' – the correct formula or convinced faith, the right baptiser or the right baptised?

Of course, re-baptism could be seen as a 'sin' against the church. To be baptised 'again' as a believer is a repudiation of one's baptism as a baby. It is to say that the church (and the clergy) has been mistaken in administering it. It is to question centuries of tradition, though it has never been the only tradition. But since when has belief in an infallible church been part of the Christian faith? The authority of the church depends on its being one, holy, catholic and, above all, apostolic (in the sense of 'continuing steadfastly in the apostles' doctrine'). When the church departs from New Testament teaching, she cannot expect to be obeyed, nor should she feel offended when disobeyed.

It is sad that very new Christians should be plunged into such controversy so quickly. It is even sadder that so many should be denied the one sacrament they so much need at the time of their 'conversion'. Baptism needs to be restored to its proper context – it is more of an evangelistic response than an ecclesiastical rite. It is a far more appropriate expression of receiving the word of the gospel than 'coming to the front', 'signing a decision card' or 'getting confirmed'. It is the only response instituted, even commanded, by the Lord Jesus himself (see chapter 7 on the Great Commission). Its vital function is to give the disciple a 'clean start' in the new life, by

281

making a 'clean break' with the old. How much longer will the church rob its converts of this important experience?

By itself, however, baptism is not enough. Baptism in water may bring the past to a proper conclusion, but should normally be a prelude to baptism in Spirit, which is a proper introduction to the future. Those who are twice-born need to be twice-baptised!

35 HELPING DISCIPLES TO RECEIVE

As with water-baptism, this might have been a short and simple chapter, but our contemporary confusion has made the whole thing so much more complicated.

CONFUSION OVER RECEPTION OF THE SPIRIT

In the apostolic days, prayer was made with the laying-on of hands, normally immediately after baptism; the Spirit was then given by the Lord and received by the penitent, baptised believer, with confirming outward evidence. As we have seen, there were only two recorded occasions when the Spirit was given and received without such 'ministry' – and there are clear reasons for treating these as 'exceptional' (see chapter 14 and 18). The usual procedure was for those who had already 'received' the Spirit to 'minister' the gift to those who were seeking. Nor is there any record of this failing to produce the desired result. Life seems to have been much simpler in those days, spiritually as well as materially (Acts 3:6)!

Consider the variations in the church today. The 'liberal' stream seems to ignore the need to 'receive' the Spirit, since he is believed to be with people already, in the world as well as the church – and some would even say more in the world than the church. The 'evangelical' stream rarely mentions 'receiving' the Spirit, believing this happens automatically, and usually unconsciously, when a person 'receives Jesus into their life'. The 'sacramental' stream believes the Spirit is received at infant baptism or adolescent confirmation, but opinion seems to be divided as to which actually achieves it. The 'Pentecostal' stream tends to teach two receptions of the Spirit. The first is subconscious and is for salvation, so it happens at conversion. The second is conscious and is for service – this happens after conversion (often a long time after) and is sometimes called the 'second blessing'. The first reception is of the person, the second of the power of the Holy Spirit (a distinction which is not easy to establish from the New Testament – see chapter 13 and Appendix 2).

None of these views is true to the total teaching of the New Testament, as we have tried to show earlier in the book. Against the 'liberal', the New Testament clearly states that the world cannot receive the Spirit (John 14:17); he is only given to the disciples of Jesus. Against the 'evangelical', the New Testament clearly distinguishes between 'believing' and 'receiving', so that it is possible to have one without the other (see chapters 16 and 20); furthermore, 'receiving' is fully conscious, with clear evidence. Against the 'sacramental', the New Testament clearly distinguishes between water-baptism and Spirit-baptism, though the two are in close association; nor would it regard a 'confirmation rite' as adequate evidence that the Spirit had, in fact, been received, however exalted the personage whose hands were laid on! Against the 'Pentecostal', the New Testament speaks of only one 'reception' of the Spirit, for salvation and service, the person and the power, as an integral element in the 'first' initiation.

This confusion has led to a striking reluctance to use New Testament language in its original meaning. 'Received' is transferred back from the third person of the Trinity to the second. 'Sealed' is interpreted as an inward and spiritual transaction of which others are totally unaware. 'Anointed' is not used at all, except of physical oil. 'Filled' is dropped, in favour of later 'fullness'. 'Baptised' is used only in theological argument and never in general preaching or teaching (and its meaning of 'soaked, drenched, plunged' is ignored). 'Poured out' ('downpour') is never used. 'Cry out' is changed to a silent 'inward witness'. 'Fall upon' is kept for rare seasons of 'revival'. The simple fact is that such New Testament terminology simply does not 'fit' contemporary church practice or experience!

There seems to have arisen, therefore, a mutual agreement to maintain a conspiracy of silence about the gift of the Spirit, especially in ecumenical evangelism. 'Converts' are left to discover for themselves the third person of the blessed Trinity, at some later stage in their discipleship (some do, much later, but many never do at all). The delay invariably makes the introduction more difficult. The very best time to pray with someone for the Spirit to 'come upon' them is immediately after they have repented, believed and been baptised. The longer it is left, the harder it usually gets!

However, there is one good feature in the contemporary scene! The 'charismatic renewal' has been affecting all streams within the church. The experience of many is now much nearer to the early church. Greater freedom in worship, depth of fellowship, release of gifts, confidence in scripture and joy in the Lord have all reappeared – to the delight of some and the consternation of others! But theology has not caught up with experience, particularly in the matter of initiation. On the whole, mainline denominations have reluctantly welcomed the experience but stubbornly maintained their former theology and practice, trying to fit the new wine into old wineskins. One of the signs of this anomaly is the development of euphemisms for the experience, to replace the New Testament terminology. Such phrases as 'release of the Spirit' (favoured by Roman Catholics and some Anglicans) and 'actualisation of gifts already received in potentiality' have attempted to create new categories for an old experience; and the term 'renewal' itself is capable of many meanings. Those who have been willing to reconsider their doctrine of initiation have usually finished up in new fellowships or 'house-churches', most of which practise believers' baptism as well.

All this may seem to be a rather academic digression in a practical chapter on 'helping disciples to receive'. The relevance of it is simply this: the first requirement for 'helping' concerns the 'helpers'! They must be clearly convinced from scripture and their own experience about the need to 'receive' the Spirit in addition to repentance, faith and baptism. They must be wholehearted in praying with the laying-on of hands and strong in expectant faith that the Lord will 'drench' his disciples in the Holy Spirit. Uncertainty and hesitation are just as likely to have a negative effect on ministry (in word or deed) as clarity and confidence affect it positively. Strong faith rests on a clear grasp of *the* faith; Pentecost itself rested on faith in the 'promise' (Luke 24:49; Acts 2:33, 39; Gal 3:14). The helpers must be absolutely sure of the promise and its individual fulfilment.

DEALING WITH FAILURE TO RECEIVE THE SPIRIT

We can now consider possible inhibitions in the one being helped. In other words, if a person is prayed for and 'nothing happens', what should be said or done next?

The most unhelpful approach is to assure the disciple that they have received, even though nothing has happened! It is disturbing to find how frequently counselling material includes such advice as 'Don't worry if you feel no different,' or even 'Don't expect to feel any different' (an expectation likely to be fulfilled!). Appeals are sometimes made to texts which imply faith must be sure of something before it is given – for example, Jesus' own words: 'Therefore I tell you, whatever you ask for in prayer, believe that you have received it, and it will be yours' (Mark 11:24; cf. Heb 11:1). There is a kind of faith-teaching, based on this verse, which wrongly encourages testimony without back-up evidence ('I know I'm healed, even if I'm still limping'); such statements can be self-deluding and lead to disappointment and disillusion. The tenses Jesus used are significant: '. . . believe that you have received [aorist = once-for-all] and it will be yours [future, so not to be understood as 'already yours']'. In other words, prayer that was uttered in the confidence that the petition was accepted in principle will be answered in practice. I have prayed over a number of people to receive the Spirit, without any immediate result; but I have felt able in the Spirit to assure them that the prayer has been heard and have asked them to let me know just as soon as the gift has been actually received, which has led to some exciting telephone calls, usually within a matter of hours. There is a world of difference between believing that it has happened without any evidence and believing that it will happen with evidence. The latter is the faith needed to 'receive the Holy Spirit'.

But suppose nothing happens after praying with such faith – what then? There is scriptural encouragement to go on asking until it does! The 'present continuous' Greek verb tense is not always translated into a full English equivalent (to 'go on' doing something). So we miss the flavour of 'Go on asking and it will be given to you; go on seeking and you will find; go on knocking and the door will be opened to you' (Luke 11:9), which immediately precedes Jesus' assurance '. . . how much more will your Father in heaven give Holy Spirit to those who go on asking him' (Luke 11:13). This cannot refer to unbelievers, who cannot 'receive'; so it is an encouragement to believers to persist in prayer for the gift of the Spirit. After all, a person who asked once and then gave up when nothing immediately happened cannot have been very serious in the first place; they would hardly be so easily discouraged over any other need, ambition or priority in life! When someone wants something badly enough, they usually hang in there until it is theirs.

Consistent failure to receive the Spirit suggests that there may be other factors to be identified and corrected. These may be quite basic (Paul checked on water-baptism, for example; Acts 19:3). One of the most common blockages is a failure in repentance, particularly in relation to occult involvement and bondage (from Freemasonry to astrology). Even faith may need to be clarified and tested. It is wise to follow the apostolic precedent and check out these essentials before looking for other 'problems'. But what else could it be?

Some quite simply do not know what to expect or how to 'receive'. They need an example and an explanation. If someone has never heard or seen what happens when the Spirit 'falls on' a person, they are at a disadvantage. The one hundred and twenty at Pentecost were Jewish, and their own history supplied examples (Num 11:25; 1 Sam 10:6); the three thousand saw and heard what happened to the one hundred and twenty (Acts 2:33). Receiving the Spirit doesn't *depend* on witnessing the experience of others (as the case of Cornelius' household shows; Acts 10:44), but it can be a great help. Seeing and believing are not necessarily contradictory, as we have already seen (in chapter 33). The average church today, exhibiting so little audible or visible evidence of the presence or power of the Spirit, hardly quickens the envy or expectancy of the new believer! It is much easier for someone to receive the Spirit in the context of a group filled with the Spirit. To be utterly practical, it is much more helpful for a group of 'helpers' to be 'praying in the Spirit' themselves (1 Cor 14:15; Eph 6:18) than 'watching to see what happens'. The person newly baptised in the Holy Spirit will then simply become part of the 'fellowship of the Spirit' (Greek: *koinonia* = common, shared). This will help them to realise immediately the corporate aspect of what has just happened (the truth of 'into one body'; see chapter 23 on 1 Cor 12:13).

The active element in 'receiving' may need to be carefully explained. Many try to be totally passive, assuming this to be the right posture. They need to be told that we do not become mechanical robots! The Spirit does not force his power on anyone, but with their co-operation enables them to say and do supernatural things. It needs to be emphasised that at the first Pentecost '*they* [not 'he', the Holy Spirit] began to speak in other languages' (Acts 2:4). The Holy Spirit told them what to say, but they did the speaking. So it is with all his gifts – he energises them (the literal word in 1 Cor 12:6) but we have to exercise them. If the Spirit so 'overwhelmed' us that we 'couldn't help' doing something, that would be a direct contradiction of his own 'fruit' of 'self-control' (Gal 5:23). His power is released when our wills are blended with his and we respond to his infilling by voluntarily overflowing.

Alas, there are many who want to be filled (inwardly and privately) who do not want to overflow (outwardly and publicly). When an individual introverted temperament is coupled with a national cultural reserve, the emotional barrier is enormous! Perhaps this is one reason why 'Pentecostalism' has grown more rapidly in the 'New World' than in Europe and in South America more than in North America. British religion has been so introverted that 'aerobic' worship is anathema. Demonstration of feeling and dignity of worship are regarded as totally incompatible. 'Hallelujah' may be said or sung liturgically but not uttered spontaneously! A person is admired for 'keeping it in' and despised for 'letting it out'. Yet this repressive attitude can be very damaging – for example, to the bereaved.

Even 'evangelical' understanding has equated 'inward' with 'spiritual' – the opposite of 'pentecostals', who often assume noise is power! Many never pray aloud, even when they are all alone, in spite of Jesus' instruction 'When you pray, *say* . . .' (Luke 11:1). The result is that many only express themselves spiritually in words when prompted from outside themselves (as when a hymn is announced) and have never learned to be prompted into speech from the inside. Others have been used to speaking only from their minds, carefully considering what to say before they say it; they have never learned to speak, or even contemplated the possibility of speaking, from their spirit (see 1 Cor 14:14–15 for the distinction). When Paul talks about shouting out spontaneously (the meaning of the Greek word *krazein* in Rom 8:16; cf. Matt 14:26, 30) the word 'Abba', this is referred to as 'the inward witness' and is assumed to be 'sensing' rather than 'shouting'!

This social pressure is seriously inhibiting when it comes to being filled to overflowing with the Spirit. The fear of making a fool of oneself in front of others is very real. At the original Pentecost the rumour soon spread that they were drunk, due to their uninhibited behaviour in public, which gave Peter a marvellous opening line for his sermon: 'What? At nine o'clock in the morning? The pubs aren't open yet!' Paul compared alcoholic intoxication with Spirit-filling as a means of having a good night out, but contrasted the results on the morning after (Eph 5:18)! Pentecost also illustrates the fact that it is much easier to disregard social restraints when others around you are doing the same – which is yet another reason for surrounding a seeker for the Spirit with a group praying and praising in the Spirit.

Some counsellors have encouraged 'babbling' as a first step. This is not likely to do any spiritual harm, but in some cases it has helped to overcome the psychological habit of thinking carefully about everything that is uttered and it has familiarised others with the unusual experience of hearing themselves utter things they do not understand (which is what they will be doing when they are fluent in an unknown language). But such 'babbling' must never be identified as the gift of tongues (which has clear grammar and syntax, whether it is recognised or not). I have preferred to encourage people to overcome their psychological hang-ups by getting alone and learning to 'shout and sing' (so frequently commanded in the Psalms) to the Lord at the top of their voices, dancing and jumping for joy at the thought of the sheer grace and mercy they have received – until they reach the point where they couldn't care who saw or heard them! A good number who have tried this found that they slipped almost imperceptibly into an overflow of the Spirit, without realising they were using a new language until they stopped to think about what was happening.

Alas, some fears have been fostered by bad teaching. If a person has already been in a church for some time, they may have had serious doubts sown in their minds by the teaching they have received – which prevents wholehearted reaching out in faith. Such 'double-mindedness' is paralysing (Jas 1:7). Two examples of such teaching are related to 'dispensational' and 'demonic' assertions.

First, some will have heard that supernatural experiences of 'baptism in' and 'gifts of' the Spirit belonged only to the apostolic age and were rendered obsolete by the completion of the New Testament. Such things were only given to attest the words of the apostles before they were finalised in written form, thus enabling their authenticity and authority to be recognised by the early church. It is a neat theory, but one without any real foundation in scripture itself. A person brought up on this teaching will be handicapped in faith and must be patiently shown that such manifestations were for 'the last days' (Joel 2:28; quoted in Acts 2:17) – which covers the entire period of church history from the first coming of Christ to his second; they will only 'pass away' when the 'perfect has come' and we see the Lord 'face to face' (1 Cor 13:8–12).

Second, some will have been warned so frequently to beware of 'satanic counterfeit' that a healthy fear will have become a paralysing phobia! This is often related to the teaching just mentioned: those who believe the 'gifts' of the Spirit are not for today will suspect all manifestations as being of evil inspiration. They fail to distinguish between divine, fleshly and satanic tongues (there are the same three types of 'faith-healing'). For every divine gift that is genuine, there is a fleshly substitute and a satanic counterfeit. Unless this is made very clear, there will be a real fear of asking for the right thing in case the wrong thing is received! Fortunately, Jesus himself anticipated this very problem. In the very same context of asking for the Spirit, he taught that a child asking for something wholesome from his father can rely on not being given something useless, harmful or dangerous (Luke 11:11–13). The only circumstance in which a satanic counterfeit might be received is where occult involvement has not been fully renounced. For the rest, the heavenly Father may be fully trusted to give what is requested.

A SPECIFIC PROBLEM: OLDER BELIEVERS WHO HAVE NOT RECEIVED

One final situation needs to be considered. What about the disciple who having repented and believed was baptised and has continued in the Christian life for many years, growing in grace and holiness, maturing in trust and obedience, being faithful and fruitful in service, and being devoted and dependable in character – yet never having had an experience which could be called 'baptism in the Spirit'? Do they need to 'begin again', as it were? Do they lack anything? Is their salvation not complete? Is their service not effective? Two points need to be made.

On the one hand, it would be quite wrong to belittle anything of the past or present. It has all been the work of the Holy Spirit. He has been 'with' them all the way through, whether they realised it or not (see chapter 12). Even before they repented and believed, he was convicting them of sin, righteousness and judgement (John 16:8–11). Everything they have learned of spiritual value has been the result of his teaching, either directly or through others. He has no more been a 'stranger' to them than he was to the disciples before Pentecost. They may, like them, have been able to perform the occasional miracle, even though none of this is what the New Testament means by 'receiving the Spirit'.

On the other hand, it would also be quite wrong to imply that nothing more is available or desirable. It is quite illogical to compare a mature 'non-charismatic' believer with an immature 'Spirit-filled' one! The real comparison is with what either would be like if they had more – more gifts in the former case, more fruit in the latter! The believer is intended to have a conscious and continuous relationship with the third person of the Trinity as well as the first and the second – and to be fully aware of the supernatural resources available through this relationship (notice the sheer 'boldness' of the early Christians, which was quite unrelated to educational advantages – Acts 4:13, 31). It is sad when a real 'saint' seems to know the Holy Scripture rather better than the Holy Spirit. When the New Testament speaks about the 'indwelling' Spirit, this refers to a dynamic state rather than a static status (see chapter 21 on Rom 8:9). The 'receiving' of the Spirit is followed by God going on giving and working miracles (Gal 3:2, 5)

There are many testimonies to the new dimensions, even later in the Christian life, that are enjoyed after the Spirit is 'received' in the New Testament way. New ministries open up to the Lord (particularly in praise and prayer), to others (healing can be given to the sick as well as sympathy and succour; prophecy as well as preaching; particular as well as general guidance) and, perhaps the most surprising, to oneself: (the prime purpose of tongues is to 'edify' onself; it is profitless in public without the companion gift of interpretation).

The only sadness such 'older' believers feel is that they did not discover such exciting dimensions of ministry years before. They now realise that the 'fullness' of the Spirit is not a reward for faithful service at the end but the equipment for fruitful service at the beginning. I vividly recall a Welsh evangelist pointing this out by reminding his audience that Pentecost is to be found in the second chapter of Acts, not in the twenty-eighth! All would agree with the old proverb: better late than never . . . but better never late!

Temporally speaking, the nearer Spirit-baptism comes to water-baptism the better; and the nearer water-baptism comes to repentance and faith the better. For the four elements of initiation belong to one another and take their meaning from one another. What God has joined together, let no man put asunder!

36   SAVED AT LAST

By now many readers will be burning to ask the question: At what point in the 'process' of being born again can a person be said to be 'saved'? Sometimes the query is directly linked to one of the four elements of initiation. Is it necessary to be baptised in water in order to be 'saved'? Must one speak in tongues to be 'saved'? Few Protestants ever ask if faith is necessary to salvation!

This aspect of the subject was deliberately postponed until the end, primarily because preconceived notions of the meaning of 'saved' could have clouded the overall thesis of the fourfold complex of initiation. The challenge must now be squarely faced!

We could begin with a list of biblical references to the word 'saved'. It is never directly connected with the element of repentance, though 'perish' and 'forgiveness' certainly are (Luke 13:3; 24:47). It is used in conjunction with faith (Acts 16:30–31; Rom 10:10), with water-baptism (Mark 16:16; 1 Pet 3:21) and with Spirit-baptism (Tit 3:5). It is therefore comparatively easy to show from the New Testament that 'saved' involves all four elements. But this is more likely to aggravate than relieve anxiety in the questioner! Does this mean that if one or more of the four is lacking, the person is still 'lost'? And, at a theological level, how does this fit the doctrine of 'justification by faith alone'?

THE MEANING OF 'SAVED'

Clearly, the first thing we need to establish is precisely *what* one is 'saved' from. Most would say that we are saved from eternal punishment (i.e. hell).

Simplistic evangelistic preaching has created a widespread impression that the gospel is basically an insurance policy for the next world. The preacher faces his audience with the challenge 'If you died tonight, would you find yourself in heaven or hell?' This may produce fear of hell, but not necessarily that fear of the Lord which is the 'beginning of wisdom' (notice in Rev 6:16–17 that the fear of facing God is greater than the fear of being destroyed in a landslide; and Jesus himself warned his hearers to fear him who can destroy rather than being destroyed – Matt 10:28; the focus throughout is on personal wrath rather than impersonal ruin – Luke 3:7; Rom 2:5).

Apostolic preaching was as concerned with this world as with the next. The kingdom of heaven was now re-established on earth; it could be entered in life, not just at death (note Jesus' extraordinary claim that the Son of Man who came down from heaven is still in heaven – John 3:13; some copyists couldn't cope with such a paradox, so the latter phrase is missing from some manuscripts). Eternal life begins here and now (John 3:36). The apostles were more likely to have challenged their hearers with the question: If you are still alive tomorrow, will you be living in the kingdom of Satan or the kingdom of God and the Son he loves (Col 1:13)? They were more concerned to get their hearers on 'the Way' (Acts 18:25f.; 19:9,23; 24:14,22) than 'over the line'; they talked less of being born again than of being fully alive.

To put it another way, 'saved' meant 'salvaged from sins' rather than 'safe from hell'. The latter was the result of the former. Jesus was not given his name because he would save his people from hell, but because he would save them from their sins (Matt 1:21). Many people want to be saved from hell; few want to be saved from their sins. Most want to enjoy the pleasure of sin and escape the penalty. Full fourfold initiation is for those who want to escape from their sins, who have really understood the gospel (offering the freedom to live right) and truly want to be 'saved' to righteousness. Though water-baptism and Spirit-baptism have some relevance to the future (note 'heirs' and 'hope' in Tit 3:7), their primary reference is to the cleansed life here and now, purified from the past and empowered for the present.

'Salvation' is therefore a continuing concept in the New Testament, not so much a point beyond which one is 'safe' as a *process* through which one is being 'salvaged' ('salvage' is much nearer the word 'salvation' than 'safety'). There is the classic story of a Salvation Army girl asking Bishop Westcott if he was 'saved'; the Greek scholar replied 'Do you mean *sotheis*, *sesosmenos* or *sozomenos*?' (in English: 'Do you mean have I been saved, am I being saved or will I be saved?')! He was gently rebuking her ignorance of the past, present and future tenses of the verb 'save' in the New Testament (Rom 8:24; 1 Cor 15:2; Rom 5:9). For no believer is the process of salvation yet complete; whether it is certain to be completed is quite a different question, which we shall come to later.

THE RELATION BETWEEN JUSTIFICATION, SANCTIFICATION AND GLORIFICATION

The past, present and future tenses of the verb 'save' are somewhat analogous to the three nouns 'justification', 'sanctification' and 'glorification'. Together, they constitute full salvation, full redemption. Through them a person is delivered from the penalty, power and presence of sin. The two questions that must now be faced are, first, When does justification take place? and, second, Does justification guarantee glorification without sanctification? To put these questions in the wording of the cliché 'once saved, always saved' – When does 'once saved' happen and does 'always saved' automatically follow?

Justification and the four elements of initiation
'Justification' is a horrible word for a wonderful experience. The Latinised English word needs 'Saxonising' before it can travel from the head to the heart. The 'Pidgin English' translation does this perfectly – 'God 'e say 'im alright'! It was originally a legal term from the law-court, and was the judge's declaration of acquittal on the ground of innocence (it was *not* a

pardon for the guilty). When God justifies a sinner, that would be a complete legal fiction unless the sin had already been atoned for in the eyes of the law; this is precisely the case, because his Son has already 'paid the penalty' (Rom 3:21–26 is the key passage). 'Justification' means that a holy God can 'accept' an evil person, 'adopt' him into his family and call him a 'saint'!

The *only* condition demanded of the sinner is 'faith' in the death, burial and resurrection of God's Son. However, an over-simplified view of 'faith' has led to an attenuated understanding of 'initiation' into faith.

For example, an excessive emphasis on justification 'by faith alone' could lead some to conclude that repentance for sin is not essential, or at least not essential at the beginning. It may be true that more repentance usually occurs after believing, but it is certainly untrue that no repentance need come before believing! Repentance is properly seen as an expression of faith; who would turn from their sins to God unless they already had some belief in his existence, character and power? It is probably for this reason that Peter recognised that God had already 'accepted' Cornelius (Acts 10:34–35); and that Jesus said the tax-collector went home 'justified' (Luke 18:14). Conversely, Simon had believed and been baptised, but was 'not right with God' because he had not repented (Acts 8:21).

Baptism is also an (indeed, is *the*) expression of 'faith', the first 'action of faith' (see chapter 28 on Jas 2:14–26), the first step in a believer's intention to 'obey the gospel' (2 Thess 1:8). It could be significant that Paul lists 'washed' before 'justified' (in 1 Cor 6:11; though even 'sanctified' comes before 'justified' in that context!). Most striking is that Paul follows a description of being 'saved' through water-baptism and Spirit-baptism with the summary phrase 'having been justified by his grace . . .' (Tit 3:4–7).

It is therefore highly probable that the apostles saw repentance and baptism as integral to that 'faith' through which sinners are justified (note how Peter made repentance and baptism essential for the remission of sins – Acts 2:38). In no way was either regarded as a human 'work' that made a person 'worthy' of God's approval.

Spirit-baptism is not so much a necessary ground for justification as the essential proof of it! How can anyone be absolutely sure that their repentance, faith and baptism have been adequate? Today, this question is often answered by an exegesis of the scripture ('God says it in his word, I believe it in my heart, that settles it in my mind'). Such 'assurance' was not available to New Testament converts, since the New Testament had not yet been written! The original 'guarantee' was not found in logic but in life, not in deductive exposition but in dynamic experience – namely, by an outpouring of the Spirit. The gift of the Spirit was the basis of assurance (Rom 8:15–16; 1 John 3:24; 4:13). When this gift had been 'received' (an inward experience with outward evidence – see chapter 5), it was certain that the person had been accepted by God (Acts 15:8) and therefore justified. The gift was God's confirmation, his seal on the transaction, his deposit anticipating all that would follow.

So faith, expressed in repentance and baptism, is the necessary condition for justification and the gift of the Spirit its necessary corroboration. It is at this point that someone invariably asks: What about the dying thief? It is assumed that his case cancels all other New Testament teaching on initiation! The answer (spelled out fully in chapter 9) is that he did everything he could under his exceptional circumstances; water-baptism and Spirit-baptism were beyond his reach and his repentance could only be expressed in words rather than deeds. He provides no precedent whatever for those who are able to have full Christian initiation. At most, his situation may be cited to the dying, but it is quite inappropriate for the living. However, if a person, through no fault or hesitation of their own, was unable to complete the normal process of initiation, the dying thief's example alone would encourage hope of an entrance to heaven.

For those who can have the whole initiation package, there is no excuse. It is exceedingly difficult to plead that 'I'm a special case' in the light of Jesus' own submission to water-baptism and his reception of the Spirit immediately afterwards. There is something wrong with an attitude that asks what are the minimum requirements for salvation; genuine repentance seeks the maximum resources available in God to live a righteous life.

Sanctification and perseverance

Whether all four elements are necessary for justification or not (I have implied they are, or at least the first three are), they are all vital to sanctification. But how far is sanctification necessary to glorification? It is astonishing how many people have the impression that justification is absolutely indispensable while sanctification is only relatively desirable! The beginning of the Christian life is thought to guarantee its ending, regardless of what happens in between.

But the New Testament writers insist that their readers 'make every effort . . . to be holy; without holiness no-one will see the Lord' (Heb 12:14). Jesus himself told a parable about the man who accepted the king's invitation to a wedding banquet, but failed to turn up in acceptable dress (Matt 22:1–14), the whole point being that to be chosen depends on more than responding to a call.

How safe is 'saved'? Does justification guarantee sanctification? Is once saved inevitably always saved? It may well be that the tension engendered in some people by the discussion of the relationship between justification and the four elements of initiation is due to the anxiety about how soon a person can be absolutely sure of going to heaven if they die. Are people more anxious to know how little they need to be safe than how much they can have to be salvaged? Has too much emphasis been put on justification and too little on sanctification when preaching the gospel? Is a place in heaven more important to secure than a character of holiness?

To ask such questions is not necessarily to fall into the trap of teaching justification by faith and sanctification by works, though that is a real danger. Both justification and sanctification are results of the work of grace and the activity of God. The gospel is not an offer of justification and a demand for sanctification; both are on offer in the true gospel, which is based firmly in the righteousness of God (Rom 3:21; 10:3). But both have to be appropriated and applied by man. Assuming that grace is resistible (Acts 7:51), what is the position of someone who has received the grace of justification but refused the grace of sanctification?

I am not eager to tread on such controversial ground! My fear is that particular schools of theology (notably the 'Calvinist' and 'Reformed') could use my comments here to dismiss the whole book, though my basic thesis does not stand or fall with this question. The relevance of this question to the whole discussion is that those who teach that eternal security depends on just one single step of faith have encouraged the 'only believe' kind of invitation and initiation. '*Once* believe and be saved' has reinforced the appeal '*Only* believe and be saved.' Both baptisms (water and Spirit) then lose their priority and slip into a secondary place, becoming at worst merely optional extras.

The question whether justification is through faith alone or through faith preceded by repentance, both consummated in water-baptism and confirmed by Spirit-baptism, is not here the basic issue. The real question is whether either route, short or long, leads inevitably, and without further development, to glory.

The bulk of New Testament teaching on the subject encourages belief in the 'perseverance *of* the saints': the Lord is able to guard what has been entrusted to him (2 Tim 1:12), to keep us from falling (Jude 24) and to complete the work he has begun in us (Phil 1:6); none can pluck his sheep out of his hand (John 10:28–29); nothing can separate us from the love of God (Rom 8:38–39). Such statements are too numerous to list.

But there are also many exhortations that contain another doctrine – 'perseverance *by* the saints', with warnings that this is by no means automatic or inevitable. We have already noted the New Testament emphasis on the need for continuity of faith (see chapter 3). There are also examples in the New Testament of a failure in faith (or in faithfulness, since both Hebrew and Greek use only one word to cover both 'faith' and 'faithfulness'). There are the unreliable steward, the foolish virgins and the unprofitable servant (Matt 24:45–25:30), whose fates can only be understood in terms of hell. There is the failure of some germinated and growing seed to reach maturity and fruitfulness (Mark 4:16–19). There is the statement that 'he who stands firm to the end will be saved' (Mark 13:13; cf. Luke 21:19). Branches that do not bear fruit will be cut off and thrown into the fire (John 15:6). Christians are in as much danger of being 'cut off' as the Jews were, if they do not 'continue' in God's kindness (Rom 11:22; this is particularly significant in such a context of divine predestination as Rom 9–11). The failure of the majority of the Hebrews delivered from Egypt by the blood of the Passover lamb and baptised in the Red Sea to complete their journey into the land of promise and rest is used as a solemn warning to Christians by three apostolic writers (1 Cor 10:1–5; Heb 4:1–11; Jude 5). To say that the danger is only 'hypothetical' is to neutralise the warning. The whole epistle to the Hebrews is an exhortation to 'persevere' and contains the most solemn warning in the New Testament about the consequences of apostasy, significantly in the context of the only complete account of initiation in all the epistles (Heb 6:1–6). There is also the hint that those who fail to overcome are in danger of having their names erased from the book of life (Rev 3:5).

Such scriptures must be taken seriously. There is a beautiful balance in the New Testament between our responsibility to keep ourselves in God's love (Jude 21) and his ability to keep us from falling (Jude 24). (In my judgement, I. Howard Marshall's *Kept by the Power of God* (Bethany Fellowship, 1969) is the most balanced book on this whole subject.)

In conclusion, I feel it is probably better to keep the word 'safe' for the end of the journey, when we finally get there, and to use 'being saved' until we do! After all, the first name for the Christian religion was, appropriately, 'the Way' (Acts 18:25, 26; 19:9, 23). It is better to imagine salvation as a horizontal line along which one is travelling from the past (justified) through the present (sanctified) to the future (glorified) – rather than a vertical line one has crossed from the 'unsaved' to the 'saved'.

Then 'conversion' will be seen as a departure rather than an arrival, a beginning rather than an end. Bunyan spoke of *The Pilgrim's Progress* (and understood that at the end of the journey there was 'a way to hell from the very gates of heaven').

Whether one believes it is possible or impossible for a Christian to lose his salvation, the distinction made earlier between 'safe' and 'salvaged' is still valid and important. The point may be made in quite a different way by asking whether it is possible to accept Jesus as Saviour (for justification) without accepting him as Lord (for sanctification), whether it is possible to trust him without obeying him. One of the most effective pleas for an integrated gospel that includes both may be found in John MacArthur's *The Gospel according to Jesus* (Academic Books, Zondervan, 1988).

Birth is, after all, only the prelude to life. A good start is one thing; a good finish is another. Patient pastors are needed as much as enthusiastic evangelists. Decisions for Christ must become disciples of Christ. When the midwife's work is done, the parents' labour has just begun!

EPILOGUE: A WORD TO THE FAMILY

Normal birth is into a family, both the first, physical, birth and the second, spiritual, birth. There is one striking difference between all other creatures and the human species, whether natural (*homo sapiens* – the 'old man' in Adam) or spiritual (*homo novus* – the 'new man' in Christ). Man takes an incredibly long time to mature and needs the greatest amount of care to do so. His very complexity, combining an affinity with earth and heaven, increases his vulnerability during the process of 'growing up'.

THE IMPORTANCE OF DISCIPLING

Birth is, after all, the beginning of life. But it does not bring with it a guarantee of continued, never mind developed, existence. A baby can be abandoned. There will always be a battle with infant mortality. Post-natal care is essential. In terms of modern evangelism, 'follow-up' is vital. There is a balance to be redressed. Because of an emphasis on being 'safe from hell' rather than 'salvaged from sin', too much stress has been placed on the need to be 'born again' rather than to be 'healthily alive'.

A return to the concept of 'making disciples', instead of 'getting decisions', will correct the anomaly. Parturition (child-birth) must be followed by education (see chapter 7 on Matt 28:19–20). However, 'teach' in the New Testament is 'manual' rather than 'mental'. It is concerned with the practical as well as the theoretical. 'Disciple' is nearer the word 'apprentice' than the word 'student'. (See Philip Vogel, *Go and Make Apprentices* (Kingsway, 1987) for further detail on this understanding of 'disciple'.) Instead of putting the new Christian with all the other new Christians in a 'class' or through a 'course' for beginners, we need to link them with older and more mature Christians (of the same sex, lest Satan gets a foothold!). Again, the eye-gate will be more effective than the ear-gate in the process of learning. A good discipler will imitate the Lord and invite the disciples to 'come and see' (John 1:39, 46). Indeed, imitation plays a vital role in discipleship (1 Cor 4:16; 1 Thess 1:6; 2:14; Heb 6:12; 13:7). A personal and intimate relationship with a true saint will teach more about holiness than all the books on sanctification!

SEARCHING FOR A SPIRITUAL HOME

Life was much simpler in the days of the New Testament, not least in ecclesiastical matters. Evangelism and church planting were two sides of the same coin. There was usually only one church in each place; conversions took place through that and into that one fellowship. There is therefore no New Testament exhortation to 'join a church', only to 'stay' in it (Heb 10:25). To be born into Christ was to be born into the church; to be baptised into the Head was to be baptised into the body. There was no search for a 'suitable' spiritual home for the new baby. Initiation and incorporation were one and the same thing.

Two developments in our day have made 'joining' necessary. First, the rise of denominations (each with its own traditions) has produced a multiplicity of local churches (in England most people with cars have a choice of at least twenty within easy reach!). Second, the rise of evangelistic crusades and other organised outreaches which are interdenominational or even non-denominational has meant that people 'come to Christ' outside the context of a local church, making it necessary to encourage the 'adoption' of spiritual babies.

Which church should be selected as a potential home for the new disciple? Denominational diplomacy can cloud the issue. A pure concern for the new baby simplifies the search: where is the best post-natal care to be found? The church with the most life and love is likely to be the best, whatever its label.

Fishing needs to be supplemented by shepherding; the evangelist by a pastor. One is a quantity person, anxious to see as many started as possible; the other is a quality person, anxious to see them finished, however few. The two functions rarely coincide in the same person, though Peter was called to do both (Mark 1:17; John 21:15–17). They should both be represented in a healthy church, in the leadership as well as the membership. Where this is the case, there should be no problem in finding a family to care for the new baby. Alas, more often the evangelists work outside the church and the pastors inside, with little liaison between them.

CRITERION FOR CHURCH MEMBERSHIP

Membership in the early church was not formal (a roll in a book) but functional (a role in a body). The only conditions for full membership were the four things discussed in this book: repentance, faith, water-baptism and Spirit-baptism. Of the four, the last was the most important for church membership; to be able to function in the body it was necessary to be 'baptised in the Spirit' (see chapter 21 on Rom 8:9 and chapter 23 on 1 Cor 12:13). There are two practical implications for church membership today.

First, nothing *more* than these four things should be required for full membership of a local church. So often, further conditions are imposed on a new convert – an extra ceremony (e.g. episcopal confirmation), a particular 'commitment' (e.g. tithing), more rules (e.g. no smoking, drinking, gambling, dancing, make-up). All these matters should be dealt with after becoming a member, not before. Reception into the body should mark the beginning of training, not, as is usually the case, the end of it. A person should be accepted because they have been justified (Rom 15:7), not rejected because they are not yet sanctified enough for a church that considers itself 'pure'. The staircase should be inside the front door, not outside! Someone who has been properly birthed will be eager to learn and often embarrassingly teachable! Of course, discipline may be necessary later, if there is wilful persistence in sins, even to the point of temporary exclusion from the family (1 Cor 5:1–13; note that this excommunication was a majority decision of the church members, leading to the recalcitrant's repentance and return – 2 Cor 2:6–7). Perhaps our distaste for such later discipline lies behind our raised threshold of entrance: if we make it hard for them to get in we are not so likely to have to throw them out! But such thinking is flawed: the church is a nursery for those who have departed from sinning, not a rest-home for those who have arrived at sainthood!

Second, nothing *less* than these four things should be required for full membership of a local church. Classes before admission should cover all four thoroughly, making sure that they have each become a matter of experience rather than a subject of education. Two groups need particularly to be borne in mind. There are those converts who have started their initiation in another context (they may have gone forward at an evangelistic crusade and had their names passed on to the church); it is vital to complete their initiation before receiving them into membership, whatever they have been told by a counsellor or assumed about their decision. Then there are those who want to transfer their membership from another church where the four things were not insisted upon, or, in some cases, not even expected. This is a more delicate situation, requiring firm but loving attention. They should be fully informed, through careful biblical teaching, of the church's conviction that these four things represent the basic minimum foundation for the corporate life of the church as well as the individual life of the Christian. Without all of them life will be handicapped rather than healthy. If they are not willing to seek such 'wholeness', it may be questioned whether their transfer should be accepted. Each local church is directly responsible to the Head of the church for maintaining proper standards, whatever happens elsewhere (see Rev 2–3, where Jesus deals separately with seven churches in the same district). The situation cannot be corrected everywhere unless it is put right somewhere. One good maternity home is better than none! Many good ones soon reduce the mortality rate.

To repeat myself, a 'normal Christian birth' is the beginning, not the end; the departure, not the arrival platform; the start, not the finish. A good beginning can make all the difference, provided it is followed through. A holistic birth into a happy family is God's intention for every human being he has made and loved. Incredibly, he has given the responsibility for birthing and bringing up babies, both physical and spiritual, to us human beings. It is a solemn trust.

I have nearly always been able to find a suitable verse by Charles Wesley to conclude a message – and this is no exception! Let the reader conclude this study by saying (or singing) aloud:

> A charge to keep I have:
> A God to glorify,
> A never-dying soul to save
> And fit it for the sky.

APPENDIX 1   INFANT BAPTISM

Baptism is almost universally accepted as an essential part of initiation into the church. In Europe the vast majority of baptisms are of babies. In England two-thirds of the population have been 'christened' (though baby-baptising denominations are generally in decline, while believer-baptising churches are holding steady or growing). In the Third World the majority of baptisms are of believers. The American scene is shifting from the European to the Third World pattern, with the main growth at the Baptist/Pentecostal end of the spectrum. As Christianity increasingly becomes a persecuted minority force in a pagan mission field, the universal trend in baptismal practice is from babies to believers.

HISTORICAL CONSIDERATIONS

How and when did 'infant baptism' begin? Why was it continued? How does it fit into the New Testament outline of initiation? What is its significance or effect when given to a baby incapable of repentance or faith?

In seeking an answer we shall use the term 'baby' rather than the ambiguous 'infant' (Southern Baptists in the USA often baptise 'infants' of seven or even under!) and we shall approach the subject historically, noting the principles behind the practice at different stages of its development. As with so many church traditions, baby baptism began for one reason, but continued for quite different reasons (or even for no reason at all except that for which Mount Everest was climbed – 'because it is there'!). It has been shrewdly described as 'a practice in search of a theology'.

Most scholars acknowledge that there are no direct references to the practice in the New Testament. Some claim to find indirect references, but the evidence is at best circumstantial (see chapter 15 on 'you and your children', chapter 19 on the 'households' and chapter 22 on 'children are holy'). The practice can only be established from scripture on general theological principles (see below), not particular textual precepts (it is never commanded by Christ or the apostles).

What has in fact happened over the centuries is that doctrinal truths, perfectly valid in their own context, have been transferred from elsewhere in scripture and attached to the practice of baptism, invariably distorting the meaning of the rite and diverting its application to those for whom it was never intended. The door was thus opened to speculation, sentiment and superstition.

The first explicit mention of baby baptism is around the end of the second century AD. By then baptism was beginning to have a greater prominence in salvation than it had previously had. Two quite opposite developments took place – for exactly the same reason! On the one hand, baptism was postponed until physical death, for fear that sinning after it would lead to hell. On the other hand, baptism was brought forward to physical birth, for fear that a baby would go to hell before sinning (understandable in the light of the high mortality rate among babies in those days). In both cases, baptism was considered the only means of salvation.

Eternal suffering in hell was later felt to be somewhat rough justice for babies who hadn't sinned and even for baptised adults who had. This is indicated by the development of two other church traditions – *limbus infantum* (limbo) for the unbaptised baby (less unpleasant than hell but just as permanent) and 'purgatory' for the baptised adult (nearly as unpleasant as hell but less permanent). What was not in dispute for over a millennium was that baptism *saved from hell*, by removing 'original', that is inherited, sin from the baby and both original and actual sin from the adult.

At the same time as babies began to be baptised (it was not universally practised until Christianity was 'established' by Constantine as the religion of the Roman Empire) there was a general drift in the church from the 'substance' of the 'new' covenant back into the 'shadows' of the 'old' covenant (priesthood, altars, 'temples', vestments, incense, etc.). Furthermore, the church structure was increasingly aligned to the administration of the Empire (many bishops to one church in the New Testament became one bishop to many churches, with regional and metropolitan hierarchies; the process reaching its climax when the Bishop of Rome took over the Emperor's title 'Pontifex Maximus' and became an international figure, a spiritual 'father', a 'papa' or pope).

'Christendom', as this church state blend came to be known, had much more in common with the Old Testament people of God, the 'theocracy' of Israel, than the New Testament church; 'priests and kings' were once again state officials rather than titles of all believers (Rev 1:6). Not surprisingly, a parallel began to be drawn between baptism and circumcision, both being regarded as a recognition of having been born into 'God's' people as subjects of his kingdom. However, in spite of this parallel, it needs to be stated that baptism was still considered an act of redemption, which circumcision never had been. Through it the baby was set free from 'original sin', was 'born from above' and thereby obtained for eternal salvation.

There are some bizarre tales of medieval (and modern) missionary expansion in which priests 'evangelised' newly discovered territory by surreptitiously baptising babies. However, it is clear that while the baptism of a baby was considered sufficient qualification for entrance to heaven, should it die, this was not enough for full membership of the church! The New Testament practice of following baptism with the laying-on of hands for the reception of the Spirit was also transferred to babies (with a 'chrism' of oil to represent the Spirit, presumably in the absence of other outward evidence). Later, this part of the rite was postponed until puberty and became the ceremony of 'confirmation' (regarded as the moment of admission to Holy Communion and church membership), at least in the Western church (Eastern Orthodox churches remained more consistent, if even less scriptural, in giving baptism, 'chrism' and communion to babies). Through the Middle Ages the focus of initiation shifted from baptism to confirmation (for centuries the 'bishop' did the baptising and the local 'priest' the later confirming; but this gradually reversed and episcopal confirmation prevails today).

Christendom had something else in common with the ancient kingdom of Israel – it was more comfortable with its kings and priests than its prophets, with their constant call to move from tradition to truth, from rites to reality, from sophistication to simplicity. The first 'protest' against the blurred boundary between 'church' and 'world' led to the formation of monastic orders, though these would remain within the ecclesiastical framework. Later, there would be many independent groups seeking to recover the character of the early church by making the New Testament their only 'rule'; most of these would restore the practice of believers' baptism. Indeed, a Catholic prelate was later to inform the Council of Trent that if these 'baptists' had not been so ruthlessly suppressed over the previous thousand years they would by then have been more trouble than all the Reformers put together!

The biggest factor in the change from small protesting groups which could be suppressed to large 'Protestant' bodies which would secede was undoubtedly the widespread rediscovery of the Bible. Erasmus' study of the Hebrew and Greek manuscripts behind the Latin version, combined with Luther's exposition and translation into German, together with Gutenberg's invention of printing enabled many to draw comparisons (usually odious!) between the church of apostolic and medieval times.

A theology based on scripture alone soon concluded that salvation is by grace alone and justification is through faith alone. The idea that forgiveness could be earned, much less bought and sold (the final straw for Luther was when 'indulgences' reducing the time in purgatory for dead relatives were hawked round Europe by Tetzel to finance the building of St Peter's in Rome), became the new 'anathema' (a proper application of Gal 1:9). Under the banner of 'The just shall live by faith' (Hab 2:4; see chapter 3), medieval accretions were swept away – including the 'sacrifice' of the mass, the adoration of relics and statues, prayers to departed saints, pilgrimages to sacred sites, clerical celibacy and a host of other pious practices without scriptural warrant.

Yet baptism of babies persisted. The Protestant Reformers had quickly realised the incompatibility between salvation by baptism and justification by faith. At first, all of them advocated a return to the New Testament practice of believers' baptism.

Since this is largely unknown, and may be widely doubted, we need to quote their own words (for these quotations I am indebted to a remarkable book by T. E. Watson, *Baptism Not For Infants* (Walter, 1962), in which he establishes the case for believers' baptism entirely by quotations from the writings of paedobaptists!).

First Luther:

Without personal faith no one should be baptised. Where we cannot be sure that young children are themselves believers and themselves have faith, my advice and judgement are that it is better to delay, and even better that we baptise no more children, so that we do not with such foolery and tricks make a mockery of or outrage the blessed majesty of God. (Sermon for Third Sunday after Epiphany)

INFANT BAPTISM

Next Calvin:

As Christ enjoins them to teach before baptising, and desires that none but believers shall be admitted to baptism, it would appear that baptism is not properly administered unless when it is preceded by faith. (*Harmony of the Gospels*, vol. 3, p. 386, commenting on Matt 28); Baptism is, as it were, an appurtenance of faith, and therefore it is later in order; secondly, if it be given without faith, whose seal it is, it is both wicked and too gross a profanation. (*Commentary on Acts*, vol. 1, p. 362).

Zwingli also maintained that baptism was dependent on faith and meaningless without it (*Works*, vol. 4, p. 191); he thought it should be deferred until the years of discretion (Vadian II, p. 231). 'Nothing', he said, 'grieves me more than that at the present I have to baptise children, for I know it ought not to be done' (Quellen IV, p. 184). With commendable honesty, he admitted that 'If, however, I were to terminate the practice then I fear that I would lose my prebend [salary].' However, his understanding that baptism, like the Lord's Supper, was purely a symbol and had no 'sacramental' value or effect, made it easier for him to change his views later.

Why, then, did none of the Reformers practise what they preached? The answer is disturbingly simple. They were opposing an ecclesiastical authority with biblical authority, but they were also relying on civic authority to help them. The success of the Reformation rested on this alliance between church and state, though the pact took rather different forms in the German and Swiss contexts. Inevitably, the confusion between citizenship of the state and membership of the church was perpetuated. It is impossible to maintain a 'national' church without welcoming into it all born within the nation. Baptism becomes a covenantal seal of civic-religious membership of a nation regarded as a 'new Israel' under God. (This is clearly explained in Johannes Warns, *Baptism* (Paternoster Press, 1957), which is subtitled 'Studies in the original Christian baptism, its history and conflicts, its relation to a State or National Church and its significance for the present time'.)

This was the 'positive' reason; but there was also a negative one. What the Reformers had preached about baptism began to be practised by others! Those who had been baptised as babies without faith now sought 're-baptism' as believers (the nickname given to them was 'Anabaptists', from the Greek word *ana* = again). At first

313

this was considered simply as disloyalty to the church (it still is!) and to those still seeking to reform it from within (they still are!). But when it was realised that believers' baptism carries with it the concept of a 'gathered' church, (as distinct from a 'national' church), and one totally separated from civic authority, re-baptism came to be associated with treason against the state, especially a state that had 'officially' become 'Protestant'. This led to a reaction against believers' baptism and the persecution of those who were re-baptised (the punishment by drowning is an ineradicable stain on the record of the Swiss Reformers).

Believers' baptism was therefore suppressed yet again, though not this time with the same success. Many 'anabaptist' groups became eccentric and extreme when forced into isolation, but they have had a lasting influence. In England and the Low Countries, the concept of a 'gathered' church, independent of the state, took firm root; attempts to suppress it there led the Pilgrim Fathers to take it with them to the New World, which helps explain why America has never had an 'established' religion, though it regards itself as a Christian nation – and why the Baptist and Pentecostal churches are so strong and socially acceptable. But we are rushing too far ahead . . .

THEOLOGICAL CONSIDERATIONS

How could the mainline Reformers justify their complete reversal on the subject of baptism, either to their own conscience or to their followers? Clearly, they had to find some biblical or theological justification for maintaining the medieval practice. Luther rather feebly argued that it was impossible to say that a baby didn't have faith, but he never really resolved the dilemma. For Calvin, help was at hand. Zwingli's successor at Zurich, Bullinger, came up with a totally new concept in theology – he took the many covenants in the Bible (note the plural in Rom 9:4), lumped them all into one and called it 'the covenant of grace' (a phrase found nowhere in scripture). The continuity between the 'old' and 'new' covenants was so emphasised that their essential discontinuity was neutralised. Most significantly, entrance to both covenants was essentially the same: normally by inheritance through physical descent from those already in the covenant. Baptism can therefore be seen as a straight trans-mutation of circumcision, to be applied at the same age. Of course, to 'stay' in the covenant requires later faith in Jesus for a Christian child, as later obedience to the law was required of a Jewish child; but both were already in the covenant by birth and therefore eligible for its physical 'sign and seal'.

Since this 'covenantal' theology has now been so widely disseminated and is so commonly used to justify baby baptism today (for example, by all Presbyterians and some Anglicans, most of whom are evangelical), we need to make some critical appraisal before considering yet other variations of theory and practice.

Covenant theology and the link between baby baptism and circumcision

The greatest problem at the theological level is the biblical emphasis on the discontinuity between the old and new covenants, the latter rendering the former obsolete (Heb 8:13 is rarely quoted by covenantalists; note also the use of 'unlike' in Jer 31:32). In particular, the old covenant was collective, while the new covenant is individual. This major shift had been predicted by the prophets of the Old Testament (Jer 31:29–30; Ezek 18:1–32; Joel 2:32), but it was even more clearly preached by the apostles in the New Testament ('each one of you' in Acts 2:38 is typical). There is a 'whoever' at the heart of the gospel (John 3:16; Rom 10:10–13). Both John and Jesus went out of their way to repudiate any hereditary rights to a place in the kingdom of God (Matt 3:9; John 8:39). Spiritual birth, not physical, is now the qualification.

Baptism is never identified with circumcision in the New Testament, an astonishing omission considering all the controversy the early Christians had about the Jewish rite (Col 2:9–12 is not an exception; see chapter 25) and in the light of the fact that both were 'physical' acts. If there were any parallel at all, it would be with Abraham's own circumcision, which came *after* he believed, as a 'seal' upon his faith, making him the 'father of all believers', whether they are circumcised or not (Rom 4:9–12; note that believers are never said to have shared in the 'covenant' made with Abraham). Later circumcisions of his descendants were not a 'seal' on their faith, coming before they believed, if they did at all; it was a token of the promise that would one day reach one of them (Abraham's 'seed', singular – Gal 3:16). Christ, having fulfilled this promised 'line', makes the rite obsolete for spiritual purposes, but it may still be sometimes desirable for social reasons (as in Timothy's case, even though he had been baptised – Acts 16:3).

Those who preach 'covenantal' baptism for babies must be expected to practise it! On the one hand, the practice of indiscriminate baptism must be renounced. The parents themselves must be believers, particularly the husband as head of the family (the substitution of 'godparents' with their vicarious vows cannot fulfil covenant requirements). Furthermore, in the light of the thesis in these pages, parents must have received the Spirit. On the other hand, those baptisms done outside the covenant, when parents were not believers – probably the vast majority of christenings in Britain – must be repudiated and repeated. The recipients must be told they have not had Christian baptism and need to be re-baptised, which should then be done. I have encountered a growing number of clergy who will discourage unbelieving parents (few have the courage to refuse) – but very, very few who will 're-baptise' the millions who have slipped through the net, showing that they still accept the validity of indiscriminate baptism, even though they do not practise it themselves.

These anomalies in both the principles and practice of covenantal baby baptism, together with the fact that the theology can be traced back to a single source only four hundred years ago, do raise the question whether it is, in fact, not a brilliant rationalisation rather than a biblical reason. If it was as clearly taught in the New Testament as its proponents claim, this view would have arisen spontaneously wherever the Bible has been studied; actually, it is only held where a person has been taught to find it in scripture by someone influenced by the 'Reformed' wing of the Reformation. The Anglican General Secretary of the Bible Society once told me that records of Bibles reaching people without a missionary interpreter revealed that the resulting Christian communities all practised believers' baptism.

The confusing legacy of the Reformers over water-baptism is not unrelated to their failure to rediscover Spirit-baptism, or even more general truths about the Holy Spirit. They were strong on the work of the second person of the Trinity, but weak on the third (in Calvin's *Institutes of the Christian Religion* there are four pages on the Holy Spirit and sixty-three on the law of Moses, perhaps one reason why his devotees are particularly prone to legalism). Since water-baptism and Spirit-baptism are so closely linked, though never identified, in the New Testament (cf. Matt 3:16; Acts 19:2–3), it is hardly surprising that the Reformers' treatment of the one led to a blind spot on the other. The wholeness of Christian initiation was not restored, leaving the matter of baby baptism open to yet further misunderstanding.

Prevenient grace and baby baptism

The last theological rationale to be considered is comparatively recent. This time the starting-point is 'prevenient grace', a precious truth in itself, underlining the divine initiative in salvation, which Calvin was right to emphasise. God loves us before we love him, seeks us before we seek him, calls us before we call on him, and sent his Son to earth so that we may be his sons in heaven. Jesus summed it up beautifully: 'No-one can come to me unless the Father who sent me draws him . . .' (John 6:44).

Baptism has come to be regarded by some as the perfect expression of this truth. It is therefore considered *more* appropriate for babies than believers, emphasising as it does that it was 'when we were still powerless' that Christ died for us (though Paul was probably referring to moral rather than physical helplessness – Rom 5:6). God steps into our life before we step into his. The account of Jesus' blessing of the children is a favourite reference-point for those espousing this outlook (though it is not always pointed out that the children were no longer babies and were brought by their fathers rather than their mothers – Matt 19:13); it is often read, sometimes as the only scripture, at the baptism of babies.

This interpretation, which is common among Methodists (see especially W. F. Flemington, *The New Testament Doctrine of Baptism* (SPCK, 1948), ch. 10) and Congregationalists, is particularly congenial to those who have embraced universalism – the belief that in the end everybody will be saved, in the next world if not in this. This sees in the cross a 'cosmic' redemption, of universal *efficacy* as well as sufficiency. The gospel is then the proclamation that the whole human race has been 'liberated'; baptism then declares that everyone born into it has a 'right' to enjoy this freedom, and, in theory, already does.

The main objection to this 'prevenient grace' approach is that the New Testament views baptism as the sacrament of *appropriated* grace rather than prevenient grace. It is the point at which grace is met by a voluntary and conscious response (in repentance and faith) to the good news of the sufficiency of Christ's atonement by a grateful sinner. It is *both* a divine and a human act, and it may not be vicariously undertaken on behalf of another (see chapter 24).

Difficulties over baby baptism

These, then, are the three basic theological reasons given for the baptism of babies: original sin, covenantal birthright and prevenient grace. The Church of England contains a mixture (some would say a typical English 'muddle') of all three. The 'high' church would retain the Catholic view of 'baptismal regeneration' (which is reflected in the liturgy of the Book of Common Prayer). The 'broad' church would emphasise the grace and love of God, welcoming the latest addition to his 'family'. The 'low' church would reflect the Puritan/Presbyterian period of Anglican history, using 'covenant' concepts to justify an evangelical presence in an 'established' church. The major practical problem facing the evangelical wing is that the other two theological positions (Catholic and liberal) inevitably foster the practice of indiscriminate baptism, so abhorred by themselves but widely advocated by the upper hierarchy. To an impartial observer, it seems that Anglicans only agree in their determination to defend the practice of baby baptism, whatever the reason which can be found to justify it! Once again, this looks more like a rationalisation of tradition than the realisation of truth. As we have already seen, it would be virtually impossible to maintain a 'national' church with the baptism of believers only – which may be the real rationale, as distinct from the rationalisation.

However, all three streams (Catholic, liberal and evangelical – both within and beyond Anglicanism) are being affected by 'charismatic renewal'. The rediscovery of Spirit-baptism is leading to a fresh appraisal of water-baptism (reversing the pattern of the Reformation in this regard). A personal experience of the Holy Spirit renews interest and restores confidence in the scriptures. The result is a widespread desire to see baptism 'restored' to its original meaning and mode – though, understandably, this has been more readily undertaken by the laity rather than the clergy, whose vocation centres on the administration of the sacraments.

The main damage done by indiscriminate baptism is to give a false sense of spiritual security to its recipients, who are often strangely resistant to later appeals or challenges (as if inoculated against the gospel). But harm is also done by the 'discriminate' baptism of babies – primarily by changing the *meaning* of the event. Whether seen as the remission of original sin, the recognition of covenantal birthright or the revelation of prevenient grace, baptism no longer carries the significance of the New Testament rite. Many 'paedobaptists' openly admit that it is impossible to apply New Testament teaching to the baptism of a baby without turning it into a purely symbolical or patently magical act. Instead of using any of the thirty New Testament passages about baptism, recourse is made to doctrines found elsewhere in scripture, particularly in the Old Testament, which never mentions baptism once.

There is an even more serious effect. Not only is the meaning and significance of baptism usually altered; the baby is thereby robbed of the opportunity later in life of a baptism with true New Testament meaning and significance, assuming the church forbids re-baptism, which it always does officially, though local conditions are beginning to relax. When a person later repents of sin and believes in the Saviour, they will be forbidden to express their desire for cleansing in a perfectly natural and entirely scriptural way. They will not therefore experience that divine cleansing which is mediated through the sacrament, and this at the very moment they most need it – and all because their parents submitted them to a ceremony involving a few drops of water and a verbal formula when they had no active part to play.

The total divorce of baptism from the will of the main participant is perhaps the most disturbing aspect of this changed perspective. The baptism of babies actually removes *all* choice! Someone christened as a baby may later become convinced that believers' baptism is right, but they are forbidden to obey their conscience, on pain of offending their church. Conversely, someone who was not christened as a baby may in later life become convinced that they ought to have been – yet there is no way that they now can be! Such dilemmas would never have arisen had the church continued steadfastly in the apostles' doctrine.

For all these reasons, there is no attempt in the main body of this book to integrate baby baptism – which Luther candidly called 'unbelievers' baptism' – into a full doctrine of Christian initiation, though it has certainly not been ignored (the reader is particularly referred to chapters 4, 19, 22, 24, 25 and 34). It is hoped, however, that paedobaptist readers will still be able to benefit from the teaching on repentance, faith and receiving the Spirit. It is further hoped that paedobaptists will study thoroughly the credobaptists' case for believers' baptism. In addition to the works mentioned earlier, the following are significant contributions to the debate: Karl Barth, *The Teaching of the Church Regarding Baptism* (SCM Press, 1948); G. R. Beasley-Murray, *Baptism Today and Tomorrow* (Macmillan, 1966); A. Gilmore (ed.), *Christian Baptism* (Lutterworth, 1959); David Kingdon, *Children of Abraham* (Carey, 1973); R. E. O. White, *The Biblical Doctrine of Initiation* (Hodder & Stoughton, 1960).

APPENDIX 2 'SPIRIT'
WITHOUT THE DEFINITE ARTICLE

The Greek New Testament does not always use the definite article ('the') when referring to the Holy Spirit. For example, it speaks of both 'the gift of the Holy Spirit' (Acts 2:38) and being 'filled with Holy Spirit' (Acts 2:4).

E. J. Young (in the preface to his *Literal Translation of the New Testament*) pointed out that the presence or absence of the definite article was itself a significant feature of the inspired word and should be reflected in English translations (astonishingly, he then proceeded to ignore his own principle when translating statements about the Holy Spirit!).

The basic question is whether the presence or absence of 'the' is purely a *grammatical* and stylistic matter, or has *theological* content in giving a particular emphasis or meaning.

Some scholars have found a rationale in the construction of sentences. For example, there is a tendency in Greek to drop the article after a preposition. The same trend is associated with phrases employing an instrumental dative or a governing genitive.

But there are some grammatical anomalies. The first mention of a personal subject or impersonal object is usually anarthrous (without the article) while subsequent mentions are not (for example: 'He bought a Rolls-Royce car' will be followed by 'He took *the* Rolls for a spin in the country' and 'He crashed *the* Rolls'). This habit, characteristic of Greek and English, is broken again and again in the New Testament when speaking about (the) Spirit.

It is true, as James D. G. Dunn has noted in his *Baptism in the Holy Spirit* (SCM Press, 1970), p. 68f., that nine situations in Luke/Acts have both forms to describe the same event (e.g. Acts 1:5 says 'You will be baptised in Holy Spirit' whereas Acts 1:8 says '. . . when the Holy Spirit comes upon you'). However, he does not stop to ask whether the different constructions could, in fact, be emphasising two varied aspects of the same event.

'SPIRIT' WITHOUT THE DEFINITE ARTICLE

There is quite a long history of biblical scholars who have found reasons for the variation in the content as well as the construction of these statements. That is, the presence or absence of the article is significant for the sense as well as the sentence!

In 1881, Bishop B. F. Westcott reprinted his Notes on John's Gospel, originally written for 'The Speaker's Commentary'. On John 7:39 ('Up to that time the Spirit had not been given . . .') he commented:

> The addition of the word *given* expresses the true form of the original in which *Spirit* is without the article [*houpo hen pneuma*]. When the term occurs in this form, it marks an operation, or manifestation, or gift of the Spirit, and not the personal Spirit. Compare 1.33; 20.22; Matthew 1.18, 20; 3.11; 12.28; Luke 1.15, 35, 41, 67; 2.25; 4.1. (*Gospel of St. John* (Murray, 1903), p. 123; transliteration mine)

In 1909, in his *The Holy Spirit in the New Testament* (Macmillan, 1909), p. 395, H. B. Swete devoted an entire Appendix to the issue. He concluded: 'Middleton's canon seems to hold good; while *to pneuma to hagion* or *to hagion pneuma* is the Holy Spirit considered as a Divine Person, *pneuma hagion* is a gift or manifestation of the Spirit in its relation to the life of man' (transliteration mine).

Dr S. G. Green, in his *Handbook to the Grammar of the New Testament*, p. 189, makes the same point: 'The name of the Holy Spirit requires the article when He is spoken of in himself; but when the reference is to His operation, gifts or manifestations in men, the article is almost invariably omitted.'

Much more recently, D. Pitt Francis wrote an article entitled 'The Holy Spirit – a Statistical Enquiry' in the *Expository Times*, Vol. 96, No. 5 (February 1985), p. 136. Classifying the eighty-nine references to 'Holy Spirit' in the New Testament, he came to the conclusion 'that "power" references (49) do not contain the definite article, but references to the Holy Spirit as a person (40) invariably do'. He claimed that 'a chi-squared test [a well-known statistical test] . . . with six degrees of freedom gives a significant value of 85.228'. In layman's terms, this means that the presence or absence of the definite article being a mere 'fluke', without any meaning or significance, is less than one in a thousand!

This distinction, common to many scholars, between the 'person' and the 'power' of the Spirit is generally borne out by the content or context of individual texts.

With the article

The Spirit descending (3x), poured out (3x), falling on (2x), sent by Father (2x), resting on, supplied. The Spirit speaks (19x), teaches (2x), witnesses (5x), searches, knows. Communicated by, signified through (2x), speaking with, revealed by. People come by, are seized by, thrust out by (2x), prevented by, not allowed by, placed by and bound in the Spirit. He can be blasphemed against (4x), spoken about, lied to, done despite to, tempted, quenched, resisted, lusted against (2x), grieved, sown to, reaped from, seem good to. A person can be sealed with, washed by, justified by, sanctified by (2x), mighty through and rejoicing in the Spirit. The Spirit raised Jesus, helps our infirmities and blows where he will. He is the Spirit of the Lord, of his Son, of truth (3x), the same Spirit (3x) and the Lord is the Spirit. The scripture speaks of the name of, the power of, the promise of, the gift of (2x), the comfort of, the firstfruits of, the mind of, the love of, the things of, the temple of, the manifestations of, the supply of, the unity of, the fruit of, the earnest of (2x), and the communion of (2x) the Holy Spirit.

Without the article

Baptised in (7x), filled with (10x; Acts 4:31 is without the article in the 'Majority' text), full of (4x), anointed with, have, have not, begun in, pregnant by/born of (4x), in Spirit (3x), Spirit in (2x), dwelling in (3x), love in (2x), signs and wonders in, demonstration of, witnessing with gifts of, demons cast out in power of, revealed by, speaking in (2x), praying in, worshipping in, instructing through, declared according to, offering self through, written with (2x), renewed by, sanctified by, partakers of, living in, walking in (2x), waiting through, mortifying by, in hope by power of, righteousness and peace and joy in, persecuted after, conscience bearing witness through Spirit.

There are a few exceptions in both lists (only seven texts in all, some of doubtful manuscript authenticity); but the general pattern seems clear.

Both forms are freely (and almost equally) used in Romans 8; these also may be classified in the same way. *With* the article (9x), the emphasis is on what the Spirit is – law of (v. 2), things of (v. 5), mind of (vv. 6, 27), firstfruit of (v. 23); and on what the Spirit does – raised Jesus (v. 11), bears witness (v. 16), helps us in our weakness (v. 26), intercedes for us (v. 26). *Without* the article (8x) the emphasis is on what we have – we are in him (v. 9), he dwells in us (v. 9), we have/have not him (v. 9), indwelling of him (v. 11); and on what we can do in him – walk according to him (v. 4 and v. 5), put old life to death by him (v. 13) and be led by him (v. 14).

Conclusions

To summarise, the presence of the definite article draws attention to the objective attributes and activities of the person, with a 'downward' direction of God acting on people; the absence of the definite article draws attention to the subjective experience and enabling of the power, with an 'upward' direction of people acting in God. The difference is one of degree rather than kind, so no hard and fast line can be drawn between the two; but the trend is clearly present.

The wrong conclusion to be drawn from this tendency would be that there are two 'receptions' of the Spirit. Both Pentecostals and evangelicals have explored this path of reconciliation; and it would provide a convenient solution to the tensions between them! To believe that a disciple receives the person of the Spirit at 'conversion' (i.e. at the moment of faith), automatically and usually unconsciously, and then receives the power of the Spirit, later and consciously (at what Pentecostals call *the* baptism of the Spirit' and evangelicals sometimes call *a* baptism of the Spirit' – another situation where the presence or absence of the definite article is theologically significant!) would be a neat solution. Some have tried to base such a dual 'reception' on the two mentions of the apostles' receiving (in John 20:22 and Acts 1:8); but it is very doubtful if they received anything on the first occasion (see chapter 13).

But the fact remains that the New Testament seems to teach only one 'receiving' of the Holy Spirit – of the *person with power*. In this connection it is interesting to note that 'baptised in Holy Spirit' is 100% without the article; 'filled with' is 92.8% without and 'receive' is 71.5% without. The emphasis is clearly on the subjective and manifest aspects. Receiving (the) Spirit is an experience with evidence (see chapter 5); though this understanding does not depend on the presence or absence of the definite article, it does find confirmation in this usage.

It also helps us to understand the ambiguous, if not paradoxical, teaching of the New Testament on the subject – alternating as it does between 'the Holy Spirit' as a personal being who thinks, feels, acts and speaks like us and 'Holy Spirit' as an impersonal force that blows like wind, pours like water and flows like oil. To be 'baptised in Holy Spirit' will therefore feel more like the influx of impersonal energy than an introduction to personal encounter. In existential experience the believer is more likely to be aware of the power before the person; in intellectual instruction it is usually the other way round!

APPENDIX 3 TRINITY OR TRITHEISM?

The major doctrinal objection to my basic thesis relates to my understanding of the Godhead. In separating 'believing in Jesus' from 'receiving the Spirit' (both theologically and chronologically), I am thought to be jeopardising the unity of the Trinity and verging on tritheism (belief in three Gods). In simple terms, the critics are asking – how is it possible to receive one divine Person without the other two, since they are all 'in' each other?

I could say that the apostolic writers themselves are open to the same charge, if my case is a true explanation of their teaching (Paul's question to the Ephesian disciples in Acts 19:2, for example – see chapter 20).

It is also a fact that, historically, the apostles came to a relationship with the three divine Persons at separate times. As Jews they had known the Father (though they would not have dared to call him that); then they met the Son (though they did not realise it at first); finally, they received the Spirit (though he had been 'with' them incognito – see chapter 12). There was even a period of ten days when they had neither the Son nor the Spirit 'with' them, between the Ascension and Pentecost. But they were praying to the Father during this time (probably in line with Luke 11:13), presumably doing so in the name of Jesus (John 16:23), who had already begun his intercessory ministry on their behalf (John 14:16, cf. Acts 2:33, Heb 7:25).

But all this is before Pentecost, and my position assumes that post-Pentecost evangelism is the norm. This must also take into account our Lord's predictive pronouncements before and after his death. For example, he said he would 'depart' and send someone else to take his place (John 16:7), yet promised them his permanent presence with them (Matt 28:20)! He said the Spirit would come to dwell in them (John 14:17), yet also promised that the Father and he himself would do the same (John 14:23)! Indeed, Jesus' statements about 'coming' back to his disciples could be applied to his resurrection, Pentecost or the Parousia at the end of the age (let the reader study the ambiguity in John 14:18f, 16:22).

The only way to resolve the paradox is to believe that when the Spirit came into them at Pentecost, the Father and the Son also took up residence within them at the same time – while remaining outside them as well. This combination of immanence and transcendence is characteristic of divine being.

In simple terms, then – *when the Spirit comes, the Father and Son also come*. In a real sense, the whole Trinity indwells the initiated disciple, who may be said to have the Spirit in him (or to be 'in the Spirit', not so common in the New Testament) and to have Christ in him (Gal 2:20, Col 1:27 where 'you' is plural; but note this is rare in the New Testament where apostles normally use the reverse phrase, 'in Christ'), and to have the Father in him (corporately and individually believers are the 'temple of God').

Since this is what I believe, why should I be suspected of heterodox, if not heretical, views of the Trinity? Because there remains a clear difference of opinion concerning the stage of initiation at which the Godhead 'takes up residence'.

Traditional evangelicalism and classical Pentecostalism persist in using the (to me, unbiblical) term 'receiving Jesus' for the *second* stage of 'believing in Jesus' (based on a misinterpretation of one verse, John 1:12, transferring its application from the historical phase when he was in the flesh to the contemporary phase in the Spirit – see pp. 59–62 for a refutation of this error). On this premise, they accuse me of teaching *two* separate 'receptions' of Jesus and the Spirit, whom they rightly say are so much 'one' that neither can be received without the other.

I agree with this last assertion but differ over the moment when this dual (or rather, triple) 'indwelling' begins. Instead of the traditional view that when Christ is 'received', the Spirit is received, I am putting it the other way round: when the Spirit is received, Christ (with his Father) is received. This makes the moment of entry to be the *fourth* stage of initiation, rather than the second – but keeps the Trinity united!

This is no mere quibble, for there are enormous pastoral implications (think of the damage done by telling people they are 'indwelt' before this is actually true!). Some readers will not even consider the possibility of re-thinking their position for fear of repercussions!

Nevertheless, it does appear to have been apostolic preaching and practice to encourage enquirers to enter and enjoy this indwelling relationship with Father, Son and Spirit by 'receiving' the *Third* person of the Trinity in an evidenced experience, as they themselves had done on the day of Pentecost (let the reader who questions this make a careful study of the exegesis in chapters 7–30). This was the climax of the new birth, God's response to those who responded to the gospel in repentance, faith and baptism.